RUNNING *and stuff*

Hope you enjoy!
All the best
James Adams

RUNNING

and stuff

JAMES ADAMS

Matador
9 Priory Business Park,
Wistow Road, Kibworth Beauchamp,
Leicestershire. LE8 0RX
Tel: (+44) 116 279 2299
Fax: (+44) 116 279 2277
Email: books@troubador.co.uk
Web: www.troubador.co.uk/matador

ISBN 978 1784622 626

British Library Cataloguing in Publication Data.
A catalogue record for this book is available from the British Library.

Typeset in 11pt Aldine by Troubador Publishing Ltd, Leicester, UK
Printed and bound in the UK by TJ International, Padstow, Cornwall

Matador is an imprint of Troubador Publishing Ltd

RUNNING *and stuff*

FOREWORD

IAN SHARMAN

The first time I met James was when mutual friends at Serpentine Running Club in London introduced us because James was about to undertake his first ultra. It was in 2007 and neither of us knew many people who considered that running more than a marathon was sensible or maybe even possible. He was fairly relaxed about it and didn't seem to take the distance very seriously, yet since that date he's finished pretty much any event he puts his mind to. This is where James has an advantage over everyone else – where they may assume that a diet of kebabs and beer would mean DNFs and injuries, he has an innate stubbornness that means he could run in ballet slippers over glass for days because it wouldn't cross his mind that it was impossible.

I've been to many races with James in the UK and beyond and he's guaranteed to make the trip more fun and have better stories to tell at the end that everyone else, partly due to his attitude and partly due to an almost masochistic choice to under-prepare. Sometimes ultras in their normal format just aren't hard enough for James so he has to add extra challenges. Therefore it's no surprise this is the man who came up with the idea of the Piece of String race, where the distance isn't advertised and runners just have to keep going until the race director tells them it's the end.

One of my favourite races with James was a trail marathon where we decided to experiment with the effects of alcohol on the ability to run 26.2 miles. After a whole night out and too many beers, we stumbled back to the hostel we'd forgotten to check into earlier. The front desk was closed but we managed to pass out on sofas in the lobby, then scrape ourselves into our running kits for the early start. In case anyone wonders, the result of the experiment was surprising – the first few miles were tough then it felt fairly normal.

Over the years James kept taking on bigger and harder challenges, driven by an insatiable appetite to out-do the difficulty of his previous race. Eventually this led to James running over 3,000 miles in the Los Angeles to New York race and even he had some doubts about whether he could finish, but the full story of that effort is brilliantly told in this book. This isn't a 'how to' book for ultra marathon training, nor is it an ego trip about how incredible James' accomplishments are (spoiler alert: they're damned impressive, but it takes someone else to say that since James won't). Instead it's an in-depth description of the highs and lows of many different types of ultras from a very down-to-earth perspective. It's readable and entertaining in the same way that a chat by the fire in the pub is relaxed and fun, full of plenty of laughing.

These races have made James into a stalwart of the UK ultra scene where his experience and stories are well-known and oft repeated, plus his blog is widely read for the same reasons. For those who know him, you may be disappointed that this book has fewer descriptions of bodily fluids than you might have thought, but that's because you'd expect a lot of mentions of those.

Ian Sharman October 2014

Ian Sharman started ultra running in the UK in 2006 where he routinely won races and set course records. He needed a bigger pond and so moved to the States in 2009 where he quickly established himself among the ultra running Galacticos of the West Coast. He shot to international fame with an intimidating 12.43 100 mile run in the Rocky Racoon, breaking a record that stood for decades. He has since placed 5 times in the top ten in the Western States 100, has broken the record for the "Grand Slam" of ultra running, running four tough 100 milers in the space of three months and continues to complete with the worlds best ultra runners.

He also runs his own coaching service [www.sharmanultra.com/] where he trains runners to win races as well as first timers to complete races. He is also the director of US Skyrunning.

Wow, that's a lot of stuff to remember. So if you only remember one thing about Ian Sharman then let it me this;

I once beat him in a 50 miler.

INTRODUCTION

Ask a teenage boy what his dreams are for the future. Ask him to imagine that he is old and he is looking back over the decades and picking out the best moments of his life.

If he is anything like I was at that age he'd be sure to say something about the time he scored the winning goal for England in the World Cup final and returned home to greet his adoring fans. Or the time he stood on stage in front of a 150,000 strong rabidly obsessed crowd while he belted out a signature guitar solo as they swayed in awe.

Or the time he became the first man on earth to step onto Mars, or the time he was awarded the Nobel Prize for Physics for finally solving that unified theory problem, or the time Kylie announced to him "I'm yours forevermore".

I want to go and tell this boy that he is selling himself short and he should aim much higher than that. I want to tell him there will be much better memories for him to cherish into his later years, to wow the people in the pub or his kids and grandkids or to sometimes just silently reflect upon some of life's wonderful moments.

Like the time he thought he was done for having run 120 miles with another 25 to go but somehow managed to get up out of the chair, staggered back into a run and all of a sudden forgot all the pain and hurt as he just glided over the path.

Or the time he climbed a sand dune in the desert and for the first time in his life not being able to see any sign of human life, only sand and stars. Feeling a chilling sensation as he tried to come to terms with the terrifying but exhilarating prospect of being the only human alive on the whole Earth.

Or the time he completely lost himself in the Canadian wilderness, crushing hours into seconds as gnarly path was swept aisde with the grace of a figure skater.

Or the time he was hallucinating while ascending a huge mountain in the USA having spent two days running through the hottest place on earth. The time he barked orders at his friends in the dark before sheepishly realising that these people were total strangers.

Or the time that he saw a mirage of his wife reflecting from the roasting hot road in Oklahoma, a gremlin from a heat battered brain as he suffered during a heatwave. Then running close and closer, seeing the mirage getting bigger and bigger and then realising that it really was her, it was no illusion, she had come to save him.

Or the time he was reduced to tears by an email from a legend of of the sport, who said "I was in bits doing this race too, hang in there, you are doing amazingly well and I'm proud of you"

I want to tell him to sod the stupid football dream, that a much better moment would be when he is staggering up a highway in New Mexico, starved from illness and wilting from the heat and in the depths of despair. Where he thought there was no hope left until another competitor came alongside him. I want to tell him the greatest moment of his life might well be the time he was sung too whilst trying not to shit himself.

I don't think he would believe that this collection of memories is worth more than the ones he has on his list. Hopefully he might read a book like this one and realise that the key to happiness is to find an activity that allows you to collect these gems to serve as your emotional pension when the time comes. That life is rarely about "things" or "outcomes" but the random and unpredictable stuff that you pick up on the way.

There is no secret or short cut to collecting these gems, you just need a big digger and to spend a lot of time clawing through the earth.

Ultra running has been my digger, and here are some stories I'd like to share.

CONTENTS

THE LOS ANGELES TO NEW YORK FOOTRACE

– JUNE 19TH – AUGUST 27TH 2011

1

ONCE UPON A TIME IN NEW MEXICO

I was looking forward to going home at the end of summer and telling everyone I made it. That I made it all the way across the United States of America on foot. I hoped to have collected some great stories along the way, great views seen and friends made, bunions and blisters, animal attacks and bewildered locals, greasy burger bars and dodgy motels. Moments of crippling depression and euphoric highs. Running into a sunny Central Park on a Saturday afternoon to mark the end of an epic journey. The best summer holiday ever. Not to mention a great big bushy beard.

But New York seemed even further away than it did at the start. When I set out from Los Angeles 19 days ago this all felt doable. Now I've covered 800 miles, crossed two deserts, two states and some beautiful mountains it feels impossible. I've already made some friends who I know will be friends for life, have been overwhelmed by the unbelievable kindness of strangers and experienced some of the highs and lows that got me into these situations in the first place. I am still a long way from the finish in New York though; 2400 miles. I am still a long way from the finish of today.

I have had diarrhoea for four days now and it is not getting any better. All the food and drink I try to consume gets thrown back out again from one place or another. I am empty; my legs can barely stand as my body chews itself up from the inside. I am shaking and sweating all the time, I don't know what my body is finding to burn but somehow it stays upright.

I can take the vomiting, the feeling of being punched in the stomach and my legs wobbling like jelly as I stagger along this highway. What I can't bear is the thought of just passing out at the side of the road, waking up in an ambulance and being told "Hey James, don't worry you are fine but the race is over for you". I couldn't bear going back and telling everyone I didn't finish.

I look up at the long and winding road to the finish; it's about 30 miles away. I can't see any of the other runners they are all too far ahead. I feel like a burden on the organisers who have to hang back to support me. Perhaps I should drop out for everyone else's sake?

No. I'm not going to drop out. Not consciously anyway. I have already decided that I was going to give everything I had to stay in this race. The problem is that now I am overdrawn. I don't know what my body is burning to keep me upright; fat and muscle? Brain? Organs? My soul?

I shuffle forward slowly, obsessing about every mile post and incline in the road. Every churned up piece of tarmac or truck passing by represents an obstacle to me finishing. I can't walk for more than 500 meters without having to throw up or worse. I am determined to get through this no matter what but fear that soon it will be out of my hands.

It gets worse.

It was still very hot and I see a dog come sprinting towards me from a small building in the middle of nowhere to warn me not to encroach on his space. I hate dogs, I've hated them for about two days now. In all other times when charged by an aggressive dog I just look the other way and carry on walking, making no eye contact until I can't hear it anymore. I've done this about 20 times in the past three weeks.

But this time I do something a bit different. As it reached

the road and started to gallop across I just froze right there on the spot and then shit myself.

It gets worse.

As the dog got still closer and the warm feeling of defecation humiliated me I just burst into tears. That dog could have just ripped me up for all I care now, this is over. Shitting yourself and then crying about it? When was the last time anyone does that? Two years old maybe? Here I am on the side of a road having done just that at the age of 31. The dog didn't even bother after that. Among the many things he can surely smell is an aura of hopelessness and feebleness that surrounds me. He just walked back from where he came having decided not to waste any of his dog breath on such a pathetic human. I have just been patronised by a dog. In my own voice in my own head I can hear the repetitive phrase:

"James Adams you are the most pathetic human being who has ever lived"

It was hard to argue.

It gets worse.

The last 30 seconds of my life slams into my long term memory like nothing else had ever done before. The folder labelled "This is your life" that currently contains the most significant moments of my life now had a new addition. It did not pass through any temporary phase, any holding area for editing before deciding whether to keep or discard. It just went straight in to the place where I store memories like my first kiss and first kiss with someone I love, finishing races, graduating, leaving home, epic holidays and adventures. A space that will contain future experiences like my wedding day, the births of my children, death of a loved one, disease, hearing "granddad" said to me for the first time, perhaps even running into New York. This just dropped straight in there and there is no way I can ever delete it.

I carry on, hoping to find somewhere to clean myself before the support team come find me again and try to get fluids into me. I am dry like a prune, sunburnt, heat-exhausted, and now with a warm feeling of a full nappy. Some end to the story this would be.

I imagine going home and my friends and family asking me what I did this summer. "Hey James, remember that time when you tried to run across America but in the end you only made two weeks and got scraped up off the side of the road in a pool of your own filth? That was hilarious".

But what others thought now paled into insignificance to the new objective I had given myself. There was no way I can ever delete or overwrite what had just burned into my brain. The only way to reduce the damage was for me to do something this summer that would better it, which would make that experience seem insignificant in comparison to something much better that I might have done instead.

Whatever motivations I had for doing this race – the personal challenge, the story telling, bragging rights, adventure, travel and exploration or whatever – I now had a much, much bigger one. I had to eclipse that memory. I had to make this summer about more than shitting myself and crying because of a dog.

The only way I could do that was to run to New York. There was no way I was going to tell anyone about the last five minutes of my life unless I made it to New York. Maybe not even then.

★★★★★

I promise you there is a perfectly sensible explanation for all of this.

So how did I end up on a highway in New Mexico with broken bowels trying to shuffle up to a finish line that I'd then have to repeat another 53 times? How did my perception of running change from training for the occasional marathon to running nearly two a day for 70 days without rest? How did this become normal? Why did I think this was a good idea?

Like with many stories of this type it was an accumulation of events and conversations after I originally got involved in the ultra-running community. I can remember the moment when I thought that running across America was a good idea but that didn't happen until I had already been wrapped up in this world for a number of years.

I can remember vividly where it all started. I don't remember the date exactly but it was a hot British summer's day, and it was a Tuesday.

2

THE EMAIL

Sometime in the summer of 2006 – a Tuesday

It was a hot British summer's day, and by "hot British" I mean about 25C. I was working in an office with poor natural lighting and yearning to leave. I was not a big fan of the sun though. The BBC website was offering all kinds of advice about dealing with such a "heat wave" such as carrying water with you at all times and always wearing a hat. The best advice I think was to just barricade yourself into a cellar with a month's worth of supplies and pray that the sun will stop its merciless attack on our great city.

I was training for a Marathon at the time, it was not my first. I had done six marathons before but this time I was really training properly for one. Training properly meant that every Tuesday evening I had a date with a running track in Maida Vale, West London. This week it was something called "Yasoos", where I beast myself for 800m at a time and somehow that should tell me the outcome of a marathon I will do in two months' time.

I thought of myself as a bit of a veteran at marathons but I wanted to get much faster at the next one and hence all this fancy training. For previous marathons I just trained by setting out of my door and running around until my legs hurt. Now I was running around tracks at various paces, running up and down hills, learning about such things as "tempo" and "threshold". I was enjoying the training.

I was still a little concerned that the temperature would be over 20°C at 7 pm when the session was due to start. How would I cope in such temperatures? The population at large have been told to stay indoors and I am about to go out running in it. I could die. I emailed my concerns to a friend who was also going to attend. I said it was not a good idea to run in this temperature, that I won't be able to have a good session and that I might end up in hospital.

His reply was less than sympathetic.

"How about this one then?" he jokingly replied to my whinging about the London heat wave. He had sent me a link to a race in the USA. It was called "The Badwater Ultramarathon". That name alone made it sound quite scary. I was vaguely aware of what an "ultramarathon" was; it was a race whose distance is more than 26.2 miles. I didn't think they went much over the 26 miles though, it sounded like it was the limits of human endurance.

But I was blown away by the distance of Badwater. It was 135 miles. ONE HUNDRED AND THIRTY FIVE MILES. If that wasn't enough it was in Death Valley, the hottest place on Earth, typically reaching temperatures of over 50°C.

I thought it was a joke. This is a fake website, something left over from April fools' day. Humans don't do that. Humans *can't* do that.

I spent quite a while looking at the website. At the time I was working in marketing and had already produced two pie charts which was more than enough work for one day. The rest of the afternoon I was hooked on this website where I'd ask so many questions to myself. How can people run that far? How can people run up hills that big? How can people run in such temperatures? What exactly does 50 degrees feel like? The more time I spent the more I realised that this was not a joke at all. This actually happens. I had to pull myself away from the site at the end of the day to go and run in the relatively cool summer night.

The training session went very well. I was told to run 800m in around 3-3:15 minutes, then spend the same time jogging 400m and then repeat seven times. I did exactly as I was told, or in other words I had a "good session". I didn't end up in hospital.

I felt the warm glow of a good hour of exercise on warming down from the session, it was still warm outside but not really bothering me now. My marathon was in two months' time and this was evidence to suggest that I was going to achieve my marathon target of 3:15. I felt one step closer to getting my marathon target and this gave me some warmth, but I was distracted.

While running around the track, alternating meticulously between 9.7 miles per hour and 4.85 miles per hour my mind was elsewhere. I could not stop thinking about Badwater. I was still suspicious that the website and all the attached stories might be some elaborate hoax designed to fool idiots such as me into believing things like that were possible. As I read more about the race these doubts disappeared and it became clear that this is a proper event that human beings do.

Which set off the following sequence of thoughts.

"Humans can do this race."

"I'm a human."

And then a few more seconds for the penny to drop.

"I could do that race."

I gave myself five years.

2A

WHY? VERSION 1

Joining a running club was one of the best things I had ever done. Since moving to London I hadn't made many friends and was quite lonely. It seems strange that in a city of seven million people it is quite hard to meet people but that is how it was for the first year.

When I joined I was not a regular runner. I liked running and had run a few marathons before but never made a habit of it. As soon as I joined the Serpentine Running Club I was mixing with a load of people who shared this interest for running and did it regularly. All of a sudden my life became more interesting. I had a hobby and people to share it with.

I naturally stuck with a group of people who ran at similar speeds to me and we went out running on club sessions and then to the pub to chat the night away, usually about running. It sounds boring but I think in the year before most of my conversations in public were about parcel logistics or the weather. Now I had something worthwhile to share and people to share it with.

It was great having a bit of structure to my life outside work too. No longer wondering how to kill time at the weekends or just lying in bed, I can go and run and make progress towards a goal I have set myself in a few months' time, a Marathon.

What made it even better was the friendly

competition between the people I'd run with. I ran with guys called Nikolai, Ben, Simon, Alex and John and we were mostly all of similar speeds (Nikolai was actually much faster). We'd tick off 20 mile long runs, intense track sessions, hill sessions and regular seven mile club runs and feel like we were more ready for the big race each time.

Then when it came to the race there was a mix of excitement, nerves and competition. We'd want each other to have a great race but we wanted a better one for ourselves. There was a joy in tracking our progress in marathon times and other distances. When I first joined I looked at other runners and thought "they will always be way faster than me", then with some training I'd be as fast as them and then with some more training I'd be faster. This made me feel good. Progress.

But not only the tangible rewards of faster times, higher rankings and bragging rights. There was the social aspect of the running. I had something in my life that was not work or boredom. I guess it could have been anything, cycling, rowing, boxing, chess, who knows? I felt like my life had some structure and direction and all because a few times a week I'd put on some trainers and run around.

That was why I ran.

3

FETCHING THE STICK – THE FERRARI MARATHON ITALY 2006

The Italians do love their marathons. There are loads of them in most of its beautiful and historic cities. I elected to do the Ferrari Marathon because it was advertised as the flattest marathon in Europe and so a personal best was almost guaranteed. The training had gone well; I had done all the track sessions, long runs, tempos, and recoveries exactly as prescribed in a colourful spreadsheet.

This particular marathon ran from Carpi to Bologna. Carpi was the birthplace of Dorando Pietri who came to fame nearly 100 years earlier when in collapsed on his way to winning the 1908 Olympic marathon in London. Eventually he was disqualified after protests from the USA and it was their runner Jonny Hayes who was awarded the victory.

I remember the anxious coach journey from Bologna to Carpi, driving from the finish to the start. I could never really comprehend in my head what 26 miles was. I have run it before but never in a point to point in this way. The coach must have taken about an hour as I watched out of the window at the road rolling by and thinking to myself that this is much further than I imagined. 26 miles is a long way to run. I was a bit nervous. 26 miles will never be easy.

I started near the back so as to not set out too quickly. The field was much smaller than the 30,000+ I had run with in previous marathons in London, Berlin and Paris. There were only around 2,000 people here and soon I was in more space than I ever had been in a marathon.

The plan to not set out too quickly did not go very well. All the space I had been given seemed to be an invitation to charge right into it. I passed the 10k point in 40:30, almost a personal best for that distance and realised I was going too fast. Soon after I ran through the half-way point in 1:28:00, faster than I have ever done that distance before. I felt pretty good and started to wonder whether I was capable of breaking 3 hours.

It was not to be though. During the second half I was passed by more runners than I could count, and the heat of the day bore down on me and seemed to magnify my suffering. Eventually I finished in 3:12:00, still well under my 3:15:00 target.

The kind of elation that I had felt finishing some previous marathons was absent and at the time I had no explanation why. Though I had paced it badly I *should* have been thinking "Blimey, imagine what time I would get if I had paced it properly". A properly paced race and another six months of training with the track sessions and fartleks and long runs etc. and I should be able to smash that time further. It had worked here: in just 6 months with a structured programme I had gone from 3:39:00 to 3:12:00 and that was despite screwing up the race.

My coach was a lot more excited about it than I was. Her help and training plans had worked a treat and she was really keen on me doing it again and perhaps taking another 27 minutes off my marathon time. All of this enthusiasm was lost on me. I had annihilated my marathon time and demonstrated that I could annihilate it again and all I could feel was, well *nothing*.

Why did I feel this way? Or rather why did I not feel anything? I did not really talk about it at the time which was hard because the congratulations were pouring in and the comments of "you could be a really fast marathon runner if you put your mind to it" were frequent. My mind was already elsewhere.

I could not articulate this at the time but looking back I guess I got as much satisfaction from getting that marathon time as a dog does when it fetches a stick. I did exactly what I was told, followed a training plan designed by someone else, fed in the inputs and got an output like a well worked computer programme. It was not me running but someone else using my body to achieve their aims. I was pleased to see that others were pleased but deep down I knew I could not do that anymore. Soon after the race the stick was thrown again. I ran the other way and signed up for my first ultramarathon.

4

TIP OF THE ICEBERG

I found out about a race online called the Tring2Town; where "Town" was London, "Tring" was a town called Tring and the "2" was obviously shorthand for "you must run from one to the other". The idea of a point to point race that was quite long was really thrilling. On finding out about it online I signed up immediately and then cursed myself for having memorised my credit card details.

I figured the best way to train for an ultramarathon was to run marathons as "training". The idea of entering a marathon as "training" seemed odd to some but I felt like I needed some motivation to get around 26 miles and doubted I could do that on my own. I signed up for the Athens Marathon which was 3 weeks after Ferrari. I was breaking the rule of thumb that you should take a days' recovery per mile raced. Fortunately I am not a thumb.

I felt fully recovered from 3 weeks before but was determined to take it easy. I started at the back and was the last to cross the start line.

Being more relaxed and less concerned about pace I managed to chat to some people on the route. Right near the start I saw some Brits wearing 100 marathon club vests. I approached and they seemed like really nice and normal people except that they each quoted a number – 104, 157 and 205 – as the number of marathons they had run. For me this was number

8 and I was proud of that. One of them said he had run 44 that year so far. I immediately calculated that to average 1 every week. Who on earth runs a marathon every week?

Within the first few miles I spotted another couple of Brits running dressed as Greek soldiers. They said they were training for an event called the Spartathlon, a 153 mile race from Athens to Sparta next year. The idea of it did not really shock me as I had already read about the 135 mile Badwater race but I was a little surprised that there were other such things out there. I was also more surprised that there were other people out there training to do the same sort of things as I was.

I wished them well. Little did I know I would meet both of them again in the future, and come to know the Spartathlon very well too.

I was having a great run, feeling really relaxed as I jogged through the field. Towards the end I saw an older chap in front of me with a Sutton Runners vest and I pulled up alongside him. We chatted and soon I discovered that he had run "the triple" the weekend before, three marathons in a weekend; Beachy Head (very hard) on Saturday, Snowdon (quite hard) on Sunday, and Dublin (not so hard unless you had done the previous two) on Monday. I was astonished. Until now I felt pretty chuffed that I was running a marathon only three weeks after running a marathon. This guy was running a marathon only 1 week after running three marathons. He was at least twice my age too.

I entered the stadium in 3.34, beating the PB I had before 3 weeks ago and not even feeling like I was trying. I had a really good run and felt even better about my chances of running 45 miles in a couple of months' time. The best thing about the race though was leaving quite humbled by what others out there were doing. Three and a half hours ago I was blissfully unaware of things such as "Triples" and the 100 marathon club. I knew of Badwater but not of the Spartathlon. The biggest realisation was that the world of ultra-running extends far beyond what I originally thought. My initial feeling that I was "unique" in getting bored of chasing marathon times was blown away by the people that I met in this race. Forty-four marathons in a year? Three marathons in a weekend? 153 miles non-stop? There were obviously lots of people doing this and lots of places to do it at. As Tyler Durden would say in Fight Club "You are NOT a beautiful or unique snowflake". I wasn't, I had just drifted onto the tip of the iceberg. It was a world so much bigger and more exciting than I had imagined. I wanted in.

December 11th 2006 and all the runners I knew were talking about one thing; The Serpentine Christmas Party. Every year 250+ people from our running club take over the Hilton in Shepherds Bush and try to convince each other that legs are made for dancing as well as running. Thus far I have seen no evidence of this but it has never stopped anyone trying. I had to get a long run done this weekend and figured that Sunday was not the best plan. Fears of a sore head, dodgy stomach and perhaps waking up in the wrong bed on Sunday meant that I had to do it before the party instead.

I chose to keep it simple, something that I would come to rely on so much more later on. I set out from my house in Ealing West London and followed an ugly route west along the A4. My plan was to run for five hours and then get a train back home. Simple.

With a rucksack filled with water, a coat and some money I set out around 10 am to see how far I could go. The A4 is filled with distractions. I ran right alongside Heathrow airport and gazed in wonder at how planes so big can get in the air. Further on I'd pass the M25 and venture onto crossings that I am sure pedestrians are not meant to go on to. Soon I passed an oddly placed strip club in the middle of nowhere. It was closed. I pressed on into Slough and then Maidenhead which marked the

26 mile point of the run and I had only been going for four hours.

Running into the unknown was liberating, I had no idea really where I was except for road signs. It was hard to comprehend just how far from home I was but I was determined to keep going for the remaining hour. I continued west on some busy roads with very narrow walkways, having to stop in a couple of petrol stations for drinks and snacks. 5 hours came and I was still on this very busy road about 4 miles away from Reading. My great concern was getting back for the party but I figured that it would only take another hour at the most to get to Reading and so I went for it. I felt like Forrest Gump. When I was hungry I ate, when I was thirsty I drank and when I had to… y'know… I went.

And so I entered Reading train station around 5 hours and 40 forty minutes after I started. It was a wonderful sight and I could have gone further but I had a party to get to. I just sat there waiting for my (delayed) train which gave me time to eat and stretch. I looked around at everyone else at the station and thought of how different this was to any other long run I have done. At the end of all my marathons there was a huge fanfare greeting you with rabid enthusiasm for what you have done. Now here I was having run 10 miles further than a marathon and no one had any idea. It was wonderful. The only reason why people would look at me was because I was doing some stretches and they were probably only really concerned with the competition for getting a seat on the train.

I got a seat, it was very welcome. The train went back to Ealing along a route very similar to what I had just run. I passed the places I had passed on my adventure; Maidenhead, Taplow, Slough, Langley, Iver, West Drayton. It took 45 minutes on the train to get back and each of these place names had anchored in me. I had run from Ealing to Reading, a map of greater London would not even cover such distances. The thought of getting from place to place under one's own efforts was exhilarating.

At no point during the run did I feel like I had struggled. I ached a bit and had blisters but never did I feel like stopping, even when I got on the train I didn't feel like stopping. The sheer pointlessness of just setting out from my house, running a long way in a straight line then getting the train back felt so significant. That was as ugly a 36 miles as you could create, yet it was beautiful.

I enjoyed the journey home surrounded by an aura of satisfaction, which I think others on the train could smell.

I got to the party in plenty of time and was actually quite good at standing up despite my efforts earlier. I don't recall doing any dancing but that's not to say it didn't happen. I told some people about my run and they just thought I was stupid but held quite a bit of respect for it. One thing I do recall was that a friend of mine had told a (quite attractive) girl about it and she was really impressed.

"Wow – you ran to Reading, that's a really long way isn't it?"

"Well, it depends where you start" I said quite curtly.

And with charm like that the problem of waking up in a different bed never materialised.

4A

WHY? VERSION 2

Finishing the Ferrari Marathon was a bit of a shock. I achieved many of the great things that I described in "Why? Version 1" yet I was not happy. I smashed my time, jumped up in the rankings, could now say "I'm faster than that guy and that guy" and I could do it all again, I was certain of it.

I could not put my finger on what had changed, until I ran to Reading.

During my 35 mile 6 hour run from West London to Reading I think I hit upon the reason I run. The pure pointlessness of it. Just running from my house along a busy road and a train track to some city miles away for no reason other than the adventure of getting from point A to point B with my own feet.

Running 35 miles made me feel powerful. It was like some magical skill I had that few others had, similar to a martial art or CPR; if I had to run 35 miles for some reason then I knew that I could do it. On that 45 minute train journey back home from Reading, I got to look out the window at everything we passed and say, "I just did that with my feet". That gave me great confidence in myself.

I realised that, on some basic level, there was something truly satisfying about running to make myself hungry and then eating; making myself thirsty and then drinking; making myself tired then sleeping. It all felt so natural.

So in my first ultra-distance race I knew I had nothing to fear as I knew I just loved running for the sake of it. The longer the better and so doing seven hours of it didn't worry me at all because I just loved it.

That is why I ran.

5

TRING 2 TOWN ULTRA (2007) – MY FIRST ULTRAMARATHON

One-way train tickets in the UK cost the same as returns, which makes getting a train somewhere and running back seem even more pointless. Nonetheless that is what I did in January 2007 when I travelled to my first Ultramarathon.

On the Friday night I travelled up to Tring with my friend Nikolai. Nikolai had been the friend who had sent me the email about Badwater that got me into all this in the first place. He was also supposed to be running, but had unfortunately sustained an injury at the Ferrari marathon a few months previously.

We stayed in a pub with lots of other runners. In the evening we attended a seminar about the race and ultra-running in general and I was taken aback again by how many people do this kind of thing. What also struck me was the profile of the people here; they were all much older than me with a few exceptions.

I was amazed by how relaxed everything was. There was an uncomfortable urgency to all the races that I had entered before and this was just a case of "wake up in the morning, have breakfast in the pub, put on some shorts and then start running". It was so wonderfully simple, so relaxed.

The race started at a pub in Tring and soon joined up with the Grand Union Canal which we were to stick to until the end.

There were over 100 runners, but I only saw six legs – and two of those were my own. Everyone looked dressed to climb a mountain and had covered up considerably. Did they know something I didn't? Would I regret wearing shorts for this? Is it heat loss? Nettles? Dogs? The Randy Old Women of Rickmansworth?

I was getting quite a lot of attention for sporting the running number 1. People were glancing at me, obviously under a misapprehension that I was any good. It was purely because I happened to be first in the alphabet, a race I had been doing well at my whole life.

The first 1.5 mile or so was from the pub to the start of the canal. Everyone spread out quite quickly. Some walked to the canal so that they would not get over excited and try and sprint at the start. My plan was nice and simple; run nine minute miles until I finish. I often have a problem with navigation, however once I was on the canal I knew the way. Run 31.1 miles and then turn left. No one could possibly mess that up? Right?

I mean Left…

I knew I could run at 9:00 minutes per mile pace for 35 miles and still feel OK. I also knew how to run this pace exactly without any need for a Garmin, mile markers or anything else. My pace was seeing me overtake a few people early on. The pack spread out neatly and I counted about 15 people in front of me. It was just a matter of time now. When my stopwatch says 7:00 I should be lifting my arms up and woo-hooing. In seven and a half hours I will be drunk.

The ground was quite hard to run on. It was like cement mixed with bits of brick; very uneven and quite hard on the feet. I'd developed a running style that involved lifting my feet only a little off the floor. Great for saving energy and going easy on the knees. Not so good if you wanted to avoid tripping over.

We were handed a route guide that told us which bridges to

cross over the canal. It was very simple, all of the bridges had numbers on and you were instructed to cross over at bridge x. However, the distance of the bridge from the start didn't seem to add up. When I crossed a bridge at 5.3 miles there was an hour on the clock. It had taken me an hour to do 5 miles? So that's 9 hours for the whole thing? I did not feel like I was going that slowly. In fact I was absolutely certain I was not. At that early stage the worst thing to do would be to panic. It wasn't as if I'd be devastated with missing my target, the thing that concerned me was how I'd judged my pace so badly. Do I run faster? Settle on a slower time? Instead I just trusted my instincts and carried on as normal. Don't panic.

More bridges came and went with the same anomaly. I arrived at the first checkpoint, 9.8 miles in 1:44:00.

The runners had become very spaced out and the only time a passer-by would talk to me would be to apologise for their Doberman mauling me. For the next ten miles I had only my own brain for company.

So my train of thought commences. The top of my thighs hurt a bit, how are they going to cope with the remaining 35 miles? OK just don't think about them and the pain will go away, think about something else. Oh, bridge number 165. It's cool how every bridge has a number, it makes it easier for Trolls to tell people where they live. What happens when a new bridge is built between two consecutively numbered bridges? It would have to be called 165a or something. They couldn't possibly re-number all the bridges could they? The Trolls would get so confused and turn up to the wrong dinner parties and everything. Oh I need a wee. Look out for somewhere where I can ... oh damn it, there's a girl running behind me. I can't go in front of a girl, it would be rude, and I'll get stage fright anyway. Must hold it for a while and think of something else. Owwww my thighs hurt...

The way to do ultramarathons (so I've heard) is to break them down into manageable chunks. I discovered this in my second long run. To make a 6 hour training run interesting I decided to run the length of the Central Line from Ealing Broadway to Epping. All I was thinking about was getting to the next station. I have long suspected that many of these "zone 5 & 6" stations don't actually exist. It's just some map drawer taking the piss. However, I can confirm that they do all exist, even Theydon Bois. Whether it was necessary to run 35 miles to prove that is still in debate.

After about 3 hours of running, I reached the 20 mile checkpoint. I was still a little behind schedule but had caught up a bit, although my pace had not changed so I was still a little confused. My groin was hurting a bit more but that was all. About four people caught up to me at the checkpoint, but I stayed to stretch a bit whilst they ran on.

"Only a marathon to go. Ha Ha." I was allowed to say it, but if I'd heard anyone else say it they would end up in the canal.

The ground turned soft. The beautiful scenery gave way to flyovers. The picturesque buildings and boats became industrial estates and car parks. The even surface turned to mud. The friendly walkers and other joggers turned into grumpy fishermen and grumpier wives. I was headed towards Uxbridge.

One of the necessary preparations for a race like this is the kit you run in. A normal marathon would just be a case of trainers, shorts and a Serpie top. For this run though there was a lot more to it. I felt like a woman does before a Christmas party. "I could wear my black trainers, but then if it rains then my toes will get soggy, unless I wear the thicker socks. But they can sometimes give me blisters. I could wear shorts, but if it's cold I'll regret not wearing trousers, though my trousers don't have very big pockets so I can fit my balms in there. Do I wear the long sleeve Serpie top or the vest with a top underneath? I could wear my white top underneath the vest, but then the white would clash with my shoes".

I passed the marathon point in 4 hours. At the same time I'd caught up with another chap who was pleased to hear that we had passed that milestone. He then informed me that the measurements were not quite right as the route plan did not include the 1.5 miles we ran to the start of the canal. I could not quite believe how I had not figured this out but it explained exactly why I was behind. I was running a perfect pace, it's just that I'd ran 1.5 miles more and hence should be about 14 minutes behind.

I had now "raced" further than ever before. I had run more than a marathon and still had 17 miles to go. My legs were quite sore but I knew that meant nothing. One of the most important things I learned in the training is how far you can actually go when not feeling great.

The Thought-Express was to sit in the station for a little while as I had been joined by some of my friends. Nikolai and Lou asked if it was ok to run alongside me for a while. I felt like Forrest Gump. This was the part that everyone said would be most difficult. Gowan was there too. He managed to be there for every checkpoint. I felt that I was cheating slightly by having all of this great support. Most of the other runners were on their own, having travelled from far on the day to run in some place they didn't know. I'm glad they were there though.

Lou is always fun to have around when running. She would often remind me that my "form" was good (it wasn't) and that I was winning (I wasn't). I felt sorry for Nikolai though as he should have been running the whole thing with me. No, that's wrong. He would have run the first mile with me then the next time I'd see him would be at the finish in 7 hours eating a burger or something. It was great to see him back running after 3 months out.

The surface was now gravel. I had several small stones in my shoe but was scared of taking it off as I'd have ended up with even more small stones in my shoe. The gravel was quite tough and my legs were getting sorer. It was great having company though, even if one of them started coming out with this:

The Strange World of Lou Reeves 1 – "*I was just thinking, wouldn't it be awful if you found a dead body while running*?" Yes, it would.

The Strange World of Lou Reeves 2 – "*I've foolishly decided to wear a G-string and it's really uncomfortable*" I wouldn't know.

We approached the turning. 31 miles in and I was looking for a left turn, praying it would be obvious so I wouldn't miss it. I knew that as soon as I saw this, I would be on the home straight. And there it was; over a bridge then round to the left. Making the turn felt like the last turn in the London Marathon at Buckingham Palace where you can finally see the finish. Only I couldn't – it was still FOURTEEN miles away! However I could see the Wembley Arch, the first recognisable landmark I had seen so far.

The stretch between checkpoint 4 and checkpoint 5 was the hardest part. I had slowed a bit and was hurting more and more. If no one was around I may have considered walking, but luckily I was in very good company and a lot of friends had come out to see me run today. To start walking would be the end of me, and the thought of making everyone wait longer than necessary eliminated these cravings pretty quickly.

At 35 miles exactly Nikolai got a call. It was Ben who informed us that Ian Sharman had just won. Less than 6 hours had elapsed, I still had 10 miles to go, I was amazed that someone could run a distance that fast and while I'd like to have said well done to him I was heading into my own world of suffering with those 10 miles to go.

There was a seminar the night before this race where lots of tips and stories were exchanged about ultra-running. For many, including myself, this was their first. There was an air of nervous anticipation in the room. The guy leading the session says that the key to success is how you feel when running. How you feel determines the outcome of your run. He asked us to take a card and to write a few words on it to say how we wanted to feel the next day. Some then read out their suggestions. "To feel strong, in control, relaxed, the sense of achievement and to have a smile for the finish line". I couldn't decide what to put at the time but I did later add something to the card. Soon after Ian's victory I thought about what I'd written, and what I wanted from the race.

Nikolai and Lou were still beside me. Nikolai had been out of action for 3 months and was just returning to running. He should have been doing this too, but after 3 months he'd changed his goals and was really pleased to be running his longest run for ages.

Lou was in training for her first marathon. If she was feeling nervous about it she was hiding it well. She doesn't need to worry at all. This was her first long run for a while and she looked fine.

They both ran 13 miles with me and both looked like they were enjoying themselves.

I thought of the guys at the end who were waiting to buy me a beer at the nearest pub. How I was looking forward to seeing them.

Gowan had been there at every checkpoint along the way. Sometimes I'd only acknowledge his presence with a grunt. I felt guilty for a man who had thanklessly driven from point to point on a canal to cheer me on for 2 minutes at a time. Then I remembered that I'd sent him a text message at exactly half way. It said "Start singing the song", a reference to the Bon Jovi song that had become the official anthem for being half way through anything. I'd forgotten to ask him if he received it. I asked Nikolai, "Did Gowan like that text?" "Yes, he loved it". Brilliant, Gowan was happy too.

I thought about what was on my card. What I wanted from this race. I had written "I hope that my friends enjoy today as much as I do". 6 miles from the end I realised that I'd already got what I came for. The pain receded, the pace quickened.

The sky started to dim. I was lucky to be finishing while it was still light. Nikolai and Lou had left me to run the home straight. Harlesden isn't the most pleasant place to run at the best of times; however it contained a steel cold beauty. Iron bridges, rail depots, dockyards, rusty boats, abandoned warehouses and idle cranes. It felt like I was running back into London.

More friends joined me at this point, Ben and Simon came out to see me in the last few miles. I think they were anxious to get to the pub. I felt stronger and faster than I had been for the whole race. I had never felt this good in the last four miles of a marathon. Navi popped up out of nowhere and started running too. It was Forrest Gump all over again. There were a couple of really steep bridges along the way, but I had spent the day exploring the four dimensions of space and time and was not going to let a slight blip in the third dimension beat me.

I could now see three people ahead of me. If I picked up the pace I could catch them, all of them. Alas there was no time. If the race had been a mile longer I would have done it. Damn the race for being so short. I finished in 10th place, and got caught up in the euphoria so much that I nearly forgot to get my medal.

Congratulations were shared with the anonymous people around me, names such as Mark Cockbain and Mimi Anderson that I would forget in the euphoria of finishing my first ultramarathon but would come to know very well in the future. After that race I felt a craving to go back and talk to the "normal" people who had come to see me finish. Nikolai, Gowan, Lou, Simon and Navi were there and were joined by Ian and Lucy who commented that I didn't look like I had just run 47 miles. It was a fair comment because I didn't feel like it either. It seemed easier than I imagined.

We headed to the pub right at the finish line and I told tales of canal running while being plied with Guinness. I could get used to this. I felt the wonderful glow of a job well done as I sat in the pub and drank beer, the feeling I had hoped for when I finished the Marathon 3 months ago that never came. What probably made me feel even better though was that, despite the achievement of running 47 miles, this was just the first step on a long journey towards something else much bigger.

For the first time ever I think I got the "post-race blues". I had done the Tring2Town, run 47 miles well and had maintained my focus with no other ultra in mind. It was a funny time for me, there was a repeat of the 47 miles again in 2 weeks but I felt like that might be too much. To do a second ultra only 2 weeks after my first seemed silly at the time and I decided against it and regretted it later.

I had a few things lined up for the next couple of months. Firstly in March I was headed over to Death Valley; not to run, but to participate in a charity bike ride for the Mines Advisory Council with a friend from work. We were cycling around 60 miles a day for five days through the valley, where the maximum temperatures were going to be about 30°C. I did not really have in interest in cycling but thought this would be a great way of seeing the terrain that I intended to run in a few years.

Death Valley was awesome although the endurance element of it was not. I did not really struggle with the physical side of things though one memory of the week was in the heat of the day my bike stuck into a low gear while I was getting up a hill. That was the most effort I think I have ever put into a bike and I had to keep pedalling to stop myself falling off. At that time I yelled in frustration and thought for the first time that as a result I might not have the mental toughness to come back here and run in the summer.

After the Death Valley bike ride, I signed up for another marathon but did not really "train" for it. The week after I came back to the UK from the States, I was on a bus on the way to the Finchley 20, one of the oldest races in the UK and popular for those wanting a long run in training for a spring marathon.

On the bus I started chatting to a chap called Harley Inder, a very quick runner, about his upcoming races. He told me that his main event for the year was the Grand Union Canal race, a 145 mile non-stop run from Birmingham to London along the same canal that I had run my first ultra on.

Wow, they have this kind of thing in the UK too? I don't have to travel to Greece or America to do those kinds of races. That went onto my small but increasing "to-do" list.

That summer I ran the Prague marathon, kind of hoping for an improvement on my 3:12 but the beer was too nice there and having too much of that the night before delayed my arrival at the finish by about 20 minutes. I ran the Dartmoor Discovery 32 mile race, the Picnic (the hardest marathon in Britain) and two marathons in two days around Cheltenham. I ran both these marathons with Nikolai and on the second day really suffered with heat exhaustion. It was July and about 30°C and while struggling in the heat I only thought of how much worse this would be in Death Valley. I was obsessed with this race.

I was now into year two of my "Five year plan" to finish Badwater and as an intermediate step I handed over a £500 deposit to take part in a large marketing event called the "Marathon des Sables" (MdS) in 2009. The MdS is a race that pushes most people to their limits. Their overdraft limits that is.

I finished the year running marathons about every fortnight just to keep the distance ticking over. In November I decided to put my name down to do the Grand Union Canal Race (GUCR) the following May. The longest I had run so far was still 47 miles and I was applying to do a race where I'd add another 100 to that.

I was in a really good place by the end of the year. For the first time in my life I felt like I had a hobby that I could enjoy on my own and with others. I had gone from recluse to social butterfly as soon as I joined the Serpentine Running Club and started entering running events and my social circle grew.

And now I was into the slightly more niche area of "ultra-running" I was enjoying it even more.

5A

GOING BACK A BIT, MY FIRST MARATHON – LONDON 2000

I entered my first marathon as a joke to amuse friends at university. There was an article in some bloke's magazine along the lines of "Ten ways to be a proper man". I can't remember what the others were though I imagine they involve drinking vodka through your eyeballs or having a threesome with twin sisters. One of these was to run the London Marathon and it told you exactly how to do it. Just go to a running shop and pick up a magazine with an application form in.

I filled in the form and posted it off assuming that I would not get picked out of the lottery. However a few days before Christmas I received a letter to say "Congratulations James, you will be running in the Flora London Marathon in 2000" along with a magazine about how to train for it. I actually thought it would kill me.

My friends were in hysterics, excited about the possibility that I might actually die. I didn't know the first thing about running. I went to the gym and got on the treadmill to see how far I could run before I wanted to die. It was four miles. I vividly remember getting off that treadmill and the floor of the gym was still moving. I almost fell forward trying to calm myself after my endurance feat. I felt dizzy and sick as the wall of the room sped towards me and hit me in the face.

I did all of my "training" in the gym and it never occurred to me to run outside until a few weeks before the event where someone said, "yeah but the race is outside isn't it?" Fair point, so two weeks before the race I went outside and did my longest ever run, 13 miles around the streets of Manchester, and felt like my legs were going to break.

I still did not know anyone else who ran, let alone had run a marathon before. I travelled alone to London on the Saturday, stayed in a hotel, and made my way to the start in the morning. I was worried about so much before I even made it to the start line: What if my chip fell off? What if I was late or could not find the start? What if they looked at me and decided that I clearly could not run a marathon? I genuinely thought that they'd have people checking to make sure you "looked" like a runner and who wouldn't let you start if you didn't.

The nerves got to me and manifested in a strange way; my nose bled. This had happened before, when I was nervous about an exam, and when I had to go to school one day having not done my homework. It seems my nose bleeds at times of great stress which was the last thing I needed.

The London Marathon in 2000 had chip timing, though it did not measure your time from when you crossed the start to the finish, but from when the gun went off. This caused a stampede as the runners at the back raced to get to the start and into the race. I was more worried about haemorrhaging blood from my nose and after 20 minutes of waiting to start and with my nose still spewing I managed to find some toilets about half a mile in. I went inside and shoved tissue up my nose in a panic to stop the bleeding. I emerged from the toilet a few minutes later to be greeted by empty streets. I was last in the London Marathon, behind the lorries sweeping up the debris.

I quickly ran in between the lorries and followed the trail of litter to the runners and started to pick my way through the field. I was overwhelmed by the support and noise and the amount of others running beside me. I think I ran about 16 miles before I felt the need to walk but everyone around was yelling at me to keep going. I would respond by stumbling on, running and walking through the last ten miles. St Johns Ambulance were there and they thrust a handful of Vaseline at me. What was I supposed to do with this? It seems obvious now, but I really did not know anything about running marathons and did what soft footballers did with it and rubbed in on my legs thinking it would keep them warm.

It was a truly amazing experience and I crossed the line in 4:55 (or 4:35 by my watch). I had no time in mind when I came here – I just wanted not to die.

There was no one waiting for me at the end. The euphoria of finishing my first marathon was diminished by having no one to share it with. I shook hands with some of the people near me but I did not know these people and I would never meet them again. I just collected my stuff and hobbled onto a train and went back to Manchester.

I did the London Marathon again in 2003 and 2004, while I was a student in Manchester and again while not knowing anyone else who runs marathons. My training for each was very random and last minute; I think the longest training runs I did for the latter two were about 15 miles and I only did those once. It was a very lonely hobby I had. I enjoyed the running but craved having someone to talk to who understood what was involved.

In 2005 when I changed jobs in London and one of the first things I did was join a running club. I was issued with my work laptop and Googled two things; "house share in London" and "running club in London". The former led me to a gay casual sex site, the latter led me to the Serpentine running club.

The Serpentine running club is massive with over 2,000 members and is based in central London. I joined and ran on their Wednesday night session which involved running 7.2 miles around 3 parks of London. For the first time in my life I actually ran with other people. It was fantastic.

I went along every week and signed up for the Berlin Marathon as a few of the guys I had started running with suggested, and then started to do some training distance to cover those 26.2 miles. We would build up our runs on Wednesday from seven miles to 20 miles and then head to the pub for a well-deserved drink. We were all of different standards and all looking forward to heading out to Germany to race. It was my first race outside of the UK.

When we got to Berlin we met with even more Serpies for dinner, there were about 20 of us there. I could not believe that, even in a completely different city in a different country, I was bumping into people from my running club. During the race I got chatting to a guy called Mike who was wearing Serpentine's distinctive red and gold, only to discover that he lived two streets away from me in Ealing. I ran that marathon in a PB of 3:47, and in the finish area I was greeted by friends and waited for other friends. It was a long way from my previous races where I just headed straight home; I really felt like I was part of a running community now and I loved it.

I did lots of other races with the club as well as club training runs and social events. In fact, races always felt like social events; you'd turn up on a Sunday morning somewhere, race a distance and then head off to the pub afterwards.

My involvement with the Serpentine club grew over the following years. I became involved in volunteering for the huge amount of races the club organised and helped out in training sessions. I started to blog about races that I had done and wrote an article in our club magazine "Serpentimes" about my 47 mile Tring2Town race. From then on I got a reputation for being a very long distance runner, often turning up to things like half marathons to be asked "Isn't this a bit short for you?" There were not a huge number of people at the club who would run further than a marathon. I liked the attention of being the odd one out but I did start to miss that community feeling that I got doing shorter races as I didn't really know anyone else who ran ultras.

All that started to change towards the end of the year when an email sent from club member Rob Westaway asking if anyone fancied the Round Rotherham 50 miler in December. I had heard about this event and was excited about getting another ultra in before the end of the year.

We travelled up on the train the night before, me, Rob, Mark Braley and Alan Hall, each of whom I'd only just met but each of whom I would get to know very well. I was not in a good state though. I had gone to a work party a few days before and picked up some nasty food poisoning which meant that I had not eaten for two days and needed to go to the toilet far too frequently. Not ideal.

The Round Rotherham 50 is one of the best known and most established UK ultras. It is a 50 mile loop in Yorkshire off-road on muddy tracks and fields. Held in mid-December there is always a lack of daylight and usually lots of rain. It did not disappoint this year. It was a self-navigation event with about six checkpoints along the way with food and drinks. We set out in the dark at about 7 am, and I quickly lost sight of the others as they sped away. I could not risk running fast in case my tender bowels would complain.

I got to the first checkpoint at 10 miles in fairly good time (about 1:30) and thought I would have a good chance of finishing. It was our club Christmas party again that night and we all wanted to finish in good time to get back down there and drink. Rob, Alan and Mark were making great time but as soon as I had left the Checkpoint my stomach started to complain and I was reduced to a walk.

I was downing Imodium like they were Jelly Babies, I must have had about 10 in a few hours. Nothing would stop the relentless flow of poison leaving my rear end. This was the first time I recall having to have a shit outdoors. My inexperience and modesty caused me to find somewhere well off the beating track to do this, modesty that would decline later on in my ultra-running life.

I reached the 17 mile checkpoint in around three hours and decided that as I could not walk for more than half a mile without having to stop to crap that I may as well quit. As I was waiting for a taxi to take me back to the school hall it started to piss it down.

I was on a lonely train journey home again, gutted for not finishing and with a lot of time to think about it. It would have been great to talk to the others about the race afterwards, talking about our shared experiences is one of the best things about this hobby. I went to the party a little deflated and didn't really enjoy myself, particularly when I had to run into the street and vomit.

But for me the year finished on a high. Not through any event as such but by knowing that I now had a proper hobby and people to do it with. I realised that I just loved to race ultramarathons and loved spending time with others who do too. I vowed next year to make the most of all the opportunities that came, and sign up for everything. The 5 year plan for Badwater was ticking along nicely but in the meantime I had another big and scary race to obsess about; I had signed up for the Grand Union Canal Race, 145 miles of canal from Birmingham to London. It was going to be the biggest physical and mental test of my life.

In 2008 I was getting to know more ultra-runners and finding out about more and more events. January and February are very busy in the UK ultra-running calendar and I was taking full advantage. I was signing up to everything and putting my races into a spreadsheet so I could keep track of what I had entered. Accidentally entering two races on the same day did happen occasionally.

On presenting this spreadsheet to my non-running girlfriend, I did spot that I had not left any weekends free for time with her. That was when it was time for us to go our separate ways – I had run out of colours anyway.

First up was the Thames Path Ultra, 50 miles along the river from Reading to Shepperton. The path was flooded and we had to divert away but not before spending some time waist deep in water, falling into the river on a couple of occasions.

The week after, I ran the Portland marathon in Dorset. This was where I met Oli Sinclair who drove me down and we debated about how much to pay for parking: "We'll be done in 4 hours won't we? Let's just pay for 4 hours". I was happy to pay the extra 50p for 6 hours parking (I ran 4:03).

The following week, I ran back to back 40 milers along the canal again. This was the first time I had done such a thing and it felt much easier than I imagined. Running the first day in 5:45 then the second in 6:15 – not such a massive difference between the two, which I was really pleased with. Maybe 145 miles in one go would be doable after all?

The next week was the Punchbowl 30 miler, organised by the Long Distance Walkers Association (LDWA) who allow runners to participate in some of their fantastic events. I felt like I was exploring the UK with the running that I was doing. The Devils Punchbowl is an alien looking crater in Surrey and makes for a fantastic run.

Next up was the Thames Meander, 55 miles along the river. This was the longest run I had ever done and again it went fine, despite getting a bit lost. I ran it in just under 9 hours and the most pleasing part was that the last 5 miles felt the fastest. Having run 50 miles I felt like I could still hammer in for another 5 and I did. I ran with Stuart Gillet who had come second in the GUCR the year before and was telling me how hard that race is. Back at the finish I saw another guy with a previous year's GUCR top on and asked him about the race. He told me that if I can run 55 miles in 9 hours I should be going for a time like 32 hours for the GUCR. I had an optimistic target of 36 hours in my head, but would be happy with a finish within the cut-off of 45 hours. I couldn't wait.

Later I did the Jurassic Coast Challenge, 3 marathons in 3 days along the beautiful but very hilly Dorset coast.

This was the first time I was doing heavy mileage on 3 days. There was a lot of navigation, plenty of wrong turns, slips and falls, walking breaks and rain, but I had the most fantastic weekend. After each day of running we'd stay in a chalet and have a BBQ. I felt like I could live like this.

On the start of the third day I got out of bed and could barely walk. The gentle downhill slope to the start was agony and I really wondered how I could even get going let alone run a marathon (which was actually more like 30 miles). Sure enough I got moving and then after a mile or so of hobbling I actually felt much better. I was tired the whole time but amazed that my legs could at least break into some sort of run.

The week after the Jurassic Coast my legs and body were pretty knackered but I decided to run the Bungay Marathon the following week anyway. At this point marathons were really just Sunday long runs and I wanted to take it easy and see what happened. I ran at a steady pace for the first half of the two lap course and had to stop a couple of times to stretch. However I cruised around the second half and came in to the finish in 3:16, only 4 minutes outside my best. It felt really odd that I should be able to do that and started to make me wonder about those months I spent "marathon training" a few years ago. This was a much more enjoyable way of getting good times.

I ran the Bath Beat 26.5 miles (the world's shortest ultramarathon) the next week, the Exmoor coastal marathon after that, and spent my mid-weeks running lots too as I tried to build up the miles in preparation for the long run in May. It was only a month away now, time to reign it in a bit and rest. I had one last weekend of fun.

In late April there is the 3 peaks fell race in Yorkshire,

24 miles of mountain climbing and fell running. There are plenty of opportunities to run in between the 3 mountain climbs but the climbs themselves are lung busting. On the up I was crawling on my hands and knees and going down I was too scared of the sheer drops to go very fast. I finished in a reasonable time and then headed down to Stratford for the Shakespeare Marathon the next day.

The plan was to take it very easy. I had just run a tough 24 mile fell race the day before and had done about 20 tough races already this year. I set out at what felt like a jog but found myself continually passing people. The marathon was very well organised, it had the feel of a big event without the claustrophobia that often comes with them.

I tried not to look at my watch too much and didn't really believe what it said but when I saw the clock on the finishing line it became very real. I ran 3:07. five minutes off my PB. The day after a 24 mile fell race. Jogging.

I wasn't going for a time and being able to say I have a faster marathon time now was quite nice. Runners are always tagged by their marathon time. "Yeah so and so, he is a sub 3 marathon runner". Since doing ultras I've stopped using marathon times as benchmarks of progress and ability. The best bit about it was that I felt in the shape of my life.

I learned so much in those 4 months it's impossible to describe. Talking to others and experiencing races allowed me to pick up so much knowledge. My understanding of nutrition, hydration, training, kit, recovery, stretching, shoes and everything multiplied. The most important things I learned were things I learned about myself. The capabilities that I had for endurance running, most notably:

- I can run 40 miles in one day then do the same the next at not much slower pace
- I can run for 50 miles and still feel like running fast for another 5
- I can wake up one morning unable to walk but still able to run 30 miles
- I can still run 26 miles quite fast the day after a hard run
- I can cope with 100 mile weeks and 20 marathons/ultras in 4 months without breaking down

I continued to demonstrate this fitness in the next two weeks, running 1:28 in a half marathon then 39 minutes in a 10k the week later. Next week was the Grand Union Canal Race.

6

GRAND UNION CANAL RACE 2008 – 145 MILES FROM BIRMINGHAM TO LONDON

I have thought about finishing this race for well over a year now. It has been the single biggest thing on my mind since I decided I was going to do it. In all the previous training runs and races I thought about the moment I'd cross the line. That always motivated me.

I thought about it when justifying what I had to do to get here. The time and cost, drifting away from some friends, stalling my career and a failed relationship. The glow I got from just thinking about finishing this made it all seem worth it. I truly hope that sometime on Sunday those sacrifices would be justified.

Birmingham

The alarm woke me up at 4am. I hit snooze and closed my eyes. Then, in an unexpected moment of clarity so early in the morning I thought, "What difference is another 9 minutes sleep going to make to what I have planned today?" Arriving at the answer pretty quickly, I jumped out of bed and staggered for the light.

Maypole in Birmingham is a strange place to put a Travelodge. I can't imagine anyone having any real reason to come here, except of course for one day of the year where the car park fills with very sedate looking men in full running/hiking gear and some equally nervous family members organising stacks of food big enough to feed the whole family for a week.

Gas Street Basin

I knew what the start looked like from the videos and photos online. When I first got there is was quite empty which felt strange. All the runners had spilled onto a nearby street, almost as if they were waiting for a coach to collect them. All were talking with quiet confidence about running this race. All were set on finishing but in reality less than half would. It didn't seem to dampen any spirits though, everyone I'm sure was looking forward to the start in their own way. I was.

The horn sounded soon after we all decided to huddle together by the side of the canal. It was a very civilised and English start: "After you sir, no please I insist". Much more respect and decorum than in other races where there is a melee at the start for the sake of gaining a few yards. A few yards don't really matter here, not in a race that I'll still be running this time tomorrow. I was in it now.

I'd not let myself think about running this race until I was actually doing it since all I wanted to think about was finishing. For as long as possible I just imagined what I would feel like when I crossed the line and only now did I start to really think about the 30 odd hour slog to get there.

I tried to resist any attempts to draw me in to thinking about actually running it. This explains why I was quite indifferent in a meeting I had with my support crew a week earlier to discuss practicalities. I didn't want to think practically about running this race, it was too hard. They wanted to know what food to bring, what clothes, estimated times, whether I'd like to sleep. I could not answer any of it. I just wanted to pretend that it wasn't going to happen.

Opening the race instructions and touching my race number made my skin go cold. Packing all the food and drink to take to the hotel made me feel sick. For so long I had described this race as a moment in the future, obsessing about the successful outcome of finishing. I could no longer think just about this moment, I had to think about getting there. 45 hours, 145 miles, 500,000 steps, 20,000 calories, one sun-rise, maybe 2 sun-sets. It was almost as if someone had rudely put these obstacles in between me and my finish.

The first few miles did involve ducking below a few low bridges. I hoped there were not too many of these later; I'm not much good at this at the best of times. I ran with Shaw Pye for the first 5 miles. After less than a mile we took a wrong turning and ran into a dead end – as if the race wasn't long enough. It wasn't the distance that mattered; if I can get lost one mile into the race with loads of other runners around in the daylight, then how will I fare when it's dark, there is no-one around, I've been running for 20 hours and hallucinating?

Apparently you lose an inch in height when you run a marathon. That meant that I stood to lose 5.7 inches by the end. I'll only be 5"4 and those low bridges would no longer be a problem.

Shaw was running a bit quicker than I wanted to; trying to keep up with the lead group of about six. Rather than openly admit to wanting to go slower I said I needed to duck into the bushes for a minute. I did and watched them slowly disappear into the distance.

Catherine De Barnes Bridge – 10.7 miles

The first checkpoint was after 10.7 miles at Catherine De Barnes Bridge. By this time I was already alone. I put on a sprint finish for the cameras and met Campbell, Ben and Simon who were 3 quarters of my support crew for the race. I felt nice and warmed up and it was good to see the first checkpoint and my crew, all looking very smart in their official supporters' jerseys.

It's funny how I now consider 11 miles as a warm-up. 3 years ago that was a long run. I'd spent the last week worrying about some stabbing pains I was getting in my legs. I was not carrying any injuries but parts of my legs were hurting for no reason. I dismissed this as my brain trying to trick me into backing out of doing something stupid. I ignored my brain which is often the right thing to do because sometimes it's an idiot. The pains in my legs were no longer there, I felt good although I was only 8% into the race.

I was at the second checkpoint at Hatton Locks (22 miles) in about 4 hours. I saw Harley Inder who had run it last year and was part of a film crew taking footage of this event. I told him that the shorts he was wearing were criminal. He said I was looking good and that I should take it easy. A long way to go.

Between 20-40 miles my support crew were getting concerned that I was not taking enough food. I was getting plenty of energy drink but the plan to eat constantly along the way was not happening. I'd advised them before that they would probably have to force feed me as I'm unlikely to want to eat much, even though I need to. I always took protein bars with me but just ended up carrying them along for another 10 miles. At about 35 miles I was treated to a battered sausage. Not the kind of food I planned on eating but it went down a treat. I think Campbell had meant to get me a sausage roll but the guy in the chip shop was a bit confused.

I'll introduce my support crew in order of appearance.

Campbell I've only just met. He runs marathons and ultras and appears to be really excited and intrigued about supporting me on this race. I'm really glad he is so enthusiastic, I am going to rely on that.

Ben I've known for a few years now. He runs the occasional marathon when he's not writing theses. Since he got a proper job he has taken a worrying turn towards triathlons. I hope that by doing this I can help convince him to come back.

Simon has always been a (very slightly) faster marathon runner than me (5 seconds sometimes). I spent a few weeks as a faster runner than him, however he beat my time again the week before. That's enough about Simon for now.

Gowan likes to get himself in situations that may result in being moaned at by me. He supported me on my first ultra and as long as he's there I know I won't be running my last. He laces cakes with Malibu and pizzas with mushrooms so I'll have to be careful what I take from him.

Around 40 miles the path became quite overgrown and the footing was a bit more difficult. Nettles and other plants had taken over the path, making it difficult to keep up a good pace, which was probably a good thing. No point rushing. I was startled for a moment when I almost stepped on a snake. I knew that there were a couple of snake species resident in England but never thought I'd encounter one in a race. I sent a message to the support to say I just saw one and for reassurance that I'm not going delirious yet – I wasn't even a third of the way in. Unfortunately I misspelled the work snake and my support then took the piss out of me for being scared of a nasty shake. Great, it was barely afternoon and they all thought I had lost it already.

At 46 miles the canal went underground and some minor navigation was required. This was the first time I took my map out of my pocket. The path basically goes up a long incline through some fields and at the top of this hill were my support team. They informed me that I was 6th and looking much better than those in front of me upon whom I was gaining. It was time I sent an update to everyone.

I set up a text group on my phone to keep people up to date with how I was doing. Partially because I'm sure they wanted to know but mostly because the replies gave me a lift. It was 2 pm and I sent "**46 miles in 8 hours. Only 99 to go** J ". I looked forward to reading the replies.

The one reply that stuck with me for some time was from Ian who congratulated me on "a good start". I suspect that although he was being factually accurate in his appraisal of my first 46 miles there was an undertone of sarcasm there. I did think about it for a while (had quite a long time to think). 16 months ago I was making a really big deal of a 45 mile race that I trained for quite a lot. I finished it and was really pleased with the outcome and wrote a story about how fulfilling the whole experience was. Look where I am now. 16 months on I've just completed the same distance, a bit slower but feeling very fresh but with 99 miles to go. 45 miles seemed enormous to me 18 months ago but here I was running in a race where that enormous distance was nothing more than "a good start". It might have depressed me, instead it reminded me about how far I've come over the past year. The start was good, now for the middle bit.

The middle bit

My Garmin usually tells me when I've run further than I ever have done before. The battery life is only 10 hours so I couldn't wear it in this race (unless I had 4 of them). I wanted to at least congratulate myself silently when I pass this longest point which would be 54 miles, however I had no way of knowing. I did not think too much about the distance or the time, I just kept reminding myself how good I was feeling in what was now the longest in both time and distance that I'd ever run,. I stayed focused on the finish. Not long after that my crew supplied me with a subway, Italian BMT, to celebrate. I should have mentioned before that I don't like sweet corn, I'm suspicious of its crunchy noise and it has no place in a sandwich. As I was ungraciously devouring it the film crew approached and asked if I wanted to be interviewed. I said yes and continued eating. I'm not too sure what I said to them at that point, it was probably great marketing for subway though.

I'd been advised by a friend that my crew would have to really force food into me. I told them as much and now I was there still I resisted food sometimes. I previously ran the Thames Meander (54 miles 9 hours) with very little solid food and at 60 miles was still not feeling hungry. It's strange how watching a film or getting a train makes me hungry but 10 hours of running does not. I was going to need them later on to get a bit more aggressive in their feeding. I was always going to say no and that would have been disastrous.

About 60 miles in I saw a runner ahead. He was going too slowly to be a recreational jogger so assumed he must be part of the race. It then occurred to me that I'd run over 50 miles without seeing any other runner. I had no idea it would space out this much. My preference was to run on my own but I'd always imagined that there would be people just ahead and just behind. I don't know why – dividing 75 people across 145 miles makes for lots of lonely runners. I chatted briefly and passed him. He looked like he was struggling. Another couple of miles I overtook another who was also struggling. They'd hit walls early on that surely I would hit later. I couldn't think about it now, I just had keep going and deal with that if/when it happens.

Around 65 miles the canal goes underground again and I had to run along some roads above to re-join it. I needed to ask for directions a couple of times and was heading in the right direction. I got the first pangs of paranoia as I followed the route given to me. Because I couldn't see the canal straight away I started walking and looking around. I followed a path with a big yellow arrow on it (I worried that this might be someone taking the piss). I jogged up this path and then for some reason turned around and ran as I was sure this was not the way, until another runner came and insisted that it was. He'd done it last year so following him was fine. Within a minute we were back on the canal.

"Don't you get bored when you are running for so long?" Is the second most common question asked of me by non-runners, the first being "Isn't it bad for your knees?" – The answer to both is emphatically no. I can't really remember exactly what things I thought over the course of this run while I still had control of my thoughts. It's as if running moves you to a lower state of consciousness where you are free to think silly things that may not make sense.

I thought about how vicious geese get when they have chicks and what my chances would be if I had to fight one. At this stage I was a good bet, later on I'd have struggled. I thought about the cow that charged at me in the Dartmoor Discovery race last year and wondered whether I could currently outrun one. I probably had the advantage due to the terrain. I tried not to think about work too much, I was here to enjoy and challenge myself, neither of which ever happens to me there. Then I got a craving for a Coke. I never usually drink Coke but I just really wanted one just then. My crew obliged.

I thought about finishing mostly, that moment of seeing the finish come into view and then sprinting for it. I looked forward to having the medal hung round my neck as a symbol of completion. Medals are nice to have as a reminder of races you have done, though I doubted I'd need anything to remind me of this race. They are nice mementos.

A GUCR finisher's medal would be my second most prized possession, the first being something I already own. Earlier in the week I'd bought a one way train ticket from London to Birmingham, a fairly unexciting piece of card. If I finish this race this will be transformed from a worthless piece of paper to my most treasured thing. If I didn't then it was going in the bin.

To answer the original question again, no I don't get bored while running because I'm not boring. I can entertain myself with my own imagination in a way that maybe they cannot. I felt sorry for them, sat at home waiting for the Eurovision Song Contest to come on.

Still feeling good I came to the 70 mile checkpoint and met my team. Gowan had now arrived so Ben and Simon were planning on going to a hotel they booked to get some sleep. Alright for some. I was interviewed again by the film crew who again commented on how fresh I looked. I was still in 4th place and looking strong. They asked what was on my mind and I said running in the dark and staying awake. They'd asked how I planned on dealing with that and my honest response was that I don't know. One regret in the training going into this race was that I'd not done any night running before. This was going to be the biggest challenge. I still had a couple of hours of sunlight though and my original goal was to get to half way by sundown. I was hours ahead.

Only about 85 miles to go

Running through Milton Keynes was more pleasant than I thought. Gowan and Campbell were planning on meeting me about every 5 miles at this stage but they missed me at one meeting place because I was still going faster than they expected. Faster than I expected to be doing at this stage. Time for another text update to my list.

"78 miles. 3 Marathons. 14 hours. Feeling ok still. 4th place".

About 80 miles in I saw Shaw ahead of me walking. He looked very unhappy. He'd sat down at the previous checkpoint to eat and done something to his hip which prevented him from running. His Dad was walking beside him. I chatted briefly and said that sometimes these things just go away in races like this. I hoped he'd get back running soon and would have liked to have run with him, especially as night was falling. Since I still had running in me I went ahead, now in 3rd place.

I didn't enjoy overtaking Shaw. I know it's a race and all that but there seemed to be something undignified about passing someone who had been unlucky as he had. Obviously I wanted to do the best I could but I wanted to be competing against others at their best. I was also worried that just overtaking him would have bad consequences for his morale. I know that if I was walking and someone passed me in that fashion it could break me.

Nightfall

The 85 mile checkpoint just outside Milton Keynes was where Campbell started to run with me. Night was falling and I was starting to feel sleepy. I'd been up since 4 am and didn't get a great deal of sleep the night before. It worried me that I was feeling this way even before the sun had gone down. I started to think about those 9 minutes I gave up in the morning.

Leighton Buzzard was the 92 mile point. We met Gowan who was waiting by a bridge next to a pub with some rather unsavoury chavs in the beer garden. They seemed disturbed by the thought of people out running at this time of night when they could be in a pub drinking hooch. My attention was then distracted by Pat Robbins and his support runner cruising past me like I was standing still. He was looking in really good form. 92 miles and still that fresh? I looked like that about 10 miles ago. That seemed like a long time ago.

I asked Campbell to run ahead of me so I could follow. The headlamps made parts of his clothing glow as he ran along the canal in the pitch black. I couldn't imagine doing this without a team of people to support me. I don't think I really appreciated how hard it would be to support a race like this, neither did I really thank the guys for giving up their time to support me. My job was straightforward if not easy, just keeping running till the end of the canal in London. Theirs was not so easy. They had to make sure they navigated to the right places at the right times without much info from me. Getting the right food, saying the right things – I wouldn't have liked to be there without them. We passed lots of houseboats and could see the TVs inside.

The next checkpoint was 100 miles and in Tring. I'd been thinking of this for a long time. 100 miles was a milestone in itself but arriving at Tring would feel like I was almost there. I've run to London from there twice now and the path from there on would perhaps seem familiar.

It just didn't seem to come though. I felt like I was running forever and Tring was getting no nearer. Several times I stopped to get the map out and confirm that we were headed in the right direction. It seems like irrational paranoia as I write this but the consequences of taking a wrong turn could have ended my race. In fact we were not running that slow, it just felt that way. Time seemed to be standing still. There were quite a few locks which involved inclines and I was in no mood to run up them. After what seemed like hours I finally arrived into the 100 mile checkpoint in 19 hours. Well ahead of target (24 hours) but had quickly gone from feeling "quite good" to "quite poor".

Harley and the film crew were there again and interviewed me as I drank hot tea. He congratulated me on getting there so quickly and still in good shape. I can't remember what they asked me or what answers I gave. I think I still managed to fool others into thinking I was still ok. I wasn't.

I met Harley just over a year ago when he was in training for this race. We were on a bus from Ealing on our way to the Finchley 20. I was aware of the race at that point but didn't know too much about it. We chatted about this, the Marathon des Sables and Tring2Town (which we'd both done a month back). It is possible that this conversation prompted me to start my obsession with finishing this race in 2008. I can't really remember where it started. That day was not so successful for me, I didn't even finish the 20 miles, I dropped out at 15. Now look at me, I've just finished that race 5 times over.

Tring2Town again

We got moving again, my chatting had died down somewhat. I yelled "GO" and "STOP" to Campbell like he was a husky dog. The plan was to meet Ben in Berkhamsted and then run 17 miles with him. I didn't really bother myself with the details of how they planned to support me; I just wanted to have my stuff as near to me as possible.

About 10 minutes after leaving the Tring checkpoint Campbell pointed out the start of the Tring2Town race, a slope leading from the main road to the canal. I was devastated. I thought I'd just passed 100 miles when in fact this was the 100 mile point. There are 45 miles to go from *here*. It shouldn't have mattered too much, it was only a mile, however at this stage the little things were getting blown up by my faltering and tired mind. This was just the start.

Berkhamsted was at 103 miles and this is where we saw Ben and Gowan. We had to be quiet as we were outside someone's house at nearly 2 in the morning. Ben was to run with me for 17 miles until we met Simon who was parked in Springwell Locks near Watford. I wanted to get there by 6 am (more than 4 hours) so that I could send my next update to inform people that I had less than a marathon to go within 24 hours.

I was in quite a lot of pain by this point. Both quads were very sore, the left knee hurt along the ITB and both ankles were sore. I wanted some Nurofen gel. When I was informed that this was with Simon 17 miles away I fumed. I wanted it even more. I asked (ordered) Ben to start running and I followed. He kept a greater distance between us than Campbell did which was probably wise. I was in a foul mood and was only capable of talking in catty remarks. I complained some more about how much pain I was in and how I needed the Nurofen and how 17 miles was too far to go. I moaned then moaned some more. Then it started to piss it down.

We passed Berkhamsted station which is where we crossed a bridge. I remembered this from before and the familiarity gave me a short-lived boost. Hemel Hempstead took an age to get through. My legs felt like they were falling apart, the backs of my knees felt like they'd been slashed. I moaned some more about Nurofen and hot food. I didn't even want to eat hot food, I just wanted to moan about it. I'd been transformed from the chirpy runner I was at 92 miles to a monster.

The key to running races like this is to be able to separate your body and mind. Your body will keep pressing on long after the mind has told it that you should stop. I felt it even before the race started and had to tell myself that it wasn't real. Some of the pain I was feeling now was real for sure but my body was really beating my brain up about it. I'd let the suffering into my mind and it spread like an infection. Within 10 miles I'd gone from mentally strong to mentally weak. My body was ready to stop a few hours before and at about 117 miles it had convinced my mind to do the same.

There were many symptoms of this surrender. I was flying off the handle at any slight obstacle, like two bridges with the same number on or lack of hot food. I was disgracefully rude to those who'd given up a lot of their time to help me through this. I started to feel cold. My mind was telling me that dropping out would not be that bad, 120 miles is still pretty good, something to be proud of.

For the first time in the race I was unable to think of finishing; only of the misery I was going through right now. Since I couldn't see the finish anymore I couldn't see the point of running. I started walking.

At about 3 miles till the next checkpoint it was getting light again. It did not have the lifting effect I was expecting. This had been a moment I was banking on to spur me on whereas it just reminded me of how little ground I had covered during the night. I told Ben to run off and come back with the Nurofen. I doubt it would have made much difference. In fact Ben had long considered giving me Imodium and telling me it was Nurofen for the placebo effect. It may have worked, but then I would have killed Ben for keeping that from me all this time. I looked on ahead for what seemed like hours. Occasionally trying to get back into a run but unable to I limped on and started performing the worst case scenario calculations. I had no idea what pace I was doing but figured I couldn't be hobbling faster than 3 miles an hour. With 27 miles to go at 24 hours on the clock that would be another 10 hours of running for a 34 hour finish – and a really miserable 10 hours at that.

I sent another update at 6 am – "**24 hours. 118 miles. Still 4th but walking now**". I guess I wanted to inform people not to expect too much from me now, I wasn't expecting much from myself.

I saw Simon running up the other way at last and he smeared my legs with the Nurofen I'd been moaning about for hours. I hobbled into the checkpoint at 120, well over an hour later than planned.

I sat down for the first time in a day. I took off my shoes and socks and discovered 3 enormous purple blisters at the ends of my feet. For about 50 miles I'd been thinking there was a stone in my shoe but could not find it. Now I knew. I ate a hot sausage roll and drank some tea. I changed my shoes and socks, though not without moaning that I didn't have my preferred shoes available. Ben and Simon commented (privately) that I was having a J-Lo moment and considered going out to get some rose petals to lay down in front of me as I ran. I'm not much of a drama queen usually, I guess it's useful to know that I only become one after 100 odd miles of running and 24 hours of non-stop movement. I hope they forgive my frivolous demands; they know I'm still Jenny from the block.

I sat for about 20 minutes in all. Stopping for so long can be dangerous in this race, you feel like you are only 20 minutes from a coma at any point. I needed to be helped out of the chair and standing up was painful. I could no longer isolate parts of my legs that hurt, the whole lot was burning. There were no photos taken that I recall and the film crew had gone to the end. I wondered how long it would be till I was there. Simon was ready to run with me for a while but I said I wanted to be alone now. The rain fell heavier as I limped down a slope to re-join the canal. *Less than a marathon to go.*

I'm no psychologist but I am aware of the presence of subconscious thought. It's what takes over when snap decisions are required, like life and death situations. It drives instinctive and instant behaviours when the body is under threat and logical conclusions of the rational mind can't come quick enough. I don't know whether this extends to longer time periods when the body is under prolonged duress. I can't explain it.

I still had plenty of time to finish this race. I still could have crawled to the end in under 45 hours (the cut-off). I still could have walked in 36 and got the time I expected in the first place. Time and place became unimportant at this point, all I wanted to think about was finishing.

I tried subsequently in the race to pick the words to describe what happened to me at this moment but I still can't do it. It seemed to happen independently of any action or decision by myself. The best I can do is to say that at Springwell Lock at 7 am on Sunday 25th May my body and my mind had given up. As I descended that small slope and the rain fell harder my soul stood up and told those two quitters to go and fuck themselves, I'm going to cross that finish line with dignity. I started running again.

The first mile was excruciating, like running through acid. I just leant forward slightly and ran straight through all the puddles. The water on my calves gave slight relief, my body still complained and my mind concurred. I didn't care; I'd fallen out with those two and was not listening to them anymore. I promised myself I'd keep on running till the end and that was what I was doing.

The slow shuffle increased in pace. It was not long before I felt like I was running again. I met Ben and Simon at 125 miles and did not want to stop. I think I was running at 6mph for the first time in 50 odd miles. I felt great, I didn't know whether it was hurting anymore because I wasn't listening. I continued to the next meeting place which was 130. I could not quite believe the turnaround. I'd won them back, sailing through 130 miles I had managed to convince my body and conscious self that I was going to do this. I stopped under a bridge to take a call from Campbell who had now re-joined the crew. I asked him to meet me at Bulls Bridge Junction (the left turn that signals only a half marathon to go).

Running long distances can take you on an emotional rollercoaster, that's part of the appeal. I recall from my early marathons the low feelings when quite a way into the race but still far from the end. Having run quite a few now I have to look to harder things to get these feelings back. The thought of starting a race that I might not be able to finish was exhilarating. I was not at all prepared for this, the sick feeling I had in the days before the race, the phantom pains, and dreams about being in the race.

I knew there would be highs and lows but did not expect the lows to be so low. 10 miles previously I was crushed, possibly the worst state I've been in my life. In the space of 2 hours that turned around into a euphoric feeling unlike anything I'd felt before. For the first time since Berkhamsted I could see the finish again, I thought about crossing the line. The emotion completely overwhelmed me, so much so that as I approached a gate I stopped, hung onto the railing and cried.

It was only for 10 seconds or so, I just leant into my arms and sobbed for a while. It came on suddenly and I didn't really care if anyone was around. This was possibly the highest I've felt in my life and I was going to savour this moment. About

9.30 am, pissing down with rain along a polluted canal towpath in a building site in Hayes, I had a life affirming moment I will never forget. It was beautiful.

Soon the nasty logical brain took over, but at least it was on my side now. “Come on James, stop being such a baby. You’re a grown man, snap out of it.” Grrrrrrr.

I was still sobbing slightly when I met Campbell and Gowan at Bulls’ Bridge. They decided not to film me, though I wouldn’t have minded. I was so glad to see them and I hoped they’d forgive my behaviour earlier. I felt so good I almost felt guilty since I can’t believe they would have felt the same. I was on the home straight now, 13.5 miles to go.

Inevitably the pace slowed again, I didn’t mind too much. The logical brain did make a good point that I have actually run quite far and there was good reason for my legs to hurt and my pace to be quite slow. We were back on speaking terms, since now we had the same goal.

With about 10 miles to go I met Dave Ross and his friend Edward who had originally come to support someone else who had unfortunately dropped out earlier. It was great to see them and I felt a bit more conversational than before (but not much). I wasn’t really ready for two way conversation, but it was nice just having them in front of me and chatting, except of course when they mentioned a 100 miler that Edward did a few weeks ago that he didn’t finish because he got back spasms with four miles to go. I have SEVEN miles to go, SHUT UP.

The rain stopped but the puddles made the run difficult. I was in no mood to dance around them so I ran through most, the water helped the pain. Dave and Edward ran on ahead as the canal started to get busy. I’d been told that the next runner behind me was “miles” behind, I didn’t really come here with a competitive finish in mind but felt that 4th has been mine since half way. I didn’t want to let it go. Quite often a fresh jogger would come up behind and overtake; I just assumed that anyone who can run faster than me at this point clearly isn't in this race. My race number did say "145 miles" and "Birmingham – London" on it, I kind of hoped that those out and about on the canal would see that.

Six miles to go I saw Simon and Ben who supplied me with a nice warm long sleeved Serpie top. This was the 4th top I'd worn in the race. I put it on and felt like I was glowing, it was the perfect temperature and dry. This is it now, still more than an hour to go but felt like this was the glory leg.

Lou Reeves met me with about four miles to go. It was great to see her as she'd been quite active in replying to my text messages in the night. She was in more of a chatty mood than I was, I liked hearing her talk but didn't really want to talk myself, so I asked her to go easy on the questions. She obliged and just chatted to herself like I wasn't there, which was nice.

The path was quite hard now which allowed for some pretty speedy running, unfortunately I could not take advantage of it and was reduced to a shuffle that couldn't have been much more than 4 mph. We joked at the start that given the shorter stride we would do this 233 km race in it would probably take half a million steps to complete it. It was suggested that we count them (and if you lose count you have to start again). I didn't, but knew I had only a few thousand to go.

I've been obsessed with this finish line for so long now, over a year of anticipation and 30 hours of pain. From talking to Harley on that bus, sending off the application, booking the hotel and train ticket I just thought about that white banner. Predicting the feeling as I ran right into a wall that marks the end of the Grand Union Canal made all the work seem worth it. It was hard to explain to others in words why I'd do something like this but I didn't care. I only needed to answer to myself.

The hardest part of the race coincided with me forgetting about why I was here; to finish. As soon as I could think about it again I felt better.

I knew exactly what the finish line looked like as I'd seen the videos so many times. The moment I'd been waiting for was about to happen. That white banner was about to appear.

It really does appear out of nowhere. My eyes were hurting as I tried to spot it in the distance but then it just jumped out after a kink in the canal. No longer did I have to imagine what it would be like to cross this line, I could actually experience it now.

Somehow I managed to break into a proper run and flew through the line. I didn't look at my watch, I hadn't even started the timer. I just knew that I started this run on Saturday at 6.00am, it was now 12.36 pm on Sunday. Simple maths would reveal my time, I was in no state to make such complicated calculations; someone was on hand to write it down. 30 hours and 36 minutes of running, and so much more.

I remained composed as I sunk my head and Dick Kearn (race organiser) hung a huge slab of metal round my neck. It was hard to get up again, it's quite big. It was really great to see so many people around the finish. My support crew produced cake and champagne to celebrate the victory. I sat down and paraded my blisters. Campbell surgically lanced them while the cameras filmed and passers-by looked on in disgust.

The numbers will always be important to me. 145 miles, 30 hours and 36 minutes, 12:39 minutes per mile average pace, 4th place and 10th fastest finisher of all time. These are the things that will appear alongside my name if you look in years to come.

By far the most important part was the experience I had doing this race. I've thought so long about the finish and how great it would feel. I was so sure that crossing the line would give me the greatest feeling ever. I was certain that crossing the line that I'd worked towards for a year and obsessed about in all my waking hours and many of my sleeping ones would lift me higher than I have ever experienced. But it didn't. That moment came a few hours before.

I find it hard not to cringe sometimes at races and holidays that say "discover yourself" and "push yourself to your limits and beyond". I guess it's time for me to get out of marketing. I can truly say that this experience has satisfied both of those claims without needing to shout about it on the website. It was something that perhaps can't be described in words, but I'll try anyway.

After 24 hours of running and 120 miles I felt like I'd reached my limit. My body was broken and my mind didn't want to take part anymore. It was rationalising the effort that I had already done and was being quite congratulatory. Most people would not dream of running 120 miles. It said to me, "Well done but it's time to leave now".

And I had done well, this was something I could not imagine myself doing a year ago and could not imagine anyone doing a few years ago. There would have been no shame in stopping at this point would there?

Maybe not, but imagine you are doing something long and hard and you have this moment when you feel like it should be over. Imagine some ghost of you appears just ahead with a brush and a big tin of red paint and says, "Well done buddy, you've done really well to get this far but this is it, this is your limit". He then starts to paint a red line right in front of your eyes.

A rational brain would say, "He has a point, I've gone quite far". However there is nothing rational about running 145 miles. This is no place for those who like living in spreadsheets and having everything planned to perfection. This is a place for emotional imperfectionists who are willing to risk the debilitating feelings of failure in order to experience the kind of highs that can not be described.

The ghost with the red paint seems like a laborious metaphor for what got me back out of that chair at Springwell Locks. I really can't describe what happened there other than to say that I got out of that chair because I wanted to kick this fucker into the canal.

So I chased him, past the line that he had just laid out and down along the canal. I got faster and faster but so did he until he disappeared out of view. That was good, I did not want to see him again. It was when

I realised that I wasn't going to see him again that day that the waterworks started.

Though I was far from finishing the race when I had my emotional moment in Hayes I realised that I had already finished in every respect apart from the running. 13 miles from the end but already knowing that I was going to finish? It is very strange but also very liberating.

My hardest times in this race came when I thought too much about the present and not about the end. The finish line was all that concerned me for so long, a year before I crossed the start line. As soon as I forgot that I also forgot why I was here in the first place and that is when I started to beat myself up.

This experience has given me so much that justifies the sacrifices that I mentioned earlier. It has given me moments that I hope I will never forget. I don't believe I'll experience similar feelings to this very often, even if I do longer or harder runs (of which there are very few, none in the UK). I'd still like to try. The GUCR isn't one of those over-hyped corporate races with flashy animated websites that add £20 to your entry fees and spouting the usual tosh of "discovering your limits and beyond". However I did just that. I hope the ramblings above give some idea to how good it felt. But I know it can't, you really have to be there.

Reflections on the significance

To say this race changed me would be a massive understatement. I expected the race to be hard, but not that hard. I expected some crippling lows and glorious highs, but I didn't expect them to be that low or that high. In the fog of the battle it was easy to take things out of proportion and make things seem much worse than they were. I remember thinking when I sat down in that chair after 120 miles that my world was about to end, that I was a failure and a disappointment.

But in retrospect I was actually in good control over my

circumstances. Sure I had a few low moments that would reveal themselves via angry remarks, private cursing or other horrible noises, but overall I was on top of it. Someone looking from the outside in would have agreed that I handled the whole thing pretty well. In fact you could go as far as to say that I was pretty good at this kind of thing. I had never really excelled in a sporting capacity before and the feeling that I could was nice. That super human race in Death Valley in three years' time might actually be achievable. By me.

Sometimes you look back on moments in your past that may have been significant to how you are today. I had an unspectacular childhood – nothing really happened in it. At school I was always very enthusiastic about sports but never really good at anything. I'd play football, hockey, softball and do athletics all day long if I had the chance, but never raised any eyebrows in terms of my ability to shine at any of them.

When our school first did cross country I was a little nervous. There were stories that if you could not complete the 2.5 mile course in less than 35 minutes then you were made to do it again. I could not really comprehend how far 2.5 miles was as the most I'd ever run before was 800m.

The time came in late spring to run the route, down about 100m of road and then into a trail, through some fields, over a golf course where some of its patrons would relieve themselves of the boredom of their sport by using us for target practice, and then back up the street to the finish. About forty 12 year old boys grouped up on the pavement for the teacher to yell "go". I figured that 2.5 miles was a long way and so I should not treat this 100m bit of road like a 100m sprint.

At the shout of go, at least half of them sprinted the first 100m. I ran at a pace I thought I could sustain and about 200m in I had overtaken most of those who had sprinted to the end of the road. By about half a mile I had settled into 3rd place and that was where I stayed for the rest of the race. There were two other guys who were very good at distance running, Mark and Duane. They went ahead and increased their leads but I was running comfortably in 3rd while those behind me dropped off. It felt like hard work but sustainable and I think the finishing times for the top three were about 19, 20 and 21 minutes respectively. There was no reason for me to believe that I would be any good at this kind of thing but by trusting my instincts and running my own race I ended up surprising a few people. For the first time in my life I felt like I was above average at a sport.

Over the next 2 years, when we ran the course again, I would improve my times but so would Mark and Duane such that I was in 3rd again. This was fine by me. I never really trained for this race but was glad to see that the first one was no fluke. I ran the other distance races of 800m and 1500m at school and was okay at those too.

I got selected to represent my school at some cross country races in the district and was usually middle of the pack. I was then selected as one of our schools three best distance runners to run in the county championships in Leicester. I was thrilled to be able to miss some school to go and run. We travelled to Saffron Lane Sports Track in Leicester and sat in the stadium seats waiting for races to start.

There were 3 "distance" races here, 3000m, 1500m and 800m. Mark got to choose first as the best and took the 3000m. Duane next and took the 1500m. I got left with the 800m. I didn't mind but made it clear that I'm not that good at the 800m. Oh well, it's the taking part that counts.

As soon as the races started I was blown away by the standard on show. Mark was by far the best runner in our school, but here he barely scraped into a middle of the pack position. Duane fared worse; I think he was one of the last finishers in his race. My heart was thumping with the thought that in a few minutes time

I was going to get exposed, in a stadium full of people, as being an abysmal 800m runner. I was scared.

It had happened twice before in the other two races. In the 3000m there was someone who was just out of his depth, a long way behind the others. Clearly he was good enough to represent his school but when all the schools got together he looked slow. We watched the laps go by and after around half way when he was about to get lapped he did something that would even make a footballer cringe, he just fell onto the ground clutching his ankle and rolled around in apparent agony. He was not hurt at all, not physically anyway. He just did not want to get beaten so badly and so feigned an injury. It was quite sad to see but you could understand. He could tell his friends and teachers that he genuinely got injured and they might believe him and accept it. I don't know whether he could convince himself though.

The exact same thing happened in the 1500m. One kid was so far behind, and again a look of pain and tears in his face as he fell down in almost the same spot as before and clutched his phantom injury. It was embarrassing to watch but I knew that in a few moments I would be in the same position.

I was called to the start line, wished all the best from the others in my team and headed down the steps to the track. I'd never run on a proper track before; ours at school was on grass and 300m long. I'd never run in front of a crowd and never felt this small. The others were chatting to each other about what their best times were, most were around 2:40 I recall. I think mine was over 3 minutes. I was definitely going to be last.

The gun went and we piled into the first lane, me last of all because I was at the back. True to form the pack sped away while I was working as hard as I ever had to try and keep up. I don't know how far the leader was ahead of me but I could at least still see the last but one runner. By the end of the first lap I was a good 50 m down on last but one as my lungs wanted to burst and my legs wanted to blow up. But I hung in there. I was still running faster than ever it was just that I was well and truly out of my league.

I didn't even think about the others watching and no doubt sniggering at me as we had done to previous last placed runners. I approached the back straight, well and truly on my own and ran into the far corner of the last lap, where there were no crowds and where the other two runners from the previous races dropped out. I could see why they chose this spot – no one was around, no one would even notice.

It crossed my mind. But what would I say when I fake limped across the grass over to the finish area? Would people honestly believe that I could have won this race but was just unlucky? I realised that I didn't have to justify coming last to anyone, not to the teachers nor even to myself. I was never going to win, and while it was certainly a daunting experience coming last in front of all these people and other runners, I could still finish this race. I was still faster than I ever had been before, I deserved to be here and I was actually enjoying the day. I entered the home straight to see the last but one guy cross the line, I did the same sometime after and received huge applause from the coaches and marshals at the end, and then further praise from my teachers. I felt like I had performed as well as I could.

The significance of that race didn't really hit me until much later in my life. When running back then as a 14 year old, I only thought of the conversation I would have to have with myself at the end. I could lie and convince anyone else but I could never lie to myself. Since I spend most of my time with myself, it is best not to try and be deceitful. If I had not finished I don't think I could have forgiven myself, not even as a 14 year old boy.

I think I felt the same thing when I was sat in that chair after 120 miles of canal running. I certainly would not forgive a 28 year old man for such a thing.

6A

WHY? VERSION 3

I felt pretty sick with fear before the start of the Grand Union Canal Race. I knew I loved running – the longer the better – but more than 24 hours? Seriously? That does not sound like much fun.

I felt pretty scared before my first marathon too, I don't know how they compare. At that stage I'd never met anyone who had run a marathon before and had no one to share the nerves with.

This was different though, this really was something else and in the days leading up to the race I felt paralysis through fear. I had great doubts as to whether I was up to such a challenge.

But in this race I overcame all of that and did it pretty well. I went into it with clearly defined limits on what I had done before (9 hours, 55 miles), however I had yet to see the limit of what I was capable of.

I thought I had reached my limit at 120 miles and 25 hours of non-stop running, when my legs had ground to a halt and my mind had given up. I thought this race had taken me as far as I could go. In all honesty, that was further than I thought I could ever go two years before. I figured that now I was running to see how far I could go, and there was a brief moment where I thought that was it.

But it didn't turn out like that. Somehow I had a complete transformation; from a crippled wreck thinking about quitting and thinking about how proud I was to even make it that far, to getting up again and doing the best running of my life, kicking all those doubts into touch and having a euphoric emotional moment.

I thought I was beaten, yet I got up and finished. This revelation took hold of me and became the basis for all future challenges. I thought my limits were finite and definable. After this race there was no evidence of that. From now on I was going to run to see what was possible.

That was why I ran.

7

THE MOOSE ULTRA (2008) – 300K IN SIX DAYS IN CANADA

It took a few weeks after the GUCR to be able to run again but I got over it a lot quicker than I expected. I was not itching to get back to running, instead I was in this wonderful position where I could think about the canal race and be thankful that I managed to experience such a thing. As soon as I was ready I was booking more events. The Summer Tanners 30 mile was a great first run back in the summer and many more marathons followed. In July I ran the Swiss Alpine K78 in Davos – 78 km of mountain running which was exhilarating. I had never been so high up in the mountains before, I felt on top of the world.

I was signing up to races left, right and centre, and enjoying every one of them. The next big challenge came out of the blue one day; an email from a race organiser in Canada.

I had been signing up to any Ultramarathon mailing list out there, and received details of a race being run for the first time. It seemed a little too good to be true, but on speaking to the race director Richard Price on the phone it seemed like the next challenge; a proper multi-day ultra.

It was advertised as the "A 302 km 6 day run on terrain that will rival most other six day events". It seemed to come out of nowhere and with a price tag of just £800 (when I was going to be paying £3,000 for the Marathon des Sables). I considered trashing it like I do with requests for my bank details from "esteemed long good friends" in Nigeria. At the time however I was developing an addiction to any run that sounded silly, and this was certainly one of those. Note to fraudsters out there – I don't play lotteries nor am I interested in making any part of my body longer, however mention some tough terrain, exotic location, uncomfortable weather, wildlife, a number (100 minimum) and explain that this is the distance I'll have to cover on foot – then you'll have a chance of clearing my bank account.

I think working in marketing has made me immune to the rhetoric that comes with any product advert. Like foods advertising "active ingredients" or drugs that have been "scientifically formulated" I just let these words wash over me. I should bloody well hope that pills I take are "scientifically formulated"; what would the alternative be? Theologically cobbled together? Most races like this I see fall into the same trap, using tired phrases like "ultimate challenge" and "push yourself to the limit and beyond". Try reading one in a Buzz Lightyear voice and see if you can do it without laughing. It's hard, probably harder than the event. The Moose advertised itself simply as a tough but beautiful event. Here's my money.

I spent the next few months getting really excited about the prospect of having a fight with a bear.

The Moose was run over the Bruce Trail, a way-marked path from Tobermory to Niagara. I expected it to be similar to some of the trail/coastal races I've done in the UK. I wasn't far off, it was only a question of scale. How many times does the UK fit into Canada? That's approximately the number of times the average British rock fits into the average Canadian rock.

Registration

We met in a hotel north of Toronto on Friday night. I had spent a day and a half in Toronto, which is probably a day and a quarter too long – it was quite boring. A big tower and a waterfall nearby is all that there is to be done there. Apart from 8 runners and Richard Price (the event organiser), the only other guests at the hotel were a group of evangelical Christians. I did not have much trouble separating the two. Both groups were nutters only one group liked shouting about it more.

We were eight relative strangers sat around a table tentatively promoting our running CVs. This happens in any gathering of runners who do not know each other. It is an interesting dynamic; you don't want to just start banging on about yourself but you do want everyone to know. Gradually over the meal it was revealed that we had 5 Marathon des Sables vets, 4 Marathon of Britain (MoB), and several Comrades and 100 mile finishers.

The next morning we destroyed the self-serve breakfast buffet and started the drive towards Tobermory where the race started. We were introduced to more members of the support cast; Al and Christa. Along the way we exchanged more stories about our running careers, my best contribution being the time I nearly slipped over on a kebab two miles into the Leicester Marathon.

We arrived at the visitors centre in Tobermory and were warned about the biggest danger we would face on this run. It was made of leaves. Slightly disappointed to hear that bear sightings were rare and that rattlesnake bites rarely kill humans, I began to worry about poisoned ivy. I was determined to worry about something during this race, I don't normally get the chance in races in Surrey.

After confirming that we each had our compulsory kit we

were sent to the doctor to have our ECG charts checked. I wasn't too sure what he was looking for from my graph, which looked like the seismograph of a very small and short lived earthquake. Apparently I had a longer than usual something and a shorter than usual something else. He also looked at my blood pressure reading and asked, "Did different people take your blood pressure and heart rate?" I confirmed that this was the case and he smirked and suggested that the person who took my heart rate was quite attractive. This was indeed the case. I hope she was impressed with my longer than usual whateveritwas.

Later that night we were required to part with our main luggage and only take with us the stuff we were going to need for the week. I was the only multi-day virgin there and it showed, my bag was about twice the size of some of the others. Not sure how the volume was made up, but they must have learned all the tricks about high-calorie low mass food and clothing. We got into the tents at about 10 pm and tried to get a good nights' sleep on our mats and sleeping bags before the first day.

Day 1 – The brutal start

I don't think many multi-day runs start with a 50 km stage. Not really a gentle start, however this was the longest 6 day footrace in the world so we had nothing but tough days. The race started and I followed the pack out of the camp, and soon we were running over very large pebbles along the side of a lake. It was hard to decide whether I should run or walk at this point. One part of me thought that this terrain is really silly to run on and hence I should walk; the other thought that I'm only 1 mile into a 190 mile race and that I was just being a wimp. The half that calls me a wimp will always win.

The rocks in the first 15 miles were absolutely brutal. After the pebble beach the course went into the forest and that's where the really big rocks started. They were huge and omnipresent. I had hoped that 4500 million years of land movement would have reduced these to a manageable size by now. Some of them were bigger than cars. I know it's a myth that Eskimos have 20 words for snow, however I soon had 20 different words for big rocks, like tw@t and c★★t.

Scrambling up and down rocks, occasionally overtaking other runners, and then overtaking them again as they or I went the wrong way, I immersed myself in this horrible rock world, just trying not to slip and hurt myself. I thought I'd be at the first checkpoint by now (they were about every 10 km), and looked at the map to see that the checkpoint involved a slight turnoff. With 1:30 hours on the clock, I was looking for every possible turn and hoping to be caught, or to catch another runner so that I could find out. I was still on the main path so the worst that could happen was that I'd just go straight to checkpoint 2 (and maybe get disqualified).

About half an hour later I passed some hikers and I stopped to ask them where I was on the map. I was halfway between 1 and 2. I was relieved that it had not just taken me 2 hours to travel 10 km, but was also annoyed that I had missed the checkpoint and wondered what the consequences were. I later was told that the reason I missed the checkpoint was because I was an idiot. Fair cop.

So I scrambled on, overwhelmed by how much harder it was to run on these rocks in comparison to rocks back home. Every now and then my foot would slip over a rock and my ankle would twist. Having run so many trail races my feet are pretty hardy to this kind of stress and usually a twist in the ankle can be run off in a couple of minutes. The fact that there were so many more rocks here meant that my feet were twisting much more than ever before, and after about 10 miles I had 2 incidents in very quick succession on my left ankle. The pain was so incredible that I actually shouted out loud for the first time I can remember. I felt my foot slowly fill with acid which then made the bones feel fragile and sore. 180 miles to go and I was one false step from a broken bone – I didn't hold out much hope for the rest of the week, but I hobbled on.

Checkpoint 2 was hard to miss (I ran straight into it). It was good to finally see someone else who was connected to the race. I mentioned my ankle and they pointed out that it was quite visibly swollen. The next few miles were on tracks and roads and I found, to my surprise, that I could actually run on them. There were not many road sections in the race but when they came they were very welcome. It was nice to get some fast running done (fast being a relative term).

I was now exposed to the sun which felt like a huge change. It was very humid and about 30°C. I overtook Andy North on the uphill road, figuring that roads might be the only bits I'd be able to run now so I might as well take advantage. After the next checkpoint, the trail turned back into the woods and the rocks returned. They were not nearly as bad as before, but I still could not run on them. Every slight sideways move for my left foot was very painful.

Time – 7:30

I finished the 50 km in 7:30 hours – not the slowest 50k I have ever done, but by far the hardest. We had been told that the first day was probably the toughest in terms of terrain, so I hoped that I could at least run for some of the remaining days.

The race village was set up in a very large back garden. I saw the medics and showed them my big ugly ankle which they strapped up. It was quite funny listening to them talk about their experience of resuscitating people and cutting victims out of crashed cars, and then their inexperience of dealing with blisters and sprains. It was very reassuring that Richard had gone to the trouble of hiring proper medics to oversee this event. Hopefully there would be no major incidents for them to deal with.

Every runner in the village looked quite shocked as to how hard the first day was. Having no experience of multi-stage races before I had nothing to use as a reference, however the various Marathon des Sables and Marathon of Britain (175 mile multi stage race over seven days) vets did the comparison and said that this was the hardest first day they had encountered. Good to start with an easy one.

To save space in my bag (which was still bigger than everyone else's), I took a sleeping bag that was practically made of foil. It was like a large crisp packet. The night time temperature was much colder than I had expected and the foil wasn't really much help, so I just lay there rustling in my own condensed sweat.

Day 2 – "It gets easier"

Day 2 was going to be easier, I was sure of it and we were told the same. I thought the really hard rocky path was going to give way to nice trail and pine needle covered tracks that would be a joy to run on. Once again I was mistaken.

We headed out in 2 groups; one at 7 am one at 9 am. I was with the latter group, although my ankle was still hurting. Running around on the grass near the start seemed fine but once I got back onto the rocks I was reduced to a walk again. Even when I had a flat bit of trail to run on I'd be limping, running flat footed on my left side. Fortunately there were plenty of runnable sections and a few stretches of road.

I was making good progress despite my injury, but just before we entered the small town of Lionshead I started to feel very light headed. I'd already realised a mistake in my food choice as I had nothing sweet with me, only savoury food like nuts, Bombay mix and pepperami. I was really craving something sugary and did not bring enough energy sachets to cover the week, another schoolboy error. I walked for a bit eating beef jerky and hoped the salt would sort me out, then when I arrived at Lionshead I was determined to find a shop so I could buy some Coke.

There was a beautiful harbour and the route cut inside and went right through the town and we got the rare pleasure of actually seeing some other humans. I saw a couple relaxing in their front garden and I asked them where the nearest shop was that I could buy a Coke. I spoke to them for a couple of minutes explaining what I was doing and then out of nowhere came a cold bottle of full-fat Coke. It was an unbelievable act of kindness and they would never know quite how much it was appreciated.

The Coke craving is a strange thing; I never drink it normally, but for some reason I desire it in races. It's a bit like craving things when you are pregnant (I imagine). In fact there are probably a lot of similarities between being pregnant and ultra-running. You crave random foods and feel like you are eating for two. You feel a lot slower and heavier than normal, your bladder is a law unto itself. You have no shame in using disabled toilets and fully expect people to get out of their seats for you to sit down. You look and feel like shit while everyone around you is telling you that you look great. Every now and then you are told to push harder.

While drinking the Coke I caught up with Justin who was

struggling with a hip injury caused by a fall the previous day. I offered him some Coke but he declined, which I was quite happy with. The course then left the harbour and through some wooded areas followed by some road. My ankle was feeling better all the time and I was glad to see some road again just so I could get ahead a bit.

I saw Paul at the 4th checkpoint, which was just before a section of road that was about 10 km. He looked in really good spirits and was walking the road sections as were most of the others, which I found strange. However I didn't have the option of running on the rocks so I had to make up for it wherever I could.

It was about 2 pm in the afternoon and the temperature really picked up. It was about 30°C and humid. I always think about the MDS and the 40+°C that are expected there, however I am reassured that although it is hotter it is in fact dry heat. I won't have to choke on moisture while running up a hill.

I made good time running uphill along a long stretch of road and reached the 4th checkpoint (42 km) at about 6 hours. There was 15 km to go with one other checkpoint, and I guessed it would probably take a couple of hours to reach the end. This was the last time I ever even tried to estimate how long it would take to do a stage.

What followed was probably the hardest and most miserable stretch of "running" I have ever experienced. The rocks came back with a vengeance.

There is little way to judge distance while in the trails like this, as I discovered on the first day when I overran the first checkpoint by miles. You can have an idea that it takes x minutes to run 1 km and extrapolate, but my estimates had been totally wrong in the race so far. The only way I could judge how far I had gone was based on the side trails that appear on the map. The route was along the main trail, but every now and then a side trail would present itself and this was detailed in the roadbook. The problem with these was that they appeared quite close together on the map, however they took an age to appear in reality.

How long is the coastline of Britain? The answer depends on how long your ruler is. The smaller your measuring device, the more detailed your measurements, and this results in the coastline being measured longer. I was suffering the consequences of a long ruler here – the lines on the map looked short and straight. Zoom in and they become longer and more wobbly. The map became a deception that I continued to use as a mile marker.

I like to think that I've done enough running now so that I'm not fazed by any situation I am likely to encounter in a race, however I was losing it here. I was looking at the map and questioning whether I had gone wrong as the side trails were not appearing. It started to rain and the cover of the forest made it quite dark. Slowly one of the trails would appear and I just couldn't believe it took that long to come. I had not gone wrong but on several occasions I turned back to check. I was not sure whether it was the really hard running or the prospect of 4 more days of the same that made me have doubts about finishing this race. It took 4 hours to do the remaining 15 km.

I was hurting all over, with huge chafing wounds. It was almost dark when I crossed the line and lay down on the ground. Rhodri and Bruce had already finished. Andy, Chris and Jo followed later. I had a shower which involved an incredibly painful downhill walk. It was spaghetti bolognese for dinner that night. I was very thankful for the extra food we were being given as there was no way we would have survived on just 2000 calories per day. It was about 9 pm when we were eating dinner and we were keen to find out how Paul was getting on. He had left the last checkpoint not long ago, and was heading into the forest on his own in the dark.

Paul was an exceptionally strong character. He still had a way to go when he reached the last checkpoint, but was determined to continue. He'd be the first to admit that he wasn't the fastest ultra-runner in the world, but made up for it with bravery. The last checkpoint was at the start of a forest section which took me 2 hours. It was dark at this point and I don't believe I would have entered the forest at that stage.

Paul finished after 11 pm having spent 16 hours out there and almost falling asleep while walking. Everyone was again shocked at how hard the day had been. Justin summed it up nicely when he said "you just shouldn't feel like this at the end of day 2." Tomorrow was only a marathon, things might improve.

Day Three – "Just" a marathon

Paul, Justin and Chris decided not to start today. Paul had barely stopped since yesterday, Justin had injured his hip and Chris had feet that looked like bubble wrap and had to go to hospital. Many races claim to be the hardest race in the world but have a high finish rate. This was down to 58% and we still had 4 days to go. Surely it was going to get easier?

The plan today was for myself, Jo and Andy to start at 8 and Bruce and Rhodri (who were now referred to as the "robots") would start at 9. I was taking my time getting ready for the start, faffing around with my kit. Then out of the corner of my eye I saw Jo and Andy starting. I had no idea it was 8 already and I frantically started throwing stuff in my bag to get going. Having got myself together I ran to the start line and Chris asked me a very valid question – "Are you taking your shoes and socks with you?" I looked down and realised that I was still in my flip-flops and my trainers and socks were on the table. If there was any doubt amongst the others that I was an idiot, it had just been confirmed.

I threw my shoes on, scrambled to the start and set off a few minutes after Jo and Andy. I sped off determined not to let Rhodri and Bruce overtake me later on, it was only a marathon after all.

Most of the day was on fairly runnable trail, but there were still rocky sections that I couldn't run on because of my ankle. It was feeling better, but would still complain after any sideways movement. Even though the day felt much easier than the previous two it was still really slow going.

The finish was in a small town called Wiarton and the approach to it was beautiful. It was along a road leading into a harbour. I was looking forward to getting to the village and going to a shop and buying sweets and coke. I put on a big sprint finish and then walked into the lake.

I was so excited about going to the shop and buying sweets. It was like being 7 again. At no point did I feel slightly embarrassed about walking around a busy supermarket in tights, vanity had long since departed. I bought coke and jelly beans and felt confident about the long day tomorrow.

The race village was a joy that night. We had plenty of time to rest and chat and get to know all of the support crew who were amazing throughout the event. I'm never really good at remembering names and got no better at it during this race, but what I did remember was not having to lift a finger once I had finished the running.

Each day we'd arrive from our adventures to the camp that had dinner already started, all the tents set up and as much tea and coffee as one could drink. I was really looking forward to the long day. My feet felt a bit better though my shoes were ruined. In retrospect I would have taken some trail shoes instead of the road shoes I had. My socks were falling apart and I had no spares.

The end of day feasts were orchestrated by "Bear" – Richard's father-in-law. Though he'd often admit that he did little of the cooking or cleaning he did ensure that everything ran smoothly for the runners. Smoother than the running anyway. He was a welcome sight at the end of each day and would spoil us in the morning as well.

Day 4 – The Long Day

I was woken from a deep slumber at 5 am. I can't remember what I was dreaming about, but I was not all that enthusiastic about getting up and crawling out of the tent onto cold wet grass in the dark and then fumbling around to get my stuff ready. Bear and Mickey were up to make us bacon and eggs for breakfast. This was most welcome and Bear actually said that he was bending the rules a bit by giving us the bacon. I didn't care though and I doubt the others did either.

Andy, Jo and I started at 6am, and Rhodri and Bruce were to set out at 8am. I had really high hopes for today; I felt much better and was feeling the benefits of a lighter pack. It was still dark as we navigated through the town and back onto the trail.

I ran ahead and made an arse of navigating several times. Jo and Andy behind followed and were happy for me to do the extra running to find their way. I didn't mind though, I was bouncing around having not been able to push myself on the first 3 days. I was ready to do so today.

The trail was not really well marked for many parts of the day. The Bruce trail is managed by several authorities and some are better at maintenance than others. The path often crossed fields of tall grass and we were not sure at these points exactly which corner of the field to aim for. It was not long before our feet were soaked.

After Checkpoint 1 we had to take a side trail which was marked in blue. This particular one was called the "Slough of Despond" trail which was funny. Even all the way out here people associate Slough with despondency. I continued along this trail and turned around at the end to see a sign calling it the "President's Path". Somehow I was on a different trail to the one I thought I was on, and didn't really know whether I was supposed to take the right turn that I thought I should. I frantically emptied my bag to try and find my compass (what I was going to do with it once I found it I did not know at that stage). The exact moment that I started to swear out loud, Andy and Jo appeared from the same place I had come from and made the turning. They found it hilarious that I'd just emptied my bag all over the place and was now struggling to get everything in and catch up. The trail was marked wrong, it was as simple as that. I was right all along.

There were a few times where I wondered whether Andy and Jo were ahead of me. The way I knew that they weren't was simple, I was still eating cobwebs. Being the first to run the path today I had the pleasure of swallowing a huge amount of cobwebs. So long as I was doing this I knew I was in front.

The route turned back into the forest and this time I was able to enjoy the trail. The path was not as rocky as before, but there was plenty there to be challenging. My foot was better and I really enjoyed being able to use it properly. For the first time in this race I felt I could let my mind wander and think about other things. I was so relaxed I wasn't thinking about how hard this was anymore but let myself drift off. There was no conscious effort on my part to place my feet or look where I was going, it just all happened so naturally. I've never run like that before. I loved it.

Time and time again I am asked if I get bored when I run. The answer is always no. Either I am trying hard to focus on the task in hand, as I had been for about 30 hours until now, or I get a chance to ponder life's big questions with a slightly altered mental state. I'd best describe it as having the hang-ups and inhibitions of someone halfway drunk but with the sharpness of mind of a chess grandmaster. It takes a while to get to this stage and it does not always happen, but when it does it's all worth it.

I never quite know when I enter or exit this zone, nor do I remember exactly what I was thinking about. I just seem to recall parts of my life getting sorted out. I guess I'd be thinking of the usual stuff; races I have done, races I want to do, what to do with my life and work, girls I like, plans to take over the world. I can make sense of books I've read and people that I know. I think about everything with heightened focus but no real urgency.

Some of the time I think about just how good I feel as I run. Small hills just invite sprinting, rocky paths invite dancing and fallen branches inspire over the top jumping. At points I was actually swinging on branches because I didn't want to stop. The pain of the last few days and the aching muscles had disappeared. I stopped thinking about how far I had gone or had to go. I didn't care how fast I was going or how much longer it was going to take till the end. It didn't even bother me when I ran the wrong way.

It was such an amazing trail and I saw a few other runners come from the opposite direction. I chatted and said I was in a race and also that I was really jealous of not getting this kind of running in London.

I made a few wrong turns, including climbing down a steep and slippy hill into a swampy area and then having to climb back out again. The trail was generally quite easy to follow and I was never really paying much attention to it. Similar to driving or cycling, the actual physical process of responding to the trail signs had become automatic so that I didn't need to think about it anymore. This freed my mind to enjoy other things like the scenery and my own rambling thoughts.

I can't remember what caused me to look at my watch, but when I did I was amazed. The last time I'd looked at the time was over 3 hours ago. I'd just run for 3 hours in what seemed like 5 minutes. Imagine starting a marathon and then finishing in what seems like 5 minutes?

I spotted the Moose signs that signalled that the finish was close and that I could start sprinting. I did just that and flew through the line again in just over 12 hours to the surprise of everyone there who were not expecting anyone back so soon. I had to redo my finish for the cameras and I had loads of time to relax and wait for the others to come in. During this time I was interviewed by a chap who was making a documentary on the whole thing. When asked why I do this I gave an answer which was a less coherent version of the story above. It was a really great day to be interviewed as this was my best day so far.

Rhodri and Bruce came in nearly 2 hours later and Andy and Jo followed later in the night.

Day 5 – A lie in

Having spent the last few days getting out of bed when it was still dark and wet on the ground I was really pleased to have more time in my foil packet this morning. Yesterday's run had meant that I was to be starting with Rhodri and Bruce this morning and setting off at 9. I'm sure I could have been with them all week if it wasn't for my injury, but now that seemed to have passed I felt more like running. I was still buoyed from yesterday and a bit sad that this was the last whole day. Still, I was looking forward to the end and amazed that I'd managed to run 4 hard ultras in 4 days on a poorly foot.

I ran with the Robots for most of the day. I don't normally like to run with others but this was a welcome break as the three of us got lost a lot less than when I was on my own. The trail was a bit easier once more, with a lot more open fields and wider tracks. This meant more running and I was trying to keep up with the two in front.

Today was great as Justin and Paul had re-joined the race and were already out there having set off a couple of hours earlier. Chris was still in a bad way and had to go to hospital for his blisters. He was given some very potent drugs though which were the envy of the rest of us.

The added weight I felt in my legs over the course of the week was offset partially by the lightening of my pack. In theory I didn't need to have any food on me now as there was no requirement for any on the last day and I could have eaten all of todays at the start.

Richard and Barreleigh spent the whole week stalking us through the forests with cameras. I'd never been photographed so much in my life. Cameras always compel me to run, even if it's uphill and slippy. They were everywhere, including one time when I was taking a leak.

Heat and exhaustion got the better of me and I let the Robots go. I was pleased to have made it to near the end with them but I was just flagging now. The last few miles were on roads which I had difficulty reading because my map had melted. There was some rocky road to finish, including some steep downhill sections. I was spent by this point and walking a lot. When I turned onto the last section of road I was told to look out for a "very pretty bridge" and then turn into the finish there. This road seemed to go on for miles (which it did I think) and I was hoping that this bridge was going to be worth it.

It was a very nice bridge and even nicer to see the finish.

This had been a really hard day for me and we all celebrated the almost end of the race by jumping in the stream nearby.

That felt like the whole thing over. With plenty of daylight left we lounged around next to a stream, scoffing whatever we had left of our food and not even worrying about tomorrow's "half marathon".

It is obviously great to get near the end of a race but it is very sad to think that in a few days' time I'll be back in the mundane. I was trying to put that out of my mind now though. I was looking forward to drinking a beer at the finish line in the Blue Mountain Resort.

Day 6 – Hardly worth bothering with

I set off with Rhodri and Bruce once more and the first half of today was an uphill section of road. It was very hot and a really straight section of road. I could see for miles and wondered how far I'd have to go up. It's hard to tell how far away the next hill was and the mirage made it more difficult. I thought of Badwater as I continued in the rising heat.

I decided in 2006 that I would run Badwater in 2011. All of this was good experience towards achieving that goal, though I couldn't even pretend that I would be feeling like this in the last 20 km. Badwater would be truly hard-core, twice as hot as this, and much more hilly. I couldn't imagine what would be thrown at me in that one, but I hoped I could use some of the experiences of this race in 2011.

We reached the top of the road in about an hour. 60 minutes for an uphill 10k in the heat with 170 miles already in me was pretty good if I do say so myself. That's almost running pace. This was the last checkpoint we would see (sob). We then turned left into the woods and made our way onto the trail via a very narrow gate (which I doubt I would have fitted through six days earlier).

I let Rhodri and Bruce run on and made my own way through the trail. We were approaching a busy tourist resort and running along what were ski slopes in the winter. There were a lot of people around who were very supportive; it was nice being able to say that I was in a 300 km race with about 5 km to go. I could almost taste the beer.

I followed the trail down steep slopes which were very painful, thinking that skis would have been useful here. I was making hard work again of figuring out which way to go, but figured that if I just continued down to the town I'd find the finish – and then just as I thought that I heard Bear screaming and shouting. I looked up and saw that Justin was a little ahead of me and about to finish.

So now everyone was waiting for me. It was quite nice to be the last to finish, it was great to see everyone on the line. As I ran towards the plaza and to the finish line I stopped and did something I'd been thinking of doing all week. I took off my shoes and socks, threw them away into a nearby bin and then put on my flip-flops. I then finished the race as I had tried to start day 3. Getting rid of those things was a fantastic feeling; road shoes just didn't cut it here, and in fact they just got cut up.

I went through the finish line with all the grace and poise you would expect from someone who has run 300 km over 6 days and is wearing flip-flops. I hugged everyone and made my way towards the beer. Coors Light, which was quite fitting as that was my Wednesday night drink after the club runs. Well-earned I think, if not for the running then for all the tomfoolery in the week.

Day 6 – 3:23
Total Time 50 hours-ish – 3rd place

There was no rush to get moving from the pub and we all just sat around and took the moment in. I didn't come here expecting an easy week but I was not expecting it to be that hard. The first 2 days left me a wreck. The long day reminded me of why I run and today confirmed why I like to run in organised events such as this one.

The organisation was breath-taking in this event. Eight runners is obviously not enough to make commercial sense but Richard has taken a brave gamble and staked his money on this one succeeding in the future.

So my first multi-day race went well in the end after a very shaky start. Everyone agreed that this was the hardest race they had done and it was not to be taken lightly, however the unique environment of the race village took away some of the difficulty you'd expect in more popular multi-day races.

7A

WHY? VERSION 4

Psychologists call it "flow". A state where you are doing something you enjoy, that's not too difficult but not too easy, that you are interested in and that in a particular moment you are giving it your entire focus. Nothing else is occupying your mind except for this activity that you love.

It does not happen often, that you can just run with some Zen-like state of higher consciousness, enabled by having all of your mental resources dedicated to one thing. Times when you are doing what you love the best you have ever done it and it feels effortless. It happens sometimes though and when it does it's pretty special.

I was coming round more and more to the idea that there is something very primal about running. We've had to do it since before we were human. In fact, running in the great African plains is what gave us an advantage; an ability to hunt in the day over long distances. It makes sense that something so key in our progress should be rewarded in some way, like sex.

Now we don't have to run. We have cars, trains, deliveries, emails. There is no reason why anyone needs to run at all now, except for fun. In fact nowadays there is no need for sex. Scientists have created all that is required to make a child from the parts of a woman's reproductive organs. In fact there is no need for men to exist anymore. Now that this is the case when will we stop having sex? It can all be done in a lab.

Will that stop us having sex? I doubt it and I doubt people will ever stop running or participating in sport to achieve mental and physical rewards that our ancestors would have got from their compulsory participation in exercise.

I realised that running was not so much a part of my life but part of humanity. In Canada I was in "flow" for three hours and it went by in minutes. I was a master of my own body bounding through harsh Canadian trail. I can't remember making any decisions I was just running up and down and turning and hurdling and climbing and scrambling. I was part of the landscape.

This is why I run.

8

THE EASIEST FOOTRACE ON EARTH (2009)

A couple of weeks after arriving back from Canada I continued as normal, signing up for marathons and ultramarathons for the rest of the year. Before the year was out I had completed the Atlantic Coast Challenge of three marathons in three days, the "triple" of Snowdon, Crawley and Dublin marathons in three days and run a lot of other marathons too. I was really enjoying the running, getting to know more and more people, do different events and get to see places that I had never been to before. Later in the year I went back to Rotherham and completed the 50 miles that I hadn't finished the previous year. That was a great feeling, knowing that I don't have to go to Rotherham again.

The end of the year I felt like I was in the shape of my life. I had accidentally run a marathon PB, nailed the Grand Union Canal Run, run my first proper multi-day race and completed 40 marathon/ultra-distances races. I finished off the year by finishing a race that had been bugging me for 12 months and then the following day running a marathon time that was a PB two years before. I was really looking forward to what was in store in 2009 – but first I had to tick a box.

There were so many things I loved about the ultramarathons I had done. I loved the loneliness of running in the middle of nowhere with only myself for company. I loved the simplicity of it all, just putting one foot in front of the other lots and lots.

I loved the inexpensiveness and how event organisers concentrated on the basics of ensuring a great experience for the runner. I loved the attitude of the people I met, so humble about doing something so challenging, taking nothing for granted but being very confident about their ability to finish. I had met so many of the hardest runners in the UK who would talk and act like they had no toughness. They were always substance over style.

Why then did I enter a race that was the opposite of all these things? A race where we were made to queue and run like cattle being sold at a farmers' market? Where corporate sponsorship and marketing were more important that the runners experience. A race that leaves a £3500 dent on a credit card or overdraft, 4 times what I paid for the same thing in Canada and 100 times what I paid for the canal run. Where you meet person after person who does not even like running but just wants to buy a medal and claim they have completed the "toughest race on earth". Where everything I came to love about ultras had been turned upside-down.

I paid most of the money ages ago and there was no going back (financially). It seemed I had no choice but to run the Marathon des Sables.

I turned up in Morocco in a bit of a bad mood. I had picked up a horrible chest infection the week before and spent most of the time coughing hard. With a week before the start I hoped there would be time for it to go away but it hung around for the duration of the race. My concern was not that I would not be able to finish the race (I was certain that I would even if my lungs collapsed – it's quite easy). My concern was that I had spent so much money on a trekking holiday that was going to be miserable due to illness.

The baking heat of the Sahara started to burn us as we queued outside to be let into the airport. We then got taken to a local 5 star hotel where we stayed for about 8 hours. I would have preferred a dorm and a £200 reduction in the entry fee. We got on the coach to take us into the desert where we would then be based for a couple of days before the race was due to begin.

On the 5 hour coach journey out there it started to rain heavily. This was not what we had signed up for (though oddly this is what all the Brits train in). At the end of the long coach journey we were transferred into jeeps with our luggage and then taken on a bumpy ride into the desert to the camp.

It looked like Glastonbury on a really bad year. All of the bivouacs were waterlogged as we were told to find somewhere and set up for the night. The next couple of hours were a melee of people trying to secure dry spots and dig trenches to stop water flowing into their sleeping bags. In the middle of the night we were then told we were going to be evacuated to a nearby hotel as the rain was not going to stop. Seven Brits got stranded there overnight.

The next couple of days were quite frustrating, hanging around in hotels trying to get information from the organisers as to what was happening with the race. I was still coughing and keeping my roommates up all night with the awful noise I was making. Part of me hoped that they would cancel the race and give a refund. I didn't want to be here.

Eventually we were reassured that we will at least start the race from day two and they were going to play it by ear from there.

Day 1 – Dunes Day 34 km

We arrived at the start by coach, which is unusual as normally we would have camped the night before at the start. This was not going to be a normal MDS year. Flooding had cancelled the first day and was hanging over the rest of the race. We were all just relieved to get to the stage where we could actually start running.

Day 1 was meant to be day 2, the dunes day. This involved at least 17 km of running/hiking through sand dunes and about the same distance over tracks. The dunes day is probably the second most feared of the MDS stages (after the long day) at it is over the hardest terrain and tests one's ability to keep sand out of their shoes. The fact that we were starting with this without the 20 mile "warm-up" the day before didn't really faze anyone; we were just so relieved to be able to start running.

The coach did not take long to arrive at the start point. We were all pushing our heads against the windows of the coach to try and see the dunes that we would be crawling over in a few hours. Finally they came, from a distance they looked quite intimidating. They were bigger than any I had seen before (in Wales) and were much more golden than I imagined.

The start line was farcical. Patrick Bauer and a bad translator bumbled through the course changes which involved very precise bearing measurements (most runners did not have a pen) and the helicopter roared above us and drowned out the sound. I thought this helicopter was here for safety reasons, its presence was actually stopping us being able to hear whatever the race director was saying. I wasn't planning on winning, so I'd have to rely on following everyone else.

After too much pomp and ceremony the race finally started, 2 years and 3 weeks since I signed up for it. A horn went and we all staggered forward over a rocky path towards the big dunes that we'd been looking at for hours.

I find the starts of multi-day races very amusing. We are all running with backpacks, front packs, things strapped to our arms, legs, shoulders and waists. Everyone is wearing varying levels of clothing and tubing that could mistake the scene for a school play about robots where the kids have made the costume. One of the most important "rules" for multi-day racing is to test all of your kit lots and lots before you actually use it in the race. No one ever does.

The first few miles are a melee of people dropping bottles, adjusting straps and rearranging stuff in their bags. I quickly discarded my front pack as it bounced around and had to carry my water bottles in my hands as they kept hitting me in the face. I didn't really have a sense of the direction I was running as there were too many people around.

The first 3 km was along a rocky track. Much of the terrain is the same; flat dirt tracks with little rocks strewn all over the place. It was a bit like running through Shepherds Bush, only instead of broken bottles and litter it was rocks. It was fairly easy to run on now but once it becomes harder to lift your legs these rocks become really painful.

We then hit the sand dunes, everyone was really enthusiastic and still running up and down quite difficult inclines. I think the rain over the previous days had made it a bit easier; steps would form in them where others had placed their feet and it was like running up stairs. There were cameramen everywhere and often you'd almost run into them as they didn't make any effort to get out of the way.

I worried before this race that the dunes would be impenetrable. I had a vision that I'd try to get up them and just sink, however they were much easier than I imagined. They were still tough and some of the downs were very steep, and this was where everyone's gaiters got tested.

The gaiters are probably the most thought about piece of kit for any MdS runner. The measures taken to avoid getting sand in your shoes is the most important thing in the whole race. I had super-glued silk ones on and added a huge amount of gaffer tape. I wasn't sure how well they were working, it is something you never know until the end of the day. Every time I ran down a sand dune I'd feel sand hit the backs of my legs and slide down, I had no idea whether it was getting in. I would just have to wait.

The sand dunes came to an end and we hit the first checkpoint. At each checkpoint you are required to run through the timing sensor and have your card stamped for bottles of water. Normally two were on offer, but most were just taking one as it wasn't too hot at that stage. The route then took us onto a fairly uninspiring long straight track. Time to pick up the pace, or so I thought.

The temperature picked up a bit and I'd describe it as an uncomfortably warm British summer's day. I was told that bone dry heat is not too hard to run in and that humidity would not be a problem. The first rain in the MDS for 15 years however made humidity a problem and I suffered.

The track was flat and not too rocky, there was no reason why I shouldn't run the lot of it and run it well. But as soon as I started running at any kind of pace I was stopped by coughing. I had hoped that some dry air would clear my cough (there was no medical basis for this hope). The moisture and the sand just made everything worse.

I'd run-walk-run-walk for about a minute at a time but the length of time I could run got smaller and smaller. I eventually gave up and started to walk the whole time. This was incredibly frustrating, not just for the day in question but for the rest of the week. I was still kidding myself into thinking the cough would go away, if only it got hotter. I had written off today and was ready to go for it the next day.

Having no expectation of finishing well I thought it would be a good opportunity to take pictures and admire the scenery. I don't normally get the chance to do this as I'm looking at the ground trying not to trip over. I had spent the last few months mocking the majority of people who do this for approaching it as a trekking holiday. This was now the only way I could do this race. At least there was something to look at on this day.

I plodded over the line in about 5 hours, I didn't really enjoy it because I don't like walking. I later joined another queue for the doctors and told them about my cough and asked for some codeine. They informed me that by taking it I'd then fail any dope tests and would be eliminated from the race. Looks like I was in for another few days coughing to get the medal for this.

The coughing seemed to get worse once I stopped. There were so many frustrating things about this event, my own condition being only one of them. Because the route had completely changed we had no idea what was coming up tomorrow, if anything. Whereas normally everything is decided long in advanced and we would know what was happening, this time we had no idea. Rumours would be rife, my favourite was that they were going to make each day longer to make up for the lost miles on the first day. Another was that the race was going to keep the same distance each day, another was that the race had just ended. I started to think about the last one and wish that was true.

At the end of each day we are allowed to join another queue to send an email home. Here was my first from day 1:

Message after day 1

"Marathon Des Aster – bet Simon already had that pun. I'm feeling pretty low now. Just walked 33k in 5 hours and feel like I've been hit by a train. My throat infection got worse and the humid sand dunes nearly finished me. The doc said the only thing he can give me would break the doping rules.

I can't run without coughing and wheezing, I had 2 coughing fits in the run and get them every night. I hope it gets better but probably won't. The long day could be very long. On the positive side I get to take lots of pretty pictures and watch the wildlife, bugs and ants mainly.

I had high hopes for this race but now i just need to finish. It's going to be a long week. Badger seems to be enjoying it though.

You may have heard the 1st day was canned cos of floods. This was the dunes day and wasn't too hard terrain wise. I'd have liked to have run a bit of it.

Anyhoo, I'll stop moaning now and try to barter for some codene, which is illegal but I'm not that bothered.

Hope you have a better week than I'm going to have".

Day 2 – 36 km

We were told in the morning that we were going to run a 36 km loop along trails. Though I wasn't feeling any better I still hoped for a good day. Alas it was not to be. Day 2 went exactly the same as day 1 minus the sand dunes. Read that again if you want.

Message after day 2

"This is no fun. Today went pretty much like yesterday, I ran for a bit, coughed then walked for hours. It's really frustrating. stage 3 was a loop of about 36k back to where we started. They are having to put the course together day by day. Tomorrow is the long stage which should be 80k but i can't see that happening.

If it did happen I'm going to take a long time. Legs are a bit sore now from all the walking though the terrain is not that bad. 60% is trails like you get in lanza/watford. there are quite a few dunes. The desert all looks the same after a while, maybe cos we are staying in the same place. Maybe we'll go to a running track in Marakesh and do 200 laps tomorrow?

Anyhoo, still hoping I can run tomorrow for a bit at least. Might trade some antibiotics for a spag bol later. Its quite warm but no where near as hot as it should be.

Have a pint for me in the wargrave tomorrow for me serpies, I'll probably still be walking in the dark.

Not dead yet."

Stuff You Should Know About The Mds
Part 1 – Training

I constantly got asked (and still do now) "How do you train for something like that?" My response was that I ran marathons and ultras most weekend and had already done something similar to this. I also would get asked about the heat and I said I was planning on running for a week in Lanzarote with jumpers on and all the kit to try and simulate the heat. It pissed it down all week in Lanza, I can't decide whether that was a week well spent or not.

This race is not nearly as hard as is made out by the organisers or the press generally. Most people finish. Though I can't comment on how to run a great race I did feel that I was more prepared that most for this. Many of the other competitors had barely run a marathon before. For me this this sums up this whole event. The majority of the people here are not those who love running and want to take that to another level by talking something really tough like a 150 mile run through the desert.

Instead most of the people are here to get a medal and then go back home to say "Look what I did" and probably never run again. It's a shame.

Despite feeling better prepared than most (though much more poorly), I would in retrospect have gone about the training in a different way. Something like this;

18-12 MONTHS TO GO
– START PRACTICING YOUR QUEUING TECHNIQUES

In total, I spent 24 hours stood in a queue during the 9 days of this event; 1 hour at Gatwick, 2 hours at Ouarzazate while the officers got confused by passports, 1 hour for hotel check-in, 1 hour waiting for idiots who were late for the coach, 1 hour again queuing for the second hotel, 2 hours queuing for kit checks, 6 hours locked in a courtyard in a hotel while everyone else registered (all nationalities) because sponsors insisted everyone was there to hear Patrick Bauer announce that the race was on (something we already knew) just so the DVD could show us all cheering, 1 hour waiting for the coach to get out of there, 30mins each day queuing for water at the start of the day, 30mins each day delayed start while the French turned up later and Patrick and his bad translator spoke for ages telling us nothing, 3 hours on the last day waiting for the coach to take us out (the Brits are first in, last out), and 2 hours at the airport. I make that 24.

I would suggest buying lots of things from the Post Office, on Thursday morning in a rundown area so that you are in amongst all the Giro crowd. This is all about time on your feet and the mental preparation of standing around.

12-6 MONTHS TO GO
– DEVELOP QUEUE MANOEUVRING SKILLS AND INTRODUCE STATIC STANDING

In the race to minimise time on your feet you will need to develop some queue pushing-in skills that some competitors seem to have a natural born talent for. Go to crowded bars with obnoxious arseholes (anywhere in the City – Camden, Soho or Shoreditch should suffice) and try and get served. Try and distance yourself from any thoughts of empathy for the others around you, they'll do the same to you. If you manage to get drunk you are doing fine.

Standing is the key here. Each day you are tormented by a comedy double act of Patrick Bauer (race organiser) and a really bad translator as they read out the list of those who have dropped out, tell you (incorrectly) how much water is at each stop, point out (vaguely) if there are any deviations from the road book, and remind you to keep your running number in full view.

I would suggest attending any local Punch and Judy events (or other children's shows) which involve standing up, craning your neck and trying to comprehend mindless drivel. I hear the Chuckle Brothers are doing a world tour next year.

6-3 MONTHS TO GO
– DOING IT IN THE HEAT, WITH BACK PACK AND INTRODUCE FORM FILLING

By now you should be able to queue for 2 hours comfortably and your head should have similar rotational abilities to an owl. Now is the time to step it up and do the same things in heat and with the kit on. Perhaps take a rucksack onto a tube train in rush hour and crane your neck a lot. You may get hauled up by the

British Transport Police for this and may have difficulty explaining all the Vaseline and freeze dried food in your bag.

To do this race you will be required to fill in a lot of forms. Medical, Admin, Security, Media, Insurance, Passport Control, etc. If it's been a long time since you were in school, then this wrist breaking activity may seem a bit daunting. Don't panic though, as there are plenty of ways of exercising your wrist. Try signing up to market research panels where they send you stuff to fill in each month about your attitudes to baked beans, or your preferences for types of tree in some park you never go to. Alternatively do what I did and sit some marketing exams. Not only do you get some intensive 3 hour sessions of hand writing but you also get valuable practice in reading and writing absolute drivel. Plus you get some funky letters to add to your name. I'm now James Adams B(Econ)Sc, MSc, CIM, Dip Digm, MRS Cert. My business cards are on sheets of A3.

Now is also the time to cut down on your alcohol intake and general frivolous spending – not because it will help you in the race but because you will soon be billed for £1500 to pay for half of the race.

3 MONTHS TO GO – DO SOME RUNNING (OPTIONAL)

Most people don't bother with this bit but are still fine.

STUFF YOU SHOULD KNOW ABOUT THE MDS PART 2 – EQUIPMENT AND FOOD.

I discovered two universal truths about this when I got out there in the desert; both were given to me before I went out there but

I disregarded them anyway and went ahead. The first one is that *everyone* takes too much food. The second is that no one has ever figured out how to drink through those bottles with the straws sticking out of the top.

My pack weighed about 9 kg, which was on the light side especially for a Brit. The lower limit is 6.5 kg and some of the elites were bang on that. Mohammed Ansul had a pack that was even less and had to add a couple of cans of red bull to get the weight up. All of his compulsory equipment fit into a tiny pot and his food was all crushed up nuts.

My food consisted mainly of nuts, bombay mix, some sweets, and expedition meals. The expedition meals are surprisingly calorific; each with 800 cals and weighing only 130 g. I also took Beef Jerky, energy drink sachets (which don't count as calories in the registration process) and some Kendal Mint cake, but the latter was dumped on the second day as it was too heavy. During the course of the week people will be ditching food. You'll be burning 5000 calories a day, but you are only required to take 2000 per day. This is enough, you may as well accept that you'll be burning off fat.

Day 3 – The "Long" Day – April Fool's day.

There were rumours going around the British camp that the French organisers like to play tricks on us on April Fool's Day. Practical jokes such as pissing in the water or moving direction signs were the most common rumours. I was already convinced that this whole week was a joke and wasn't really worried.

This is the day (or two days) that most of the entrants fear. Few people run this far at all let alone in the middle of a week of hard running. There is a 36 hour cut off for covering about 50 miles. It seems like crawling but so many fear it.

The night before we were told by our concierge to expect a run of "between 70 and 80 km". I had doubts they could do a long day as the weather was still unpredictable. Later on, at night, we were told that the actual distance was going to be 91 km. This was the longest the MDS have ever done. Despite still being ill I was looking forward to this. This was going to be the bit I enjoyed more than the other stages.

It started really well. I had started near the back this time but was making good progress at getting though the field. For the first time since I'd been here I felt like I was running through a desert. There was still some residue from the rain but the whole run was punctuated with things to see rather than a track against what may as well have been a TV studio backdrop.

I was determined to keep running for longer today as I wanted to take advantage of the "rest" day tomorrow. All those who can finish this in one day get to spend a day at leisure. All those who cannot have to suffer all week.

The first 40 km was really nice. The weather was picking up and the course consisted of paths winding their way through trees (yes there were many more than I expected) and large salt plains against a glorious rocky backdrop. This is what I paid my money to do. The feeling of actually running in a desert probably kept me going for longer than I could do on previous days.

We hit a minor sand storm going through one of the passes. There was a huge salt flat in between two gebels. The sand hit me but it was fine, I started to feel good about the day and ran on. There was a checkpoint after about 40 km which was partly hidden. I did the usual stamping thing and carried on.

I prematurely got excited about how far I had run and that I was not coughing yet. I was at the checkpoint for 40 km in about 5 hours and thought I could get this whole thing done in about 12 which would be a vast improvement on the previous days. I wasn't too bothered about my times or positions anymore, I had come expecting to finish in the top 100 just by running most of it. But, like most of the field, I was reduced to walking large sections of it. For the first time the sun started to make it hard work and we headed out of the checkpoint into a long straight stretch.

My previous excitement turned to frustration as soon as I jogged out into the open terrain. I inhaled my first lungful of sand and had to stop to cough it out again. I spluttered on like a car on its last legs but to no avail. It was like having shards of glass in my lungs and making my lungs do more work than was essential was very painful. I tried putting my buff over my mouth but that just restricted my breathing which had the same effect and the sand was already in.

I had kidded myself on both days previously that this would not last for the rest of the leg and each time I was wrong. It was the same here; as soon as I get this flat winding bit out of the way I'd be fine. Obviously this did not happen.

I walked along as many people walked past me. I had not done any walking training as I had not planned on walking any of this and was abysmal at it. There is a technique to walking which I did not have and the dozens of people walking past did, kicking up more sand as they went by. I had several coughing fits where I'd have to stop and hold onto something and cough. One time I coughed so hard my nose started to bleed.

I sat down on a ledge facing the runners coming past and tried to stop the bleeding. I watched a small pool of blood and snot form right underneath me and then insects gather round to feast. It didn't look very appetising to me but I guess there is not a huge amount of food in the desert. By chance I looked up to see the Ansul Brothers running straight at me and then passing either side. They looked very comfortable running and I could not get a "well done" out in time. They started 3 hours after me and this was the first of a succession of runners who cruised past me. I had hopes of being in the top 50 at the start of the race but now I was looking at last 50.

My nose stopped bleeding and I continued, being overtaken by faster walkers and even faster runners. Hopes of getting this done before midnight had evaporated, unlike some of the moisture that was still in the air. I had some time again to admire the scenery and it really was spectacular. There was a huge ridge to my right that I would normally have loved to try climbing. It looked like we were going to go round it but then as the sun was starting to disappear behind this magnificent piece of geology I saw the path and a line of walkers heading straight into it. Fuck.

It wasn't the biggest or the hardest climb I've had to do but the idea of getting myself up any vertical distance seemed a struggle. As I started to climb I saw the two Chris's, people I was sharing a bivouac with. They were both doing quite well in the race and I knew at this point that I was at least in the top 3rd still, despite the walking. As we climbed into the dark pass we switched on the glow sticks that we were provided with. The climb was horrific. There was no sand in this crevice but the effort of scrambling up was still so hard to take. I would climb on my hands and knees and then have to stop every few seconds to try and extract oxygen through some pretty violent coughing. My legs were trembling too. I had to stop and plan the next few steps of any climb, taking into account what would consume the least energy and oxygen so that I could at least get to a higher place and stop again. I would have to think about where to place my hands, what I could grab hold of and where to fall if I needed to. I fell several times. Fell runners do a similar thing when bounding down hills at lighting pace, they carefully (but very quickly) consider where exactly they are going to plant their foot each time. The costs of getting it wrong for them could be broken legs but they take that risk because those races are won on the down hills. I had less time pressure but the cost of getting this wrong for me was that I'd still be in this crevice come sunrise.

There was no one else around me while I was making this climb. It almost felt like people were standing back to watch. I could see glowing at the top of the pass but luckily there was no one immediately behind for me to fall on. I can't remember how long it took or how many times I stopped or slid back down. I do remember getting to the top, falling down on my knees and thinking about whether I'd make it to the end.

I spent about 10 minutes sat at the top looking back down at what I'd just climbed which is probably a silly thing to do. I looked back down on the short but significant climb that just nearly broke me, I should have turned the other way, like when someone gets pulled out of the water, the first thing you do is make sure they are facing away from the water while you do all the other stuff. Stops them panicking. I'm glad I was facing back down though as I saw a chap skipping up the rocks. I was not hallucinating at this point, it was in fact one of the elite runners. He got to the top in a fraction of the time I did, stopped to say hello, asked me to activate his glow stick and then skipped on. It was only at this point I looked the other way and saw what was coming up.

I watched the glow stick bounce down a path similar to the one I had just climbed and then continue and join this amazing line of other glow sticks that spread as far as the eye could see. It was a spectacular sight that I tried to get a picture of but it wouldn't come out. A photo wouldn't have done it justice anyway, it was truly amazing.

I was drawn in like a moth to a flame, wanting to join this army of glowing walkers lifted me out of despair and got me climbing back down onto the sand. The next 10 km or so were over sand dunes.

The next few hours were also incredibly tough but for a short while I managed to forget about the discomfort I was in and concentrate on moving forward. My head torch would show the grains of sand flying across my head, it would also reflect against the others ahead of me. If I turned my head to either side I could see nothing, there was no life here, nothing for the light to reflect off. The sand dunes varied in height and incline, some were much easier to get up than others. I think I was still coughing but by this stage I think it had become an unconscious action. I no longer had to think about coughing, I was just doing it.

The tops of the sand dunes are concave, like volcanoes, which means you can't see what is immediately beneath. I'd be looking ahead at the huge line of dim light ahead and when I'd start climbing a dune this line would disappear. I could still see the one behind me but then when I was on top of the dune the whole lot would disappear. One time I was on top of a sand dune I felt like I was the only person in the world, I could not see any humans or any sign of civilisation for 360 degrees. I've done plenty of races where I feel like the only one around even when there are people right next to me; it is a strange but liberating feeling. This time I felt alone because I *was* alone. It was an amazing 5 seconds or so before the isolation was broken by someone else clambering up the dune. From then on I tried to recreate that moment by adjusting my speed so that I was ascending them alone. It never happened again, it was always spoiled by the polluting light of others trying to make their way towards the next checkpoint. I wished they would all disappear.

I was quite calm during this section, between 60-70 km. The feeling of isolation and the fantastic sight of all these anonymous glowing backpacks crawling through the desert made this a new experience that I was enjoying enough to forget about the struggle. I would still find myself short of breath getting up the sand dunes but when that happened I'd just stop, sit down and look at the stars. It was a perfectly clear night and looking at the stars in the sky was a very relaxing and calming thing. I don't get to do this very often in the smoke back home. I thought about how people would have used these to plot their course instead of the glowing way markers that we were following. I counted myself lucky that I got to see such a thing and started to feel like the expense and the faffing around was worth it.

The next checkpoint came a bit quicker than I was expecting, probably because I no longer had any sense of time. The checkpoint looked like a refugee camp, there was a medical bivouac and a sleeping one. All of a sudden I became very aware that I was covered in blood and coughing like a dying man on an anti-smoking advert. I feared that I may get pulled from the race if anyone saw me like this so I held my breath and walked past the marshals and headed for the sleeping tent. Just after getting there I saw Dan Afshah, who was one of the leading Brits but was not having the best of times either. He took a power nap of about 10 minutes before heading off. I stayed for about 45 minutes, hoping to catch my breath before heading out again.

The terrain from 70-80 km was more of the annoying rocky path of the previous days. By this stage I was walking pretty slowly and had no walking skill. I think I tried running again but it just wouldn't work. I started to feel pain in my heels, something I'm not used to as I had never walked so much before. I knew I had some blisters on my heels and each step was pretty painful. My legs did not hurt at all. I wish my legs did hurt though, that would have involved some running.

I was starting to get really frustrated and angry with myself and everything. The path was flat but had loose rocks the size of bricks strewn everywhere. When I was walking I felt like I was tripping over every one of them. Each time I did I would stop and curse. Sometimes I'd kick the rock out of the way, once

I even picked it up and threw it. I was staggering from side to side, in pain from the blisters, still coughing and most of all frustrated that I was having such a bad time and could not see how it could get any better. I left the previous checkpoint about 9:30 pm and thought I should not take more than 2 hours to walk this stretch. There was a huge green laser pointing out from what I thought was the end of the stage. I could not see the source but its light seemed to curve right over where we were running.

Edging slowly forward felt like it was using an incredible amount of energy, each step was an ordeal and all I could focus on was the time passing and the checkpoint not coming. The 2 hours I'd given myself came and went. At 11:30 pm there was no sign of the checkpoint, at midnight there was still no sign. The green light now was directly above my head and it felt like I was walking through a tunnel, the sky only a few feet above me. The rage I felt from kicking bricks turned into an admission of defeat. By now I was no longer angry at these inanimate objects in my path, I just accepted them and tried to move on. My brain felt like it was frying. It gets quite cold in the desert at night but I didn't feel the need for long sleeves. I had put on my warm top but overheated after a few minutes and went back to the T-shirt.

12:30 am came and went, still no checkpoint. I'd been on this stretch for three hours and in this stage for 15 and a half. I was thinking about everything and nothing, like some nights when you can't sleep. There was something nagging me inside my head that I couldn't get out. It wasn't important but it was consuming me, like a broken record playing the same three seconds of barely audible noise over and over. I was not physically tired nor did I feel sleepy but was really struggling being in the state of awakeness. I lost hope of finding this checkpoint, I thought all the others around were going the wrong way too. I'd never felt this bad in a race before, I had long forgotten the moments I enjoyed just a few hours before. 1:00 am came and finally I could see something up ahead. I could not believe that what I'd just travelled was just 10 km, nor could I really believe that the checkpoint was finally here. I saw the source of the green light which I thought would be at the end. I collected some unneeded water and headed for the bivouacs.

11 km/7 miles to go. This is quite a significant distance for anyone who belongs to the Serpentine running club. 7 miles is the length of the most popular club run "the 3 parks" which involves a lap around Hyde, Green and St James' Parks. It is also significant as many will use this to reference the last 7 miles of a race that they are in. I know for many a marathon I have reached the 19 mile point and said "only 3 parks to go". The same applies in longer races and the longer the race the more potent the effect. 43 miles into a 50 miler or at Perivale in the GUCR I can easily visualise the end of the race because all you have left is a distance that you have done 100 times before. I can take myself out of wherever I happen to be (a canal path, an Alpine trail, Canadian forest or Rotherham) and put myself at Speakers Corner in Hyde Park and think about jogging around familiar surroundings with people that I know and looking forward to the pub at the end. This always helps, but in this instance it just didn't occur to me.

I could not think of anything apart from whatever was rattling through my brain, I could not get it out. I had not slept well all week and felt sleep deprived but not sleepy. I knew that one of the key functions of sleep is to clear your brain cells of all the crap they build up over the course of the day. The cells build connections which normally get reset when you sleep and those that don't become memories. Right now I was building up bad memories that were clogging up my head and stopping me from functioning properly. My head was being poisoned and

I could not stop the flow. I felt mentally weak. It still seems ludicrous to this day but with only "3 parks to go" to the end of the long day I got my sleeping bag out of my bag and crawled inside. I needed to sleep, just to forget.

It wasn't the first time I'd woken up still wearing my shoes. I didn't take them off for fear of not being able to put them back on again. I looked at my watch and it was around 4 am. I'd been asleep for 3 hours, completely out of it. I could have stayed there longer but for the first time in ages remembered why it was that I was there. There was a stage to get to the end of and I had to get up and walk it again. It was still dark, I was still coughing and it was cold. I was pleased that it was cold, it meant I was no longer roasting myself from the inside. I left the checkpoint as anonymously as I arrived. Funny thing this race, there are hundreds of runners and organisers and no one really gets to know anyone. It felt like I was just leaving some service station in the middle of the night, no one cares where I've been or where I'm going, I just got up and walked.

The participants (none of them were runners by this stage) were spread out much more thinly now. I had to start looking out for the occasional markers to make sure I was headed in the right direction. I knew this was going to be a long and painful finish but I at least felt myself again. The track was the same as before and as the sun came up I could at least see in front of me and not trip up on all the rocks. I hadn't imagined that I'd be finishing the long day in daylight. I was looking forward to this day more than any other. I had nailed the long day on my only other multi-day race, but this time the long day nailed me. The sun was starting to heat up the desert floor again as I crossed the finish line. I felt nothing as I walked through the banner, collected my water and headed for my tent. Half of the people were already there, some sleeping and others just milling around. I wasn't sure what to think about what I had just done.

That was undoubtedly the hardest day of effort I have ever had, 21 hours of running/walking/staggering and sleeping.

Day 4 – The Marathon Day

This was to be the last day. Normally the last day is a 10 mile showboating exercise but instead it was going to be quite a long run. I was looking forward to getting it over with. There were a couple of marketing things we had to do for the DVD in the morning, one was to stand around for ages in a roped off area that spelled the number "24" to denote that this was the 24th MdS. Also we were given new running numbers to put on as it was considered important by the sponsors that their name looked nice and clean for the many photos that would be taken that day. I kept my blood splattered number I'd been wearing all week and threw the others away. I could not be arsed spending my time making sure that the DVD looks good and that the race organisers looked like heroes.

After the usual start line nonsense and the French turning up late again we set off on the final stretch of the MdS. I started this day as I started each day, running and expecting the moment to arrive where I could no longer do this. The marathon day actually turned into the best of days; I could run for most of it. The terrain was quite challenging but all great to run on. There were plenty of smaller sand dunes, a few rocky passes, some tracks and roads, and lots to look at. Finally we got some of the heat that we had been threatened with for 2 years. While running and enjoying the atmosphere of the last day I felt a strange sensation that I had not felt at any stage in the race until now, I was sweating. The combination of the heat and my running actually convinced my body that I was in need of cooling down and was making me sweat. It was lovely.

There were quite a few spectators in this leg, at least 20, more than I am used to in other races I have done. I wondered where all these kids came from, there were no houses nearby. I wondered what sort of curfew their parents imposed on them? How far were they allowed to wander into the desert before they had gone too far?

Towards the end of the stage there was a significant climb up a rocky pass. At this stage kids were around telling us that there was only 2 km to go and asking if they could have your water bottles/hats/buffs etc. They were not aggressive or anything but at that stage I didn't believe that there was only 2 km to go and kept hold of everything. Then at the top of the climb I saw the finish – it really was just 2 km away. I scrambled down and started my final approach, still running. This was the only day where I ran most of it and was the day I enjoyed the most. As I got to the bottom of the slope I had to give some water to a Spanish guy in distress, he looked pretty dehydrated and I could only give him warm water.

As soon as I got near the end I gave the fastest sprint finish that I have ever done for a race though it was missed by all of the cameras. I got a lot of cheers and comments afterwards. It's a shame there is no photo evidence of my finish, just one of me looking exhausted. I reckon I'd have given Usain Bolt a good race in the last 100 m of that one. As I steamed through the finish a loudspeaker was playing "Won't get fooled again" by The Who.

So there it was, all done. Well, all that we were given to do anyway. It's hard to sum up this week but it was hard for so many reasons that have nothing to do with the challenge of running. I felt like I was taking part in a corporate challenge rather than a test of endurance, everything about this race reeked of marketing and PR. Fair enough there is little they could have done about the flood but the focus seemed to be on making a great DVD rather than putting on a great race. I didn't like all of the faffing and queuing involved.

This became more of a challenge for me because of the illness. It was one of the least enjoyable weeks of my life and even at the end I felt nothing. No cause to celebrate or sense of relief, just a feeling that I'd ticked a box and could get on with other runs that I really wanted to do. It's hard to see this as anything more than a large dent in my credit card. There is other stuff out there; harder, better organised, less pompous ceremony and a lot less expensive. I still didn't feel like I had finished, I knew two more days of queues and hotels awaited. I wasn't going to consider this over until I was back in the UK. Plenty of stuff to look forward to, a running race along a canal then a running race around Greece.

It did not take too long to get the Marathon des Sables out of my mind, though it took much longer to get it off my credit card statement. The week after, while feeling mostly recovered from the cough, I ran the London Marathon in 3:18. Not a great time but I was pleased to get back to some kind of normality. Really the only thing I had on my mind was the GUCR again next month. Having done it before I figured I could only improve. I was about to learn a very important lesson.

9

GRAND UNION CANAL RACE 2009 – NOT A DODDLE

"But you've done this before so you know what to expect. It should be a doddle this time"

This is a line I heard from every other person I spoke to about this race this time. In some respects I was inclined to agree. I remember vividly some of the darkest moments of last year's race and even more the euphoric ones. I have relived and retold my experiences time and time again to all that would listen. There was a part of me that nodded in agreement at the thought of this being routine. I've done it before, I've done a lot since, what could go wrong?

Then again, what can be routine about a 145 mile race? 30+ hours, 500000 steps, 15000 calories, sleep deprivation, hallucinations, exhaustion and pain. Anything can happen in that time. Many people succeed several times then don't make it. Many more just don't make it. Each year this race indiscriminately eliminates 60% of all those who turn up at the start line.

I could not decide which one I wanted to be true. An easy 145 mile jog back home leaving half of the sunny bank holiday left over to enjoy beer and lounging like everyone else seemed appealing. However if I really wanted that then I wouldn't have bothered turning up for this, would I?

I felt a lot less sick in the morning than I did last year. I was getting a lift down to the start with Nick, Drew and Nick's girlfriend Amy, who had signed up to support him all by herself. That was going to be a tough job. I couldn't imagine staying awake that long unless I was running. I didn't get much sleep the previous night. The sickness soon came though as soon as I scoffed two McDonald's breakfast meals. The guys serving us seemed a bit confused that we were walking through the Drive-Thru.

I recognised a lot more people at the start this time and had done in the pub the night before. It seemed a bit like a family reunion. I got at least one "J-Lo" comment. Dick Kearn had sent my race report of last year to all entrants and insisted they read it beforehand. It was nice to hear that so many people enjoyed reading it.

I looked ahead waiting for Dick to sound his horn, recalling fondly the low bridge straight ahead that you have to duck under, which can get a bit crowded with 85 people heading for it. Off it went and so did we. It's amazing that I've only been here once before yet every bridge seemed familiar. Not so familiar that I didn't go wrong within the first mile again, only slightly though and this time 6 people followed me. I did warn everyone not to follow me and most of them obliged, running off ahead.

This'll be a doddle

The first few miles of long distance races are usually a collection of brief conversations with people you don't really know until you run out of niceties and then want to speed up/slow down into your own run. There is plenty of time. The running order of questions is always the same too. Have you done this before? That's great, when did you do it? Wow, how did you do? Cool, what was it like? Oh my God, and yet you are back here doing it again? Brilliant, my name's Dave by the way, what's yours? Kind of like a clichéd chatting up conversation; Do you come here often? Oh, so what do you normally do then? Wow, I find [boring thing she just said] really interesting, how did you get into that? Oh excellent I find [thing she just said but can't quite remember because you weren't really listening] is really tough on the elbows, what do you do about that? I prefer the ultra-running conversations though, I rarely get slapped in them.

I stopped to fill my barely depleted water pack up, eat some cheesy biscuits and move on. As I did I noticed water dripping down my back. I took my bag off and made sure the cap was on the water then carried on but it still dripped. I took it off again and gave it a closer look to find a large but neat gash in the top of it. My water pack was now useless and I had to run back to the checkpoint, passing everyone as they left. I had a hard time explaining to all those that I passed in 0.8 seconds or less what was wrong. I laughed it off and said my bladder had burst, people were genuinely worried that something bad had happened. I got back to the checkpoint and asked Dick if he had any water bottles spare. There were none so instead he emptied a bottle of lemonade and filled that with water. A flimsy 2 litre bottle was to be my water carrying device for the rest of the race. I am very grateful to Dick though – there was at least 15p worth of lemonade in that bottle.

The complete loss of my hydration system was a good cause to panic. From now on it was going to be an inconvenience to have to unload my bag every time I wanted a drink, but I was really quite good at keeping it under control. I was very aware of how easily little hic-cups can snowball into huge mental neuroses and then potentially end the race. I just laughed it off. 10 miles in and my race could be fucked already, ha ha ha.

Don't Panic

The sun picked up as I started out again towards the third

checkpoint which was another 13 miles away. I started to feel a bit knackered and hot and had forgotten to put sun cream on when I had my bag at the checkpoint.

I couldn't remember many of my split times from last year. My "Plan" was to get to 100 in 19 hours like last year and then not fall apart in the last 45. It became clear even before mile 40 that I was not going to achieve this. I recalled from the previous year that there was a hill after about 44 miles which I ran up with ease. I was told by my team that I looked in a better way than those ahead and I felt that I had not even got started yet. This time it was the opposite. I staggered up this time and someone overtook me looking very fresh. That was me last year. I continued down back onto the canal and had to come to terms with the fact that I was not even a third of the way into the race and I was already exhausted.

I'd been running for nearly 10 hours. Chances are I'd have at least 24 hours to go if I wanted to finish. I tried to completely detach myself from this being a race now as 24 hours more exertion is something I could not come to terms with. I didn't even try the good old "chunking" method of breaking everything down into smaller pieces because I would never be able to forget just how many pieces there were.

I think that ultra-running over the past few years has allowed me to distance myself from the panic button, not just in running but in other situations too. Not many things get me worked up nowadays and I have events like this to thank for that. In years gone by, the bladder incident at mile 10 would have been still on my mind and grating through my brain but instead it was almost forgotten. I knew I felt bad right now but knew in time I could forget about it. I just needed to keep running and it would sort itself out. Don't Panic.

The sun was merciless, hanging in the middle of the sky unobscured by clouds and bearing down on a canal that also had no cover. The humidity was high next to the water and it was really taking its toll. I would frequently overheat as I ran in the sun and would stop to guzzle water. I would explode in sweat regularly and have to stop to cool down. I felt like I couldn't breathe properly, like I was trying to run with a sock stuffed in my mouth. I spoke to a guy who suggested that I ran all the sunny sections and walked in the shade to cool down. This seemed crazy to me at the time – why would you put in more effort in the sun? It was the perfectly sensible thing to do and I tried it. There were stages where I could not run more than half a mile without having to stop, drink and cool down. I'd forgotten the sun cream again.

On the plus side the sun meant that the canal became a carnival all the way down. Everyone was out enjoying the weather, drinking, BBQing and walking. I get comments all the time about the boredom of canals but this was great. Every now and then I'd get a comment asking what I was doing. Typical conversation goes something like;

Boatman – "Hey, are you in a race?"

Me – "Yep"

Boatman – "Where did you start?"

Me – "Birmingham"

Boatman – "F**king hell, where are you running to?"

Me – "London"

Boatman – "Jesus. Whereabouts do you sleep?"

Me – "I don't"

Boatman – *Falls off boat.*

I was running and walking at this stage, stopping frequently to drink out of my lemonade bottle and trying to force myself to stay awake. I'd never felt like this in a race before, it was actually an effort to stay awake. Sometimes I'd drift into the centre of the road and have to force myself back and walk a bit to regain my composure. I was not even half way in and I needed to go to bed. How on earth was I going to make it through the night? And then run on the next day? I tried not to think about it, which was easy to do since my brain was falling asleep and was thinking of those random abstract things you think about just before nodding off.

Don't Panic.

I arrived at the Grand Junction Arms, the 70 mile checkpoint, just as night was falling. Last year I was here about 2 hours quicker and I didn't stop. As soon as I got onto the bridge I slumped into a chair and held my head back and closed my eyes. I could have stayed there all night.

There are not many rules in the Grand Union Canal Race. That's what I like about it, it's all about the running and not the admin. The only rules are that you have to stick to the route, always have your number on the front and that you are not allowed to stop for more than 40 minutes at a checkpoint.

I was ready to go to sleep. I could probably have just napped for 3 hours and then been right as rain. I wasn't sure why I was so tired, I suppose I didn't get enough sleep the week before. I was about to fall into a deep slumber when I received a prod from an organiser.

"You want some hot food?" he asked as I was scanning the scene, not quite sure where I was. The food was very welcome.

Of all the moments in both of the years I have done this race I think this was the point where I was closest to quitting. I was not even half way and I could barely open my eyes. It was very different from last year. I thought about how I got out of the chair at Springwell Locks (120 miles) the previous year. Back then my body had been broken, but this time it was fine. Nothing hurt, I just could not stay awake. When I had been prodded a few moments before, I was half expecting to be on the tube at Heathrow Airport, or West Ruislip, or some other place I may have ended up because I had drunkenly missed my stop.

I was looking forward to passing the half way mark, even though I wouldn't really know where it was. For a while I forgot to be tired and started running along again at quite a pace. During the next 10 miles I overtook 5 people who looked like they were suffering going into the night. I was bouncing. *Boing boing boing boing.*

The etiquette on overtaking runners differs according to the race. In normal mass road races, I would just ignore anyone who I overtook or who overtook me unless they were a member of my club. With trail marathons and ultras I tend to be a bit more friendly and say a few words at least. Often I'll run for a few minutes with someone and then let then go ahead/fall behind. This is easy when there are not too many runners in the event.

I'd always maintain that this is unlike any other "race" that I've done in that the competitors are not really "racing" each other. It would be disastrous to try and run someone else's run in an event like this, to try and keep up with someone who is going a bit faster than you. However it is very similar to a race in that you have an effect on other runners as they do on you.

I was aware of the potentially destructive consequences of just bounding past someone like I wasn't even trying. I was enjoying a rare moment of free running as we were heading into what many find the hardest part; the sunset. It can certainly have an effect on someone when they see another runner looking in much better shape. I know it does on me sometimes.

I didn't want to appear rude as I went past people but nor did I want to lose any momentum as I knew this wouldn't last forever. These moments are among the best in running, when you find reserves you didn't know you had and can really get moving. I overtook them without really saying much, and was fairly certain that I was not chanting "boing boing boing boing" as I went.

It got darker and I started to recognise some parts of the canal that I thought were quite nice from last year. I stopped to ask someone how far I was from Milton Keynes and he surprised me by saying I was already in Milton Keynes. I'd run 7 miles in no time at all. I had passed half way and was almost at the 3 marathons stage feeling quite good. I got to 80 miles and saw another runner's support crew on top of a bridge. I said hello and carried on, by this point almost into complete darkness. I was putting off wearing my headtorch, but now I had to, otherwise I'd be falling over.

I put on the torch and couldn't quite believe what I saw. The light was reflecting off moisture coming off the canal that almost blinded me. It was as if the canal was on fire and I could not see for more than 5 meters. The sun had long since stopped beating down on my neck but its presence was still here in the dark. Not only was it giving me a hard time from above but it had also had been drowning me from below. I just couldn't believe how much moisture there was in the air, there must have been even more earlier in the day. That would explain the sock in my mouth, I could take it out soon.

I left the next checkpoint almost against my will and was thrown back into the darkness, still wanting to fall asleep. At this stage everything looked like a bed. The benches outside the pubs and in the parks, the grass at the side of the towpath, I would even look at spaces in the bushes. I was not concerned at all with getting wet, bitten or hypothermia from lying down on the ground, but I avoided the temptation because I was worried someone would see me and think I was dead. After only a couple more miles I just sat down on a pub bench and set the alarm on my phone for 15 minutes then collapsed into my hands.

I'm not sure what I was thinking here. What difference would 15 minutes make? At least in the MDS I had the option of sleeping as long as I'd liked so long as I made the finish before the cut off. Potentially I could fall asleep for hours and get pulled out of the race. I guess I just needed to get the fact that I was tired out of my mind. It was stressing me and probably making me more sleepy and slower. I was woken up by Nick catching up again before the 15 minutes were up. He thought I was a tramp.

Nick was still looking amazingly well, he was run walking 5 on and 5 off. I walked for a bit and let him run on.

Running ultramarathons gives you a weird sense of romance for places that are otherwise shit. I was not running through Machu Picchu, looking at the Great Pyramids or taking in historic sections of the Great Wall of China. I was not in the wilderness, on a glacier or in the middle of a jungle. No I was in a Tesco car park in Leighton Buzzard. The Tesco wasn't even open. This was the place last year when I realised that I was struggling. About 90 miles in I was starting to feel the damage and about to start on the night section. This time I was already well into the night and had been struggling for a long time. This place has become a reference point for me marking the stark difference between the two races. I'm sure some of the residents of Leighton Buzzard have a sense of romance about this place too, and I suspect that many a young boy has put his hands somewhere they hadn't been before in this car park.

Hallucinations are a very normal thing to happen in this kind of event and I don't get freaked out by them anymore. In fact they happen to me quite a lot when I wake up in the dark. You get presented with objects that you don't instantly recognise and your brain organises them into what seems to be the most logical thing at the time. For example I sometimes wake up in the middle of the night and see some shapes in the corner. My brain usually resolve these into living things like someone watching over me or a dog. After (sometimes a few minutes) I gain my focus and see the objects for what they are, which might be a guitar with a coat hung on it. At this stage I've woken enough to realise that I was silly to think it was someone in the first place. The exact same thing happened here as it did in Canada. I'd see things along the canal and think they were something else; I saw flowers that turned into Oompa-Loompas and I passed lamp posts that I thought were other runners. My headlight would reflect on the water in a way that made it look like a cavernous drop. I'd get a bit worried that if I fell in that I'd plummet 30 meters rather than hit the water.

Hallucinating is different from completely disconnecting with reality, which is something I often do while sleeping. I sometimes enjoy short moments when I know I'm dreaming and then use that to get away with things that I wouldn't normally get away with. Usually jumping off tall buildings or killing sprees. I have yet to suffer that kind of lapse while awake, and running...

I arrived at Tring in good spirits and terrible pain. I'd made a schoolboy error of not putting enough Vaseline on and stride by stride I was grating parts of my anatomy off. I had to run in a waddling style so it hurt less. Every now and then I'd feel 10,000 volts shoot up right through me. I'd never had anything like this happen before, the pain was incredible and random. A constant grazing which depended on how fast I was moving and the occasional shock which knocked me sideways then stopped me each time.

I took my time at the checkpoint again and enjoyed a bacon sandwich. I knew that I had hours and miles to go and I knew that I was in for a hell of a lot of pain but I didn't let that get to me at all, I let go of any idea of finishing this well, I just wanted to finish. I wanted another medal.

The marshals at this point commented on me being quite chirpy in comparison to all the other miserable gits who had been in so far. I felt quite good about that. Despite the sleepless night, sun stroked head and shredded bollocks I was still keeping a stiff upper lip. I ate a bacon sandwich and then saw the marshal was taking a call about who not to expect at the checkpoint as they had retired.

I plodded on and felt at home as soon as I passed the 100 mile point proper. I was now running on canal that I'd done lots of times before. Berkhamstead and Hemel seemed to pass a bit quicker than they did last year. I laughed again at the point where

I remember Ben trying to feed me some warm salad pitta thing. I don't think I found it funny at the time but was laughing now.

I was struggling without a support crew, that much was certain, though it is impossible to say how much. While running the next 20 miles however it was like I had a ghost support crew. I'd remember certain points from last year, such as the salad pitta incident. I remembered chatting to Campbell before getting to Tring and the buildings that looked like scary robots as well as the two sharp uphill paths by the locks and some very steep downhill bridges. I remembered being shushed as we stopped outside someone's house for a food break. I remembered the exact bridge where I came off the canal last year to look at a road sign to see if we were out of Hemel yet and then being disappointed. I remembered blaming it on Ben.

Many of the people I knew were doing the Green Belt Relay that weekend which involves running 6-13 miles on Saturday and then something similar on Sunday. They would all just be getting up now and probably complaining about having to run again, poor things. I was hoping to have this finished before many of them started their run. In fact I would finish after their second run, having started before their first. I saw some early morning walkers and dogs. Another day was about to start. I'd been on my feet now (mostly) for 24 hours and still had at least 12 left. At least I didn't feel sleepy anymore.

It's funny how simple maths can feel quite difficult when you are exhausted. I remember, back in the days when I cared about what pace I was running marathons, the difficulty of extrapolating pace into times. "I've done 16 miles in 2 hours and want to break 3:20, then the remaining 10 I need to do in, ermmm, 8 minute miles, oh but shit there is that stupid 0.2 at the end". Simple maths like that is hard.

It was the same here except I was using distance measures to work out how far I had gone. Braunstone Locks is about 44 miles into the race. From then on there are distance markers saying how many miles it is to Braunstone. So, it's pretty easy to know how far you have gone, right?

44 plus whatever you read equals total distance. It would seem easy, except for when the numbers are over 66, or are odd.

There were a few times when I thought I was 10 miles behind of where I was because I forgot to carry the 1. Only for a second though. 44+59=93? No wait, I've just passed 100 that can't be right.

Don't Panic

There is no skill to finishing a race like this, no natural talent or tactical mastery required. All I think are needed are a genuine love of running combined with a lack of fear. Nick has both of these in spades. There are many runners I know who choose to be afraid of everything they can. Worryingly there are "runners" I know who fail the first thing too.

I was 125 miles into 145 but knew that more had been added due to a diversion around Southall. Whether it was 20 or 23 didn't really matter in the grand scheme of things but it was something to think about. After more than 30 hours of sleep deprived movement you are limited in the sophistication of what you can think about. When basic addition eludes you I would suggest that now is **not** the time to be asking yourself "Should I go long on basic fixed income derivative hedge funds?" or "Is all this stupid running some latent manifestation of suffering earlier in my life that I subconsciously want to repeat?".

Instead you allow yourself the luxury of thinking about things that really don't matter, such as "How often to canal boats crash and is there canal rage?" or "Why does the circle line have only one stop with disabled access?". Trying to guess the extra distance I'd be running through Southall was a pointless exercise but a low level distraction.

I was just ambling along the canal, enjoying my car crash of a race but looking forward to getting it over with. Continuing to dwell on the things that really don't matter I decided to get my phone out to bore the world via Facebook on how I was doing and check my messages. I opened a message from Nick saying "I'm done".

This knocked the wind out of my sails. Well, not so much a wind but a barely recognisable breeze. Whatever it was it felt like it had just been turned the other way. I stopped, sat down and tried to call him but there was no response. I walked on for a few minutes and called again but again no response. I was devastated for him, and for me too, I was looking forward to his finish so much.

Around now was a good time to think about what I had done today (and yesterday). I came here much less nervous than last year, much less afraid and with as good a chance of winning a race as I would ever likely have. I'd been stung badly by lack of preparation and some bad luck. Now I was paying for it, every step was still painful. I was hoping to have been finished long ago but I still had 10 miles to go and they were going to take up to 3 hours.

I started to think about how I'd "sum up" this experience to anyone who asked but was short of time. For this I'd usually reference some inspirational quotes from historical figures or other runners. This time I thought about 2 quotes from one of my favourite films – Apollo 13.

Gene Kranz (played by Ed Harris) is the head of operations for the Apollo 13 mission and is being grilled by his superior about this "failed" mission whilst the astronauts are still up there and in danger. He says "This could be the worst disaster NASA's ever experienced" to which Gene replies "With all due respect sir, I believe this is going to be our finest hour".

And this is what it felt like now. Lots of things had been thrown at me to get me off of this canal; some my fault, others not. It wasn't going to look as polished as the previous year and it was a hell of a lot slower, but getting to the end of this was going to be my finest hour (or 37). I wasn't going to accept that crossing the finish line was a failure of any kind.

It was turning into another glorious day and people were out on the canal in force. I felt like I was getting in the way of toddlers wanting to weave around on their bikes. I started to get messages from Lou who was going to meet up with me with Gavin. I was looking forward to that – she promised ice-cream. I was trying to explain to Lou where I was on the canal. I said about 4 miles from Bull's Bridge Junction, which meant nothing to her. For the first time in the race I got my map out to try and find where I was so Lou could find me, then I took a photo of a sign and sent that.

Crossing the North Circular was another romance in a shit hole. Everything about the whole scene is wrong, however I started to appreciate the unique sound of London. I'd spent nearly two days running through the unfamiliar and now I was almost home, literally as my house was about two miles away. I passed a runner called Jan and another chap who had been walking since 2 am. There is not really much you can say here, it won't matter as he was so close to the finish. I just said "we are sooooo close to the finish". I knew I was about 100 meters from the finish. There it was again, less of a surprise than last year but no less welcome. I didn't speed up for a sprint finish, I just plodded through. It seemed fitting to the whole race.

Shaking Dick's hand at the end of this run and having him hang a huge slab of metal around my neck was worth every minute of the pain and suffering. The mass of the medal is probably equal to the amount of flesh I discarded along the way. I wouldn't for a second suggest that he was Shylock, quite the opposite, the man is a Saint as were all those who helped make this event possible, even Henk who made sure I got up and finished this.

I fared much better in the post race drinking this time, I managed two pints of Guinness without feeling sleepy. Last year half a pint put me in a coma. I'd lost the need to sleep which was great, when you are feeling this good the last thing you want to do is fall into your subconscious. There are times for that during a race but certainly not afterwards.

And so it ended quite unlike how I expected. I thought long and hard about how this matched up to expectations and that got me thinking about the guys in the spaceship again. There is another scene in Apollo 13 where the media are treating the whole exercise with indifference. It's not really headline news. One of the journalists asks Jim Lovell (played by Tom Hanks) "Isn't this all a bit routine now?" Jim replies "There is nothing routine about space travel". Here I was trying to rate my race based on expectations and then I realised that expectations mean nothing in a race like this. It's so big and takes so long that each time I do this it is a new experience. For that I am glad. I see myself doing this run another dozen times in my life, it's incredible. I don't want any time to be the same as the last, regardless of times and positions so long as each time throws up something new and I still finish I'll regard that as a success.

I got bored of road running for a number of reasons, one of which is the repetitive nature of it. Whether it's a 26 mile road through Paris, Berlin, Deptford or Luton it's still the same. You can compare races all around the world directly with each other. Here you can't even compare the same route I ran only one year apart with itself.

I loved the disorder and unpredictability of this year. I was so pleased that the race had so much more in it this time than last time. The extra 7 hours. The sun induced delirium. The night-time hallucinations and narcoleptic moments. The crippling pain in sensitive areas and constant thirst and dehydration. Feeling drained, hot and bursting out in sweat while nearly wandering into oncoming cars. Yes this year was a lot more difficult with a lot of bad things thrown in, but it could have been much, much worse. It could have been a doddle.

I learned so much from my second GUCR. I was slower and in worse shape but discovered that I had a tolerance for suffering and an ability not to panic. I came here with a better time than last year in mind but also to use this as a reference for another race I wanted to do in September.

I certainly did not achieve that better time but I became much more confident as a runner, a feeling that I can deal with hardships that will inevitably come my way. That meant more than times and positions.

During the summer I continued to run as much as usual, it was quite a hot summer and I loved being out in the heat and running lots of miles. It was a great summer of running but also made better by meeting a girl at the running club who I started dating. The first words she said to me on the stairwell at our running club were "Get those hideous blisters off Facebook!" My profile picture was one of my big purple blisters that I got at the end of the GUCR in 2008. It got lots of reactions but didn't think it would lead to me landing a girl.

It was the first time I've ever gone out with a runner, Gemma was not an ultra-runner (yet) but it was great to share time with someone who understood what running was about.

9A

WHY? VERSION 5

I wrote this the day after finishing what I thought at the time was the worst thing I had ever done.

Sunday September 29th 2009

I really don't know why right now, there is no point to what I have just done.

There are low points and high points to every big race I have done. They can come before, during or after the race. Last year's GUCR I crashed pretty badly sometimes but hung in there and felt pretty awesome at the end. I spent the days after just glowing whenever I thought about what I did. I was absolutely sure that this was the case in every big challenge that I'd put myself up against.

Last night I couldn't sleep. Despite being close to collapse on more than one occasion during the 35 hours that I was plodding towards a statue, I could not drift off. My body is broken, right foot swollen worse than I have ever seen, right shin feels splintered and smashed. I cannot lift my leg off the ground and the left is in no position to help out. Somehow I got a kidney infection which requires me to get up very frequently and go to the toilet. When I do it feels like I am pissing razorblades and

I am also pissing blood. The journey to the toilet is horrific. Several times I consider not getting up at all.

All the clothes I wore in the race are in the bin. Two pairs of trainers, Three tops (including Two Serpie ones). I feel like I need to burn them to cleanse myself of the race. Gemma is worried about me. We've only been going out for a few weeks but she can sense that I am really unhappy now, even though she is 2,000 miles away.

The pain was more than that though. I had spent 15 hours of Saturday battering my brain trying to calculate whether I was going fast enough to finish, working out worst case scenarios or "the point" where I could walk and still finish. Even after I had I still was going through all this in my head. What if I got the injury earlier? What if the sun came out on day two? What if, what if, what if?

I've found that ultras have a way of breaking you into little bits and then the effort of finishing builds you back up into a greater person than when you started. This was certainly my experience in previous races, but right now I am still in pieces. I look at my injuries and cannot see how they are going to get better. I try to think about some of the high points of the race but cannot find any. The start line seems to already be etched onto my long term memory even though I have barely slept since then. It seemed like an indeterminable time ago.

I find it hard to accept all the congratulations I am getting from the people I am around because I still haven't come to terms with what has happened. Everyone pats me on the back and I just want to tell them to fuck off. I am feeling no joy or satisfaction from what I've done in the past 48 hours, only pain and a fear of not recovering. It's not the kind of pain you can just laugh off with your friends and know it's going to get better. I hate feeling this way so much that I have vowed never to return. I thought I loved running but how can something I love make me feel this way?

Painkillers don't help. I consider asking for rat poison instead. I went to hell and all I got was this lousy wreath and lump of Perspex. I just cannot decide whether I had beaten this race or whether it had beaten me. For the first time in my life I said "never again".

Why do I run?

10

SPARTATHLON 2009

We got a bus down to the Acropolis in Athens at 6 am on Friday. The race was due to start at seven from the historic centre of town. The sun was rising on what was going to be two hard days of running. I knew from the start that this was going to be the hardest thing I've ever attempted and that more lay between me and the finish line than in anything I have ever started before. 153 miles of non-stop running through rolling hills on Greek highways from Athens to Sparta. The temperature can get very high and there is little shade. This is unremarkable for some of the big hard ultras out there – others can boast better extremes. Badwater is run in a furnace; WS 100 and UTMB have their hills; the GUCR has Milton Keynes. However the Spartathlon is unique in enforcing a time limit which eliminates many of the field each year. 36 hours and strict cut-offs in between. In any other ultra you can go through a bad patch and slow down/stop and "take it easy". Not in this one. You have to keep going, otherwise you are out.

I didn't let these things worry me from the start though. I was in good spirits. John T (4th Spartathlon) made a comment that I looked blissfully unaware of what was coming up, like a happy dog being taken to the vets to be put to sleep, stroked and fussed over like a "good boy" before being given an injection. I had an inkling of what was up ahead but little more than that.

I spent the 2 days before the race feeling like "Junior".

Everyone I met here was doing their umpteenth Spartathlon. Not only that but "Badwaters", "UTMBs", "Western States", "Hardrocks" and "Trans-US" were just being thrown into conversations without any hesitation or even much acknowledgement from others. It was typical for someone's running CV to read; "5 Badwaters, 4 Western States, 8 Spartathlons, a Trans US and some other fun runs". My two canal runs felt a bit pedestrian. These were both shorter than the Spartathlon, flat and with all the time in the world to complete them. No pressure in the big scheme of things. Over the past 18 months I had got used to being one of the more "experienced" runners in events that I did, but today I was the baby. John Price, an American I met had been running ultras since before I could walk. It was great to be in such good company though.

The race started bang on 7 am to a countdown from 10 and then off through the cobbled path of the park and into the city. The roads are all closed to traffic while 300 odd runners heave through the city. They all seemed much more patient than I thought they'd be. I chatted to John T about his previous attempts. This was his fourth attempt and he was hoping for a second finish. I mentioned that I'd only ever been to Athens before for the Athens Marathon in 2006. He said that he thought he had run that one too. After some more chatting I said "I'm going to let my youthful exuberance take over" and ran on ahead wishing him luck. I went ahead and suddenly a thought popped into my head:

The Athens Marathon would normally be such a forgettable race, except that it was a landmark in my own journey as a runner. It was the day when I realised that there is so much more to running than marathons. I spoke to many people along the way including a couple of British guys in fancy dress who mentioned a race they were training for called "The Spartathlon". I asked what it was and they explained and I dismissed this as idiocy. How on earth can someone run that? As soon as I looked it up it became something I had to do, but would need several years to get up to that level. I wondered whether it was John who I spoke to? Was he the person responsible for getting me into this?

Soon we were joined by traffic and headed out of Athens along a very busy road. The heat was starting to rise and the cars whizzing past would have made it worse. I was running close to Peter Leslie Foxall (14th Spartathlon) and Mark Cockbain (4 Spartathons, 4 Badwaters, 1 double Badwater, Trans 333 and more ultras than I've had hot dinners). We were running at a similar pace but spaced apart. It was nice to have some familiar faces around.

The heat was rising, I was wearing my stupid looking sun hat I got from the Picnic Marathon. I commented at the start of the race that I was wearing nothing that would identify me as being British, other than just looking like a dickhead. The other Brits agreed, I did look like a dickhead, and hence I did look British. The hat was actually very, very useful. Each checkpoint would have a bucket of water with sponges in, and I would just dunk the hat in and put it back on. I remembered to plaster my body in sun cream, which I had forgotten to my cost on the canal in May. It did get quite hot (34°C) but I was dealing with it well.

The first marathon was completed in about 3:47

Exactly 4 years ago I ran the Berlin Marathon in exactly the same time, and that was a PB and I could not move any more after that. I've changed somewhat since that time when I nervously took to the streets in Berlin. I like thinking about things like this. I imagined going back to me 4 years ago and saying at the end of the Berlin Marathon that in a few years I'll carry on running, for nearly 5 more marathons, without stopping. Back then I would have choked on my Weissbeer, now I was doing it. And loving it.

The first marathon was pretty flat, but soon after the hills began. I had a "plan" to break this race down into three 50 milers (ignoring the 3 miles at the end for now). My dream race would be to do the first 50 in 8, the second in 10 and the third in 12 hours. The third 50 had the mountain and would take a lot longer.

At around 28 miles there was the first significant incline that I could recall. A winding road through some industrial estate with rail tracks everywhere. The day was still young and everyone was still in the mood for running. I only saw one person walk up the hill. I was still near Mark and Peter as a camera van passed me and then started to record me running up the hill. I felt the urge to run faster and shout things. By the top of the hill I had a stitch but didn't want to stop as I'd look like (more) of an idiot. Mark caught up at a checkpoint and ran straight through it. I was stopping at each one only to drink water and dunk my hat.

I chatted to Mark and he vented his frustration of the first 40 miles of the race. "They are really boring, I just want to get through the first 40 then it's OK". It was true, the first miles were not much to look at. It was all on roads, though now we were on a quiet one. There was no cover from the sun though which was taking its toll on some. I was right about giving the niggles 30 miles or so, after that my legs felt great. On about 35 miles I decided that I was feeling good enough to up the pace a bit as I'd slowed over the hills.

In all long ultras I have done I've experienced "purple patches", pockets of time in a race where running just feels really easy. My last one was after 70 miles of the GUCR this year where I felt like I was flying through the miles. It happened before at 125 miles, there is no reason to it. When your body appears to be working in harmony though I think it's good to take advantage and I did this after 35 miles. I said goodbye to Mark and ran on ahead, keeping a good pace for the next 15 miles.

I could see what Mark was on about; after 40 miles there were no more industrial estates but a road along the coast. The heat was still bearing down, but with a slight cool breeze from the Med coming across the running was a bit easier. There was still no shade though, and we were always exposed. There was a rare bridge or bunch of tall trees that I would slow down in to cool down a bit. I was still dealing with the weather quite well and the dickhead hat was doing its job. I tried the best I could to not hang around at the checkpoints. I'd been warned that many failures in this race are due to hanging around the checkpoints too much. I've been told many times in many races to try and minimise times at checkpoints as you end up stiffening up and finding it really hard to get going again. This can affect your ability to run and potentially endanger your race. However the single biggest reason not to stop at checkpoints in the Spartathlon is because you just don't have the time.

Each checkpoint was furnished with a big board with some numbers on; the checkpoint number, how far you had gone, how far to go, distance to the next CP (all in km) and the closing time of that CP. This number is the most important for many runners, it could almost be a bus timetable. At that time a bus will come and collect anyone who happens to still be there. This in non-negotiable, you can't say "It's OK, I'll wait for the next one". If you get caught by this bus it means your race is over.

CORINTH – 50 miles 7:37

The ancient city of Corinth sits on the 50 mile point of the race and is a massive landmark of the race. The cut-off time of 9:30 hrs is quite challenging for many, and represents a decent 50 mile time in its own right. It's as if the organisers want to really push people at the start to eliminate those who may intend on running a constant and steady pace for the whole race. I suspect it is to clear the busy roads of runners before evening rush hour really kicks in. I got there in around 7:37, well inside the cut-off and probably faster than I had ever run 50 miles before.

Corinth was the first major aid station, but it looked like a finishing area. There were chairs everywhere, food and water, massage tables, cameras and medics. This was the first point where those who had a support crew were allowed access to them. I sat down for 10 minutes and ate some rice before standing up and walking on. I just had to do that twice more, plus a mountain.

After 50 miles, the route took a more scenic turn and went through vineyards, although still on roads. The runners were spaced out enough now that sometimes I couldn't see anyone in front. The route markings though were incredible, sprayed on in permanent orange paint on the road. It just shows how important this race is where the markings are made permanent. There were even big lines and crosses on turnings that you were not supposed to take. It was very hard to go wrong, though I did once and had an Italian runner to thank for shouting me back in the right direction.

I think I made 100 km in about 10:30. A 10:30 hrs 100 km is required as a qualification time to even make it to the starting line in Athens. At this point I was running with a French guy who had never run further than 100 km before. He said there was no way he was coming back to do this next year, it's just too far. It does sound crazy, 100 km into a race and you know you haven't even started yet.

I never ran alongside anyone for an extended period, which was my preference. I couldn't imagine running for so long and listening to the same person, plus all those around me were foreign and it can be hard to understand exhausted English. I was however always within sight of others and we would shuffle past each other regularly, usually pausing to say a few words. I spent some time running near a Japanese and a Korean lady as well as an older Italian man. I could not really think of much to say. I decided I was going to hold off on saying "well done" or "keep going" and similar comments until a certain point of the race. I thought about this a bit; when, say during a marathon, is it acceptable to say "well done" and "good job" etc? At least half way surely? It can feel a bit patronising when you hear "you're doing well" at 6 miles into a marathon. I decided not to say such things until it got dark, which would be around 80 miles. After that it wouldn't sound patronising.

The weather cooled and the route continued through small villages where the children were out in force. Kids would run up beside us with pads and ask for autographs. I signed a few and they all seemed really grateful, their parents just sat in porches smoking and waiting for the sun to go down. A nice relaxing Mediterranean evening for them. Not for the rest of us.

There is a carnival atmosphere at the larger checkpoints which are positioned in bars or cafes in villages. There are lots of people (normal people) sat down eating and just watching the spectacle of runners coming in, throwing themselves into a chair and getting "mothered" by the helpers there. I was still trying to resist the mothering at the checkpoints but it was hard to refuse sometimes. I didn't want to offend those who had gone to the trouble of being there and making food.

The sun started to set. We were surrounded by mountains

and the sun disappeared very quickly. I left my headlamp at checkpoint 30 along with a long sleeved Serpie top and vest. The path starts to wind up a long hill which I was still able to run up. In fact I was having another one of those purple patches where it all seemed easy. For the first time the route went off road onto a gravel track. I passed a few people along the way as I tried to make the most of the diminishing light.

There were several miles of roads with trees packed at either side. From the trees I could hear growling and barking, it was quite loud. It reminded me of a race report I had read a while back about a runner being followed for 10 miles by a dog. I was warned that dogs "go a bit crazy" when it's dark. Greece has a lot of feral dogs which make a nuisance of themselves but don't cause too much trouble. When faced with a dog you realise how vulnerable you are; I wasn't in a position to fight back or run fast if the thing jumping and growling at my side decided to go for me. I was less worried about it hurting me and more worried about catching something. Did they have tetanus and rabies jabs at the checkpoints? This happened several times. I think with dogs you are just supposed to carry on as you are; don't run towards them or away, don't show fear either 'cos they can smell it. Luckily I only smelled of sweat, piss and cheesy biscuits.

It became pitch black quite quickly as I was still running on a gravel path with pot holes. I had a small hand torch as well as a head torch to light the dark path. There were lots of pot holes, so very often the ground wasn't quite where I expected it to be. A landing of just one extra inch really hurt, and I started to get complaints from my right shin. This was going to be unlike the GUCR because there was a lot more night-time; about 12 hours from 7 pm until 7 am, rather than the 6 hours in England in May. It was hard to make much progress in the dark.

Comparing my time and conditions to the GUCR was a constant theme in this race. In May I staggered across the finish in 37 hours. I was really pleased to finish what was a really difficult race for me and took a lot of positive learning from it. However, I realised that in that form I wasn't going to finish the Spartathlon; I had a lot of work to do. It became natural for me to compare my times to the canal race. After 40 miles in May I felt exhausted whereas after 50 miles here I felt fine. It took 24 hours to stagger to 100 in Tring whereas I was going to get this done comfortably under 20. All signs pointed to a good finish; I was a different runner than I was 4 months ago.

With 90 miles clocked up, there was a long descent towards the mountain. I had managed to run for most of the route so far but was now walking out of checkpoints and stopping sometimes to sit. I thought I'd built up a sufficient lead so far to take a rest every now and then. The long shallow downhill was where I realised that the day was going to be much longer than I had hoped. My quads would hurt as I went down and anything steeper would have to be walked. I had a short lift when the "KMs to go" number dropped into double digits. Less than a 100 km to go? Almost there? Not at all. For 60 miles I ran towards a load of mountains and wondered which one I had to climb. Now I was nearly there I could not see the mountains tops any more, just walls of rock. There were quite a few sharp downs and ups into villages but it was pretty much all downhill to checkpoint 47 at 97 miles.

There was a small camp at the bottom of a road with a hairpin that ran up one of the mountains. It lasted for about 2 miles and could be run if I wasn't already knackered. I was starting to feel sleepy and needed my first coffee of the race at the CP. I left pretty quickly and started a slow walk up the slope. I could see the distant light of other head torches in the distance and more behind.

I left a drop-bag with a change of shoes and socks just before the mountain. I sat down on a bed in the medical tent to change and there was a guy who looked out of it lying next to me. I asked someone if he was having a nap and carrying on or waiting for the bus. They didn't know and almost as they said that he just turned over and vomited, still sleeping. People rushed to clear him up and make sure he was okay. I didn't see him again.

350 runners started this with 350 strategies for how to get through it. Mine was the simple 8/10/12 split which was falling apart now as I struggled through the middle section. Others would try to reach the cut-offs just in time. Afterwards I spoke to someone who was getting to the checkpoints within minutes of the deadline; upon reaching this one with only minutes to spare, he gulped some water and food and raced on – only to stop and be sick. That was the end of his race; not the vomiting but the time wasted doing so.

The path had no lights but there was a constant stream of support cars going up. It was comforting to have such a safety net, all the drivers were well aware of the condition some of the runners may have been in and were driving up very slowly, stopping occasionally to cheer. It was useful to have the headlights behind me for a few seconds, that was a few seconds I would not have to use the hand torch to light the path and look for pot holes. The lightening of this mental load was welcome, although it only lasted a few seconds.

100 miles – 19:30 hours – Base Camp

It takes a sadistic race director to decide to put a mountain climb in a race after 100 miles of rolling hills. 100 miles marks the end point of what many ultra-runners will do; something about that big round number seems so satisfying. It was a landmark for sure, but at the foot of that large climb I tried to get out of my head that I was sleepy, hurting and feeling sick and still had to run 53 miles.

On getting out of another chair at the checkpoint, I was pointed towards a barely visible path that departed the road. The climb was about 3 km of loose rock up to an altitude of 1200 m. As soon as I was on the path I was taken aback by a sea of green and red light that lit the place up like a Christmas tree. I could always see which way to go but often not the path I was treading on. Mark had mentioned before the race that the mountain was a hands and knees scramble. I hadn't believed him until this moment. Some of the rocks needed intervention from the hands to get over.

At least this woke me up a bit, as having to concentrate on every foot landing as I scrambled up the mountain energised me a little. I was still physically tired but had a brief adrenaline spike that made this task seem easier than I thought it would. I was still going slowly and getting overtaken frequently by the European mountain goats who get to play on this kind of stuff in their back gardens.

According to the legend this is where Pheidippides met the god Pan. He went over the mountain to avoid Argos, whose inhabitants were hostile towards Athens (and also because he had no need for a new toaster). I wondered how on earth he could scramble up this mountain 2,500 years ago without the lighting that I was enjoying. If he carried a flame he would have had only one hand to stop himself from falling, or maybe he just ran in the moonlight. Perhaps he fashioned a head torch somehow? That would be a health and safety hazard waiting to happen, particularly as he had long hair. Distractions like this meant I got to the top quicker (in my head at least) than I expected.

I stopped and stepped aside a few times to let people who were much faster than me get up. The path was barely wide enough for one person and I'd often kick rocks as I scrambled up then look back to make sure it hadn't hit anyone in the face. Some of the rocks would bounce off the side. I had no idea whether they would hit someone at the bottom.

At the top there is a CP where you are grabbed by a helper, sat down and then covered in blankets. I struggled to free an arm to drink a very sugary strong coffee and just spent 5 minutes looking back at what I'd just done. I could see for miles. I could see the long road path up to the mountain and some dim lights crawling up. I could see at least 3 villages in the distance that I'd run through and that would be alive still with the arrival and departure of others in the race. It was a breath-taking and humbling site to look back and see so much of the course that I'd just struggled over. Turning to my right I could then see the course on which I'd yet to struggle, including a treacherous downhill section.

I'd spent a few hours now wanting to be sick. I wasn't sure whether it was going to happen, it never had done before. I tried to induce it sometimes by downing coke, coffee, soluble aspirin and all sorts. As I got out of the chair to start going down a guy scrambled up to the top of the mountain, went off to the side and puked everywhere before holding his hand up and yelling "OK" and then running on. I found it quite funny. Vomiting is a norm in this race, you have to eat salty and sugary crap constantly and it can take its toll on the stomach. I didn't let my sick feeling stop me from eating; to stop eating would guarantee a DNF, to vomit would just be a minor inconvenience.

The downhill was tougher than the up. My quads were screaming and my footing was uneasy. I slipped a few times and had to stop quite a lot. I got overtaken by about 20 runners on this, though I wasn't bothered by the positions, just the fact that my abysmal downhill was being exposed. I knew that only about 150 runners would finish this, so long as I was in the top 100 I felt like I was going to make it. If I'd dropped outside I'd start to worry. The fastest time I could expect to finish this in now fell from 30 to 32 hours.

One of the runners who overtook me was Peter who looked in good spirits. He was with Lisa Bliss who looked quite strong also given the circumstances. I can't remember what I said other than "Oh, Hi Peter". I don't think I let on that I was suffering a bit and I didn't want to either for two reasons; I didn't want to make myself feel any worse and I didn't want Peter or anyone else to feel bad for me.

Running in a race like this can feel a bit like being stuck in a lift. The feeling of being trapped and not knowing how long until freedom starts to grate on your mind. Everything becomes an invasion of your personal space, people in the street, cars, animals and even inanimate objects. By far the biggest of these invasions is the presence of other runners.

When doing a race of such magnitude there is little worse than watching someone bound past you like it is no effort, particularly if they want to chat to you about it. Only just worse than that is someone suffering more than you and complaining about it. It's hard to know what to say to people who look worse than you do.

But it works both ways. When Peter overtook me he looked fine and I felt rubbish. I didn't want to contaminate his race with my own suffering so put a brave face on it and didn't really say much. There would later be times in the race where I was on top and people around me were crawling. In these cases I would try my best not to rub it in, even feign suffering.

The bottom of the mountain seemed to take too long, the course went back onto the road and still carried on down. Eventually I arrived at another village and was again smothered by helpers giving me coffee and soup.

I got quite a lot of attention for being British at the CP's.

Everyone would have kids running around asking where I was from, I'd say London and they'd get all excited. For most of the race I was the first Brit through the checkpoints and always got into conversations about other family members who lived there.

"Nobody should ever run a race where they are lapped by the sun"

I was lapped as I ran on some very quiet roads surrounded by trees on all sides. I managed to get back into a run (which from the outside looking in was more of a shuffle). I wasn't too concerned at this point about my pace so long as I felt like I was moving forward. I was trying to give myself as much time for the last marathon as possible. I'd feel comfortable when I knew that I could just walk the rest of it. Right now it was looking like 10 more hours. I could crawl a marathon in 10 hours surely?

As it got light it started to rain. I had left my sun hat behind at the checkpoint where I picked up my head torch. I had not left a replacement at any of the CP's and worried a bit about coping with the sun if it came out like it did the previous day. I had an idea to swap my head torch for a hat with some kid in one of the towns when it started to get hot. Fortunately it just pissed it down for 12 hours.

The sky was not the only thing that was pissing. I felt the constant need to go to the toilet and would stop every 5 minutes and mostly produce nothing. When it got lighter I discovered that I was pissing blood. The dehydration of my organs combined with the constant shocks of the impacts combined to shake them into bleeding. That had never happened before.

Back in daylight and in drizzle we were running on quiet roads cutting through farms. I had settled into a group of about 6 others who were shuffling at around the same pace I was. With 32 miles left I saw Peter again, I was surprised that I had caught him but he still seemed in good spirits. We had about 10 hours to make it to the end, Peter was setting off for a brisk walk and confident of making it. 10 hours to do 32 miles? Should be fine.

With about a marathon to go I stopped at a CP near a house. By this time all of them were kitted out with chairs and all had runners sat down and covered in blankets. I never could tell which ones were having a break and which ones were waiting for the bus. The bus was gaining on all of us. I saw a guy from Brazil with his head in his hands about to give up. He was convinced that the time we had left was not enough for him to get to the end. I then saw a German guy who I chatted to a bit kneel beside him (a manoeuvre that must have been hard in itself) and say to him, "This time last year I was here and an hour behind where we are now and I walked to the finish". He said something else which I didn't hear as I was away in my own world trying to get straight how I was going to finish. The Brazilian got up and walked.

There are times when it is sensible to pull out of races. I'm not so stubborn that I'd finish any race whatever happened, risking months of inaction or worse. If I'd had been feeling like this much earlier on, say before the mountain I may have called it a day and waited for next year. However I was far enough into it now where I'd be devastated by not finishing. Watching the Brazilian guy get out of his chair and walk into the distance brought the issue into sharp focus. There were only two ways out of this race; one was kissing a statue and the other was getting bundled onto a bus. A bus that was gaining all the time.

I overtook both the Brazilian and German and wished them luck as I passed. Now was the time to lavish each other with positive comments and pats on the back. I was constantly aware that the bus was catching up. I would run only to earn myself walking time. I had no idea how much more running I had in me but wanted to make some more gains on the cut-off before it got to the stage that I had to walk. The repeated argument in my head went as follows: "The more you keep on running now, faster than 4 mph, the more you can walk near the end. But you are not going to walk because you can still run, so it's irrelevant. But just in case you need to walk, you have to run". Kind of made sense at the time, now it just sounds nonsense.

The rain was welcome (at least for me as it reminded of home), however soon after my feet were blistered. I stopped on the highway to take my shoes off and put them back on again. This often works (possibly like a placebo), but didn't in this case. I had something on my left little toe that forced me to run on my left heel. I had a shin splint on the right side which meant I couldn't land on the heel. I'm not sure exactly how I managed to keep running. The toe blister would later take about half of my toe with it.

I also seemed to need to piss every 5 minutes. I was suffering a constant sensation of needing to stop to go to the loo. Most of the times I went I did not produce anything. There was a stinging sensation whenever I did and I realised that I must have picked up some sort of infection. The only positive was that as long as I was thinking about pissing I was not thinking about getting caught, for that was the most miserable and hardest part of the race.

It would go something like this:

I would see a checkpoint that told me how far I had gone and how far I've got to go. I'd then covert the kms into miles (with great difficulty – by this time I can't do division but I remember that 10k is 6.2 miles and a half marathon is 21k). I'd then try to work out what pace I would have to run at to finish in 36 hours by only using the number of whole hours left (to make things seem worse than they were). After arriving at a number (usually around 3 mph) I would then try to work out how fast I was going but by then I'd have forgotten how far it was to the next checkpoint and could not measure this. There were km road signs which I'd try to use too but some of them were missing. Then when another checkpoint would arrive I'd look at how far it was to the next but then forget what time I'd left.

This would spin around in my head like a sleepless night. I could not think about anything else, my mind was not allowed to wander into the usual silly things that usually get me through the hard times. I could not put this simple but impossible calculation down but neither could I get it right. One time I would work out that I had hours to go and could probably start walking now, another time I'd think I was going so slow I was going to be caught by the cut-offs for sure. I'd sometimes just work it out wrong, sometimes I'd have stopped more and sometimes I just thought the checkpoints were further away than advertised. I suspect the latter was not true at all.

Most people in the Spartathlon are racing against the clock. Only those right at the front can look at the checkpoint times and say that they have loads of time. For everyone else there is a constant fear that the cut-offs are gaining. Even if you get 2 hours ahead this still isn't a long time. Later on when the fear and exhaustion take over this collection of cut-off times transform into a very real thing chasing you. Between each point you compare whether this thing has gained on you or whether you have gained on it. It feels like death chasing you. Being told at the check point that death is an hour behind me was of no comfort. It drove me crazy. Sometimes I'd look behind to see if I could see it. I never did but rued the waste of time and feared more that I'd given it time to catch up.

I didn't feel like I was going slower but I clearly was, the time between me and the closing times of the checkpoints was getting shorter. I knew it was only a matter of time before my leg would give way and not allow me to run any more. This happened with about 10 km to go.

The last miles into Sparta were all downhill, really hard on my shin that felt broken. I was capable of a swift hobble which soon deteriorated into a limp. I could not lift my right leg off the ground and had to slide it along, like Keyser Söze from The Usual Suspects. I wasn't sure whether I was going to finish. I knew I was a couple of hours ahead of the closing times but now they were closing in on me. The rattling of my pace and time tore through my head worse than ever.

Mark said to me after the race about feeling "trapped" once you have started. The difficulty of this race is forgotten over the course of the 12 months since the last time, then after about 80 miles it comes back, "Oh yeah, now I remember. Now I'm stuck". If I was hurting this much before the mountain I would have given up since there was no way I would have been able to walk the rest. I was still adamant that I'd only stop if I was stopped. Now this was looking more likely. I had a lot of time left of looking over my shoulder.

It got hotter as I slowed down, the rain disappeared and we came back down to sea level. I was still wearing two tops and becoming slightly more uncomfortable with the heat but not wanting to part with any clothes as I worried I might get cooler. I didn't want to waste time taking layers off, as I did not have much of it left.

The last 30 miles were on a highway that gets busier and busier as the day progressed. I wouldn't ever dare to run on such a road normally, particularly against the traffic. There was a hard shoulder for most of it but there was the occasional blind corner and no shoulder which I'd have to cross the road for. I remembered the green cross code as a child but now even getting to the other side of a road seemed like solving a riddle. Despite their speed most of the traffic saw the line of runners shuffling down the highway and would give plenty of space, and honk. Normally the honking would really annoy me but it was keeping me awake and alert.

CP 73 was next to a petrol station. It was supposed to be

about 2.8 km from the previous one but it took over an hour to get there. I could not get up the kerb onto the pavement and had to look for the ramp. On getting to the table and having more coke and water I got the impression that the people there were quite concerned about me. On leaving the CP a lady took my arm and helped me down the step to get back onto the road and head for the last checkpoint. It was 1.4 km to the next one then 2.5 to the end. 3.9 km, with well over 2 hours to do it in. I couldn't fail now surely?

The highway went on but was now in town with buildings each side. I tried to visualise 1.4 km in my head. It's about the distance from my house to Ealing Broadway station, a journey I have successfully completed many times, often when stupidly drunk. I was trying to figure out whether I was walking as slow as I would at my drunkest. Normally a 15 minute walk may take 20 if I am staggering from side to side. Can I really be going that slow?

I looked down a straight bit of road and thought that it was at least 1.4 km to the end of it. I stared into the distance and limped on. I was getting overtaken by lots of runners keen to get the race finished, every single one of them would shout something or slap my back as they passed me. Seeing them run so fast (relatively) made me feel like the end was really close.

I'd look over my shoulder for the other Brits. I recognised a lot of people as they went past me, we'd shared lots of miles before and now they were in better shape than me and eager to finish. I too was eager to finish but my leg was not cooperating.

The first Brit to pass was Mark Woolley. He looked like he was absolutely flying, by far the fastest and most comfortable looking of all those who passed me. I said I was looking forward to kissing the statue and he said my time would very nearly come to do that. I didn't really know Mark beforehand but I found out this was his third attempt and was going to be his first finish.

Despite overtaking me only 1.5 miles from the end he finished 30 minutes and 33 places ahead of me. Just shows how slow I was going.

I got to CP 74, which was in the middle of an island of traffic. In 34 hours I had seen 74 identical tables of coke, water, figs, biscuits and chairs. This was the last one I was going to see and didn't make a big goodbye of it. I stayed as long as it took to cross the road.

I walked into a very busy street with people and cars. I was deafened by honking and cheering of cars and people. I was looking over my shoulder again to see if Mark and Nick were there, if they were going to finish they were cutting it fine. Then I saw Mark and the tall German guy coming up behind me with enormous smiles on their faces. Both were shuffling along slowly but twice as fast as I was. "Is this a race or is this a race?" said Mark as he hobbled alongside me.

It felt really weird to think that I last saw Mark near the beginning of the race, yesterday.

Mark said if we jogged then we were about 20 minutes from the end and able to finish before 35 hours. I explained that I could not jog and let them go ahead. I was glad there were people ahead, as for the first time in the race I got worried about getting lost. The town was so full of screaming people and cars it would be easy to take a wrong turn. Fortunately I didn't. I took a turn and started on the home straight.

Up the slope I saw people, kids on bikes, runners and support crews all waving and cheering. I still could not see the statue but I knew that it was buried under a huge concentration of people. I watched Mark and the German guy head off and then disappear into the pile. I was there now, the threat of getting timed out was gone. It felt like a huge weight lifted off my shoulders. I was still walking like I was dragging a ball and chain but at least the ball and chain in my head was gone.

For the first time in about 10 hours I could relax and start to think about what I was doing and why. Long races give you lots of time to reflect on things, usually about running but often not. Inevitably you spend a lot of time trying to justify why it is you are putting yourself through this, what are you getting out of it? If I were to remember one thing about this what would it be?

I had these moments before in races. Alone they can make a race seem worth it and worth coming back to do it again. I was trying to think of what it was in the Spartathlon and could not come up with anything. The pain and mental torment seemed too much. I looked ahead towards the finish and knew that the end was going to merely be the end of my suffering rather than a moment of elation. I felt nothing except pain and tiredness. I was just looking forward to stopping and never having to go through this again.

About 20 hours earlier I made a decision about whether I'd do this race again. It would have been based on one of three scenarios: If I didn't finish I would return every year until I did; If I did finish and loved it then I would return just to experience it again; If I finished and didn't enjoy it I would come back and do it again just to make sure. Right now I was suffering the last scenario but had changed my mind. I wasn't coming back.

It was a shame. I never thought there was a race out there that could do me over such that I would not want to do it again. This is how I felt now. Despite the cheering crowds and sight of the finish I was thinking only of lying down and sleeping. I had thought about that a lot since before the mountain climb. Then, right before the end my mind was flipped again by the moment I will take away from this race and remember forever. It summed the whole event up perfectly.

As I limped up the slope towards the statue to roaring support and seeing some people I recognise, I was grabbed firmly around both shoulders from behind. I was startled and for a moment thought it could be some crazy person from the crowd, or a policeman apprehending me or worse still a marshal pulling me out of the race.

His grip was strong and it seemed to last for ages. I turned around to see that it was the Brazilian guy. 25 miles and about 8 hours ago I saw him dejected and as far as he was concerned out of the race. I watched a German talk him out of his chair (in English) and then both of them head off into the distance. Before my eyes I watched a broken man get back up and carry on and now I was going to watch him finish. I could see how much it meant to him as he practically sprinted the last few meters and kissed that statue. That was the best bit of the race.

My own finish was less spectacular. I limped on and saw some familiar faces in the crowd. I saw Nick, John, Stuart, James and Peter. On seeing them I felt a combination of joy and sadness. I hadn't seen any of them for a while and for the first time I felt like I was back with people I knew and who knew me (a little). However I realised that they were not going to get to kiss the statue. I asked Nick how he got on and he refused to tell me, saying this was my moment now and pointed towards the statue. John shoved a British flag in my hand and I waved in in the air, confusing some around me who thought I was Spanish.

I thought about kissing this statue for a long time. I'd watched videos of it in the weeks building up the event, it was practically pornographic. To now be here and about to do what I had seen in the videos was amazing. For years I'd wanted to run in this unique race, for the past few months I thought about having the olive wreath placed on my head, for the past few weeks I thought only of kissing that statue and for the past 15 hours the thing that motivated me the most was just for the hurting to stop.

I crawled up the steps and tasted the metallic rain soaked foot of Leonidas, splattered over the past 13 hours with the sweat and tears of the 102 runners who got there before me. I drank the water from the river given to me by the Spartan girls and then the race director placed the olive wreath on my head and shook my hand as our photo was taken.

DONE

As soon as the ceremonies were over I was taken by the arm by a nurse and escorted to a medical area. I had a choice of sitting or lying down. I was in the minority who decided to sit in a chair while my shoes and socks were removed, my blisters were lanced and then dipped in iodine. I was then given a pair of hotel slippers to hobble away in.

I looked into the tent and saw runners who had only overtaken me minutes before. Some of them were lying on the beds completely motionless, like they had just been pulled out of a plane wreck. It occurred to me that the level of medical cover in this event wasn't a precaution "just in case" something happened. I'd heard so many stories about runners passing out in the race and being picked up by other supporters or the bus. Mark told me about passing out in a lift after his first finish, half in half out with the doors closing on him. The stories of vomiting, hypothermia and collapsing are more common than stories of statue kissing. The reason why there are so many medics at this race is because passing out is normal. On completing the race they are *expecting* you to collapse.

I was helped up by Nick and then took the shortest taxi ride of my life, 200 m to the hotel. I had to use my arms to pick my legs up into the front seat and then out again about 30 seconds later. Nick had to hold open the lift doors as I was unable to get in before they started closing. I was then taken to the room that

I was sharing with Mark and a Polish guy who could not speak English but would nonetheless shout at us quite loudly.

I slumped into bed and waited for one of two things to happen; either I wanted to just fall asleep and not have to suffer the pain of it any more or I wanted the point of the experience to sink in. Neither happened and I just lay there sulking in pain. My legs hurt so much that no position was comfortable to lie in. I had to go to the toilet so often and was now pissing blood. It took so long and hurt so much to get up that I considered not getting up at all. When I did piss it felt like razor blades.

I didn't sleep that night. A combination of leg pain and the whirling of the pace calculations was still keeping me awake and making me sweat. Any dozy moments were quickly met with a feeling of still being in the race, still having to calculate how fast I was going and whether I was going to make it. I'd wake up from the slumber and then get reminded that my legs hurt so much and that I needed a painful piss.

The next day was no better. I could not lift my right leg off the floor and I was still tired. I struggled through everything, and looking around at the others I was convinced that I was the worst one. Everyone was sporting some sort of limp but few were as immobile as me.

I spent the day after with about 4 other Brits and a few Americans. Between the 8 of us there was only one finisher. Whenever someone came to our table and asked about the race I was pointed out as the one guy who got to kiss the statue. Normally I'd feel a great amount of pride, satisfaction, embarrassment and humbled at being revered by such great runners. Instead I felt nothing. Absolutely nothing, like I was without life. The only thing I did feel was physical pain, I could not stand or sit in the same position for more than a few minutes, my right foot and ankle were enormous.

For the first time ever since I started running I was doubting why I did it. I've never suffered the "never again" cliché. As soon as I finished my first ultra I was signing up for more, as soon as I crossed the line in the GUCR I said I was going to be back next year. I just thought "why the fuck would I go and do something like this to myself". I suffered the pain, collected a head piece and felt nothing, not even after 24 hours, not even with everyone congratulating me. I was keen on getting out of there, heading home and being thankful for finishing for no other reason than it meant I didn't have to come back. There was no way I was coming back.

Could it be that this race had actually beaten me?

The Next few days

The days passed, the foot got smaller, the right leg started to lift, I caught up on sleep and ate lots. The blood gave way to clear urine, the stinging became a tingle and the doctors gave me some drugs for it. I started to think a bit more clearly about what I had just done, I wrote down all the details I could remember and tried to recall them here.

The events I enjoyed and suffered during the race came spilling out and I could finally stand back and see what I had done. I'd just completed one of the hardest races in the world.

My limited (and I would not have used the word limited before Sparta) experience of ultras was that they can have a way of breaking you into pieces and putting you back together again in a better way than before. It is normal to feel in pieces during a long race at some stage, feeling like you are not going to finish or you can't finish. My experience had taught me to remember these moments but not to succumb to them. Races are so much more satisfying when you can look back on the moments when you felt terrible and in despair and say that you got over them and finished the race.

For days after I'd finished I was still in bits. If I was to compare my excitement and nerves before the race to the feeling I got from finishing I'd probably have opted to go back to the start and not bother.

The next few weeks I exchanged war stories and read a lot of race reports from others who had been through the same thing I had. I read reports of success stories from those with experience of not finishing. I read tales of those who didn't make it and their vows to come back again fitter and stronger and not making the same mistakes.

I spent weeks talking to people who had done several Spartathlons with varying levels of success and also some who had attempted it for the first time. People don't just do this once, they do it again and again, putting themselves through all that misery. I could not figure out why anyone who had "beaten" this race would come back to prove themselves again.

It was a truly amazing race, very well organised and flooded with amazing runners who were a joy to be around. This is a reason to do it but maybe not to do it again. The risk of failure and pain is too high. Then I realised that this is exactly why people come here again and again, because they know that one day they will be beaten by it.

For the first time as a runner I had found a race which I am sure will one day leave me wrecked by the side of the road and tasting the bitter taste of defeat. I have yet to experience this. I'm not looking forward to it but know that it will happen one day, and more than likely it will happen here.

Within the next 20 years I imagine myself attempting this race 10 times or more. Right now it's James 1 Spartathlon 0. After 10 goes if I have won more than I have lost I will consider myself on top. One result is not enough though.

Next time more than anything I want to run up that last straight like I was finishing a 10 km. I want to bounce up onto that statue and kiss those feet. Next year is the 2,500 year anniversary of the original running of the Spartathlon. It would be rude not to wouldn't it?

11

FIVE YEARS BECOME FOUR

It took a while to get over the Spartathlon, mentally and physically. I tried to run a "triple" 6 weeks later (Beachy Head, Greensands and Dublin marathons) and fell apart only 5 miles into the first one. I completed the first 2 but did not even attempt Dublin.

I had nearly 2 years to get ready for Badwater and felt like I was making great progress. I had run three 145+ miles races and done some heat running and felt even more like this was going to happen. I had to decide on a few races to do in 2010 though and decided to put my name in for the Western States 100.

The Western States 100 is probably the most prestigious and competitive 100 mile race in the world. Originally a horse race until Gordon "Gordy" Ainsleigh ran the course on foot in 1974 after his horse pulled up lame the year previously, it has become the "world championship" of 100 mile racing. As a result of its popularity it is now very hard to get in. I registered my name in the lottery, as did about 25 Brits, knowing that our individual chances were only about 1 in 10. I did not hold out much hope of getting in and did not feel too worried about it. There was always next year or the year after.

I watched the lottery live on the internet, it was the day of our club's Christmas party (I always seem to be involved in some ultra-running thing on these days). I watched the names come out one by one, hundreds of people I didn't know and only one person who I did know, Ian Sharman, who had recently moved out to the States from the UK. The lottery closed and I was not selected. C'est la vie.

To my surprised I was actually really gutted. I had fallen in love with the idea of heading to the States and running this race and now was told that I was not going to be able to do it. I think it was the first time I was rejected from running a race and it hurt more than I imagined it would. I knew there was only a 10 % chance and it was not even one of my "A" races to do, so why did I care so much?

These thoughts troubled me for weeks as I tried to make sense of them. I applied and got into the Ultra Trail du Mont Blanc 100 miler in the Alps the following August but this felt like little compensation. Why was I so bothered?

Over the years ultra-running has become more popular, and its most popular events are becoming oversubscribed. All of the US 100 milers have 10 people entered for every space available. The 55 mile Comrades ultra in South Africa sold out on its release day in 2010. The UTMB had just become a lottery, the GUCR was now too. To do the "classic" events now required luck as well as ultra-running experience.

With this in mind I wondered what would happen if I applied to Badwater in 2012 and did not get in. Details on how many people apply to run Badwater are not available but I imagined it would be at least as competitive as some of the other US races. For so long I had wondered what it was like to run in 50°C up those hills in the sun's glare and now I was thinking about how practically to get into the race. What would I do instead?

And so in February 2010 when the call for applications for the race later that year came out I replied. I put my name in the hat a year earlier than planned.

The entry process for Badwater was unlike anything I had

done before. You needed to satisfy qualifying criteria (two 100 mile races) just like in some others, but you also needed to provide an essay as to why you want to do this race. These applications are then looked at by a committee who decide on the 80 people they are going to admit. Again the exact details of how each application is "scored" remains a secret.

In the application form I listed all my details and wrote an essay about wanting to do the race. It felt like those silly personal statements I had written to get into university. It was a hard thing to do. I wanted to say just how much I wanted Badwater, but did not want to sound like a nut. I wanted to say that I was ready to take on such a tough ultra without sounding arrogant.

There was a competitive element to getting into this race in the first place. I like to avoid competing against others but in this case I had to compete just to get to the start line. I only had my past ultra-running experiences to put on the form and I had no idea whether this was enough. I read into the reasons why runners get turned away and worried. Not that there was anything I could have done about it. Part of the battle of the big and hard ultras nowadays is getting onto the start line.

In preparing your application, keep in mind the standard reasons that generally lead to some applicants not being invited:

The applicant only just met the minimum standards.

The applicant's credentials are only recent, i.e. not a seasoned ultra-endurance athlete with a breadth of experience.

The applicant's credentials are only old, i.e. all or most of the credentials are from too long ago and may not reflect current ability.

The applicant has no experience in extreme heat or on the Badwater course as a pacer.

The applicant didn't "prove" his or her claims (i.e. they said they paced at Badwater but no letter of recommendation was received, or they claimed they finished or won any number of major races but didn't provide any proof of that).

The applicant submitted a "thin" application – not only few qualifications were listed, but not much time was put into the preparation of the application itself. (Sometimes the applicant assumed "we've already heard of him/her" and therefore didn't provide the necessary details. Applicants should never assume we've heard of them or have heard of the events they mention in their application.)

There are always A LOT of applicants, all "qualified," and thus some applicants must inevitably be turned away.

I worried about my experience only being recent, and the lack of heat experience.

This is what I wrote:

Why do you want to run the Badwater Ultramarathon?

It was hearing about this race 4 years ago that got me into ultra-running. I have been thinking about this race since I first got sent a link to it what seems like an age ago. I was still a young runner who was concerned with plotting my next attempt to run 26.2 miles on a flat road in a temperate climate faster than I had done previously. I did this successfully a few times and the satisfaction was small and short lived. Getting marathon PB's and not really caring about them made me wonder whether I was in the right sport. The variety and challenges of ultra-running answered that question unequivocally. Ultra-running has liberated me from judging my running on what a man at the end with a stop-watch might say. I no longer let that guy decide whether I've had a good run or not, I do it myself. Ultra-running has put the fun back into the thing that I love and has given me personal experiences that I would not trade for the world. And like I said, it was this race that inspired the start of that journey.

The last three years have been an amazing journey, from my first ultra (45 miles in 2007) through to the Grand Union Canal Race (145 miles in 2008) and more recently the Spartathlon last year. What I love most about these races (though it usually is some time after when I fully appreciate it) is the way they try to break you down and stop you finishing. Whether it is the mountains and hills, the sun or the rain or just the sheer distance of it there is always something there that is trying to stop you getting to the finish. The greatest of victories is when you are smashed to pieces and on the floor in a race and it seems all but over. Then you hold onto yourself just enough to carry on moving. When you do things seem a little easier and you remember more why you are there in the first place. These are the experiences I want to take to the grave with me.

I have written about my running in my blog for the past 3 years. I write more to preserve the memories than for anyone else but hope that you get a chance to read it.

So back to the original question in why I want to run Badwater. Aside from my 4 year obsession mentioned above I feel that this is the only "step up" for me. Having finished the Spartathlon last year I don't believe there are many more races out there that are harder to finish and hence will give me those physical and emotional breakdowns which I crave.

I am now confident that I will finish this race but am fully aware of the fact that it will take more that I have had to give before. Races like the GUCR and Spartathlon have taught me that I can rely on things that I don't even know I have at the start line. I love starting a race feeling "ready" but not entirely sure how I'm going to get through it.

People keep asking me "how will you train for something like that". Fact is I don't know. I know I can run for 40+ hours, I know I can run well over 100 miles in one go, into night and day and night and through pain. However I'm not entirely sure, after 35 miles of Death Valley when my body and brain are fried from the heat and I am struggling to remember who I am and why I am stood at the side of a molten road with 100 miles to go, how I will deal with that. But I know I'll think of something.

I was to find out my fate on Feb 19th. It was a sickening feeling for a few days. I was injured at the time with a stubbed toe (I thought it might be broken but it was just a nail that went right in). I could not run for a few weeks and was getting frustrated so the wait for the outcome was a distraction at least. On Friday 19th Feb I stayed at home to make sure that if I did get in I could send off all the paperwork as soon as possible. The USA was 8 hours behind so I knew nothing was going to happen until the afternoon. It got to midnight and still no email. I went to bed and just tried to forget about it.

The feeling was like waiting for exam results, there was nothing more I could do about the outcome I just had to open an envelope. In fact, it was more like waiting for a return call from a girl. Checking my computer every 5 minutes just to make sure there was nothing new. Do I email them and make sure they got my last message? Does that sound a bit desperate? Would they change their mind and reject me for being a bit clingy? If I didn't would they assume I was not interested?

I woke up about 3 am and was surprised that I had even fallen asleep. Normally I'd just drift back off but I went to switch my computer on and have a look at the email again. There it was in all its glory:

"Congratulations! You have been accepted to compete in the 2010 Badwater Ultramarathon".

I didn't go back to bed.

The next few months I was a mess of nervous excitement and fear, like I was with my first marathon and the first ultramarathon. It was great to be here again, genuinely excited about what was up ahead, however the stakes here were much higher. This is not a marathon that I have been training three months for. It's not the ultramarathon I'd been training only three months for. This was something I had been obsessing about for four years. I had never "planned" for anything so far in advance. I was scared of it going wrong and then taking another four years to put right.

During that summer I flew out to Spain to see a friend, Mark Woolley, who lives out there and who passed me with great pace at the end of the Spartathlon. Tim Welsh also came out and we spent a few days running in the heat. At the time the World Cup was being played and England crashed out after another dismal performance and as always blamed it on injustice. I am not really into football but it struck me that those players would feel like they wouldn't be able to redeem themselves until the next World Cup in four years' time.

In all likelihood, if I failed to finish Badwater then I would have difficulty getting in again for a few years at least. Four years is a long time to live with that disappointment.

12

BADWATER 2010

"When is the heat going to kick in?" Mark Woolley quipped at around the 5 mile mark. It was just before 9 am, we had started at 8 and were still laughing and joking with the people around us. "Doin' this for the first time? Good man" echoed around the floor of the world's hottest place. It was true, the heat had yet to kick in, it was merely 40 something. Within a few hours it would be over 50. This was the time to enjoy a few miles and the unique experience of running arguably one of the world's toughest and most prestigious events.

I chatted to Mark about what we were about to do today (and tomorrow and possibly the next day). What we wanted and why we were there. There were 80 starters in the 2010 Badwater Ultramarathon and with that there were 80 different stories as to why they got to the start line and then 80 more about the race. I had read so many reports from others that had made an attempt at this race and was talking to Mark about how we were going to remember this experience as we both had for the Spartathlon the year before.

"I don't really know what I'd write about this race?" said Mark. I was about to correct him with the obvious when he interrupted to do it himself. "I guess that's because the story's not been written yet?", he quickly responded to himself. Spot on. Along the famous white line of the road through hell there were 80 unique chronicles of the event being typed as we ran.

I started in the 8 am wave at the Badwater Basin. We drove down to Badwater along a 17 mile stretch of road from Furnace Creek, where the pre-race HQ and all the runners stay. We drove carefully as the runners from the 6 am wave made their way back up to the top of the road. I felt sick as we slowly descended to 282ft below sea level. I wasn't sure whether it was pre-race nerves or the heat already getting to me.

The ceremony is huge; about 30 runners, 30 support vehicles, 150 support crew members, 50 race staff and dozens of media people. The event is immense and the majority of the people here were not here to run but to get a runner to the finish. There was the familiar 10-9-8 countdown and then everyone broke out of the crowd and formed a single line along the road, rather like the start of a 800m race, though a little slower.

Almost as soon as we started running we saw a coach tour coming the other way. I can only imagine what the tour guide was saying. "We are now approaching the Badwater Basin, the hottest and most evil place on earth. And on the left you'll see a load of idiots, who think it's a good idea to run through it".

I found the first 17 miles fairly comfortable, we all took it quite slow except one guy who was half a mile ahead after a few miles. The first section ascends slightly back to sea level then drops again into Furnace Creek where the first checkpoint is.

It's amazing what you can find on the internet nowadays. I managed to find a crew of four people who I had never met before but had committed to kicking my arse from the start line to near the top of Mt Whitney. The rules state that each runner must have a minimum of two support crew and one vehicle. Most people have between 4-6 crew and two cars/vans. Only one vehicle can be leapfrogging you at any one time and typically would do so at mile intervals.

My amazing crew consisted of Laurie, who had crewed twice

before, Debra Haaland who was keen to see Death Valley and Debra and Dave who were friends of Laurie. I was thrilled that people who had never met me had agreed to take this on. I was going to get to know them a lot more over the next 2 days or however long this was going to take.

I said before the start that my needs were fairly simple. I can pretty much eat and drink anything which is an advantage with this kind of race. I gave no instructions on how I wanted to do the race as I didn't know myself. All I said was make sure they put electrolyte in everything I drank.

I stopped briefly in Furnace to use the facilities and ate a few turkey sandwiches that Debra made. They were very nice indeed. It was now around 11:30 and the heat was really picking up. The 26 mile stretch from Furnace Creek to Stovepipe Wells is often regarded as the most critical part of the race. It's hot, flat and with little breeze. Most people manage to make it to Stovepipe, however if proper care isn't taken during these miles it can have dire consequences later on.

The roads through Death Valley are deceptive. It's hard to tell whether you are going uphill or down. Looking ahead gives you no idea and looking behind makes everything look like uphill. I'd sometimes be aware that I was working a lot harder for some reason but it was hard to separate whether it was an incline or a sudden increase in my body temperature. Whenever I saw the crew I would be sprayed with water and given more to drink. My temperature would have been up and down all the time. Adjusting your own pace is so difficult when you don't know what kind of slope (if any) you are running on. If I do this again I'm bringing a spirit level.

I passed the first marathon in around 5 hours. I thought I'd gone much further than that but I decided not to make anything of times and distances here. I was not even wearing a watch and I rarely asked for the time and was only vaguely aware of the distance. Just put one foot in front of the other, and don't die.

Not long into the race I got a headache. It was painful enough to be frustrating but more worryingly it was a sign of dehydration. I was checking the colour of my urine and it was holding up ok, but it was clear that the sun was beginning to do its work, and my right side was burning. I had not put sun cream onto the parts that were covered with my UV50 running top but now was the time to do so. I started to wonder why this place has been picked as the place for the sun to hate. All over the world the sun brings life and vitality, here it just scorches everything and we were no exception. Soon after I passed Tim Welsh who I'd met in Spain a few weeks prior. He was in good shape and was part of the earlier start two hours ago. Mark and I discussed that Tim had the best chance of finishing this. Seeing him fearlessly climb Spain's highest mountain as night fell after running 45 miles on roads without any suggestion of stopping made it clear to us he was going to do ok here. I had decided that day not to do the mountain; I slept in the car.

It was early afternoon and the heat cranked up to 50°C. A few hours into the race I was starting to receive ice-bandanas to rest against my neck. I could not even feel ice against my skin, it was too hot. Every 3 miles or so I would remove my top and dunk it in ice cold water and put it back on. If I did this in the UK I'd probably pass out with shock but here it felt so nice for my skin to be so cold, for about 10 seconds. Half a mile later it was dry again.

Every mile I'd get a fresh drink that was mostly ice. I was drinking about 500 ml every mile and alternating between water and Gatorade. I started measuring the temperature by counting how long it took my bottle to stop rattling. Early on it wouldn't stop for the whole mile, but after about 2 pm the ice would melt pretty quickly. Water and Gatorade were starting to get a bit tiresome so I tried a protein shake. It's important to take protein when going for this long but it was not really the temperature for milkshake and beef jerky. I tried anyway and felt sick. I ran for a few miles feeling sick and gagging before I finally threw up. It felt so good I've never been sick in a race before. Recommended.

I continued running with or near Mark until just before Stovepipe Wells where I went ahead. I decided to stop a while and lie down out of the heat. I got in and went to the poolside and lay down in the shade where my crew covered me in wet towels and cloths.

Around 3 years ago I cycled through Death Valley with a group for a landmine charity. It was in March and was not difficult at all. In all honesty I signed up because I wanted to see the place that I hoped to run in 3 years later. It was all coming back to me, these random towns on a road in the middle of nowhere. Stovepipe has a nice pool, a saloon, gas station, general store and rooms. It was only founded in 1923.

I recalled having lounged by this pool before, at the end of a day of cycling about 50 miles. Here I was, having run 43 miles and with 92 still to go. I was going to be on my feet for at least another day without sleep. Last time I was here at a similar time of day and was just lounging by the pool to wait for the bar to open. No such luxury this time. I did have a can of Coke though, my first treat so far (apart from the turkey sandwiches of course).

I generally try to avoid looking into race maps and profiles before I have to do them. I just turn up and do whatever is there. I don't usually know how high a hill is or how far it's supposed to go, I just carry on. Having studied this one for four years though it was hard to not take in some of the facts and I knew what was up ahead – a 5000 ft steady climb over 18 miles.

A shallow incline would normally not be an excuse to walk, but 18 miles is quite a long way to go so I would not imagine I would run all of it. In the heat of this race any slight increase in exertion will cause your own temperature to rise and increase the possibility of overheating. "You can't control the sun" was a key message from the briefing. Going up a 5 % incline uses about 20 % more energy than on the flat, so it would be easy to overheat. This was not the main issue in this climb though; it was the wind.

Badwater has its fair share of stories and tales that may have been exaggerated in their re-telling. So far I had not had the massive feet swelling that is warned by many who tell the story, nor did my shoes melt for not running on the white line. I was hoping the same was true of the "hairdryer" hill that I was about to ascend up to Townes Pass. Alas no, it was by far the hardest conditions I have ever run/walked in.

The wind was strong and hot. It would just blow right down my throat and dry me from the inside as well as the outside. The temperature was still 50°0C but I could no longer protect myself from the heat, it was going right inside me. I drank so much water but it did not stop my throat burning and my lips and eyelids were drying out. Only the elites were running up this, everyone else was staggering and stopping regularly to get hosed down. It took 9 hours to run the first 43 miles, it took about 7 to do the next 18. It was really frustrating as I still had a lot of energy and wanted to press on. At this point Pam Reed went past while I was stood at the car. I yelled well done and that I loved her book. I plodded on, and started to think about my old cat.

I must have been about 10 when I have this vague recollection of my cat getting put in the tumble dryer. I remember the noise it made for the few seconds it was getting spun around in a heated blast and now finally I can appreciate what that was like. Then I wondered, how did it get in there in the first place? I always thought that it was resting on some clothes and the door was just closed without really looking in. But why would it rest on wet clothes? And if the clothes were dry I can understand why the cat would sleep on them but why then would the tumble dryer be turned on? This confused me for a little while before I decided not to think about it anymore as it was too hard. I just wanted out of the tumble dryer.

At 7 pm we were required to wear hi-vis jackets and blinking lights. It's still very light (and hot) so it can feel a bit silly but the darkness does fall quickly. The sun could disappear behind one of the large rocks that surrounded us in an instant. The sun finally set, having done its job on me for the day, and the stars came out. I thought I had come off quite well but only time would tell; the effects of dehydration and heat exhaustion could still hit me in the night.

I finally arrived at the top of Townes Pass (61 miles) sometime in the night whereas I'd hoped to be there in daylight. After climbing 5000 ft over 7 hours and 18 miles in a tumble dryer wind in a furnace, it was then time to undo all of that and almost run back down to sea level. 9 miles of downhill were a welcome reprieve from all the walking. I asked the car to only stop every 2 miles or so now as I was going to try to keep moving.

Panamint Springs was the next stop at 73 miles and I was going to have another prolonged stay there. The sun had made me sleepy and I thought a powernap, a shower and a complete change of clothes was in order. I could see the lights of Panamint from miles away and a stream of car and runner lights leading to it. I was keen to get there as soon as possible and started overtaking some other runners. "Check you running up the hills" I heard. I had no idea I was running up a hill, it was those deceptive roads again. I really needed that spirit level.

On arriving at Panamint I was taken into the car park and

the roll mat was set up. My idea of having a shower quickly evaporated as I realised I had to climb over a load of people sleeping on the floor in the dark to get to it. There was no way I was going to be able to do that without falling on them and waking them up. I settled for a change of clothes and asked my crew to wake me up in ten minutes.

I first power napped during the GUCR 2009 and it worked a treat. It does not cure exhaustion but it can help snap you out of a malaise. I was suffering with bad thoughts of the things that were not quite going right in the race, complaining that my water was too icy and feeling pain in my feet more. My throat was still dry and sore from the wind and I was having to go to the toilet a lot. I hoped that a quick nap might flush all this out of my head but it didn't. I got up again and still felt quite grumpy. It didn't even occur to me that I'd long passed the half-way point. I had another large climb to do now; 4000 ft in 13 miles.

I've always had plenty to think about when slogging through some difficult races. Stupid question #2 when I tell people about this kind of stuff is "don't you get bored while running?" or "what do you think about?". I had never got bored while racing before, I had always had Badwater to think about.

Every single race and run I have thought about this end. Every struggle I've fought through thinking that it could be much worse when I came here. When I ran the Marathon des Sables with a chest infection I figured, "well you could end up coughing like this in Badwater, and you are not going to drop out of that are you?" Last year I was suffering heat exhaustion and fatigue on day one of the GUCR. While struggling to stay on my feet and coming to terms with the fact that I had another 24 hours of running left I thought about Badwater. Every shit moment I've suffered but got through in a race has been to finish Badwater. HTFU.

Even the races that went well I thought about how they were going to add to my chances of finishing this. The last day of my 300 km, 6 day race in Canada was on an uphill stretch of road that looked alive with a burning mirage. After 180 miles of running in 5 days I wondered if this was like the end of Badwater. After my first ultra of 45 miles I thought after the finish that all I had to prepare myself for was another 90 miles, and quadruple the temperature. And add hills. After finishing the GUCR in 2008 I was overwhelmed with my ability to step up like that and go from 55 miles to 145 miles with relative ease. That was the time when I realised I could finish anything, and by "anything" I meant Badwater.

However what was I supposed to think of when actually running Badwater? There was no "next" for me here, nothing to go onto. This was it. I had nothing to look forward to after the finish line. That made it hard for me to think myself through the race, and made it easier for the demons to get in.

It became very dark. I decided against using a head torch as I find them a distraction and only had the dim glow of my flashing red lights to show me where to go. There are a lot of twists and turns on the ascent and for some moments there is no unnatural light at all, like you are the only person in the world. I love this feeling of isolation. The huge rocks beside me became invisible and all I could see were the stars and the road. This made me think that I was running on a road suspended in space. I feared falling off the road as I thought I'd end up floating off into space so I ran in the middle.

I loved looking up at the stars; there were so many. Somewhere around one of these there must be another planet similar to ours with intelligent life. And if there was intelligent life I am sure they would have discovered the joy of ultra-distance running, which probably comes somewhere between the spear and the wheel on the order of invention. I thought about another being way up there struggling along as I was, in a similar race in similar extremities on his own world. I'll never meet him or even know for sure that he exists but nonetheless I wished the space alien good luck and got on with my run.

Whenever my mind did wander I would start to stray to the side of the road and I really didn't want to fall off and float away, not sure whether my support crew had bought a long enough rope. I was getting frustrated by the slow motion up the hill and was worried that I might not be able to get into a run again when it flattened. I waited and waited for just a small let up in the vertical so I could try a run but it was not coming. I continued to worry and it took its toll until I had a great idea. I just turned around and ran down, only for about 20 meters. I *could* still run, that made me feel better, that made me go faster.

As day broke I was still climbing up the slope. There were more cars now and I could hear their engines struggling up the hills. I had not seen many other runners for a while. The sun barely made it over the rocks before it started burning me again, I was not glad to see it back; it was trying to kill me.

The Panamint pass ended at around 90 miles and there was another checkpoint on a junction in the middle of nowhere. I was starting to get frustrated by not knowing how far I had gone. Was it 86 or 88 miles? By now I was getting really hot, feeling the heat much more than I had on the previous day. This was making me grumpy and I just wanted the CP to come so that I could sit down and have my blisters dealt with. I felt quite a bad one on my left heel and left instep.

At this point I saw a lot of James Elson's support car and figured he was only a couple of miles behind. He started 2 hours after me in the 10 am wave and I was looking forward to seeing him as I had not managed to see him before the race. He had his luggage lost on getting into the US and was doing incredibly well to scrape everything together to be able to even start the race.

It had been a long time since I saw Mark and I was worried. I knew from my support crew that he stayed a while in Stovepipe wells (43 miles), but thought he would have caught up with me by now, or at least I would have seen his support car at some point. Half of my crew went back in the spare car and I asked them to find out about Tim and Mark as they did. On finally getting to the CP at 90 miles, I sat down and was told that Tim was still going strong and was not far behind, but Mark had needed a prolonged stop and left Panamint 8 hours after I had done, having lost 11 lb since the start. The race organisers weigh everyone at the start; I was 186 lb. The only other time I was weighed was at Stovepipe where I managed to put on 1 lb. My hydration was generally very good and Mark had a lot to do with that. When Tim and I visited him in Spain a couple of weeks before I had never used any electrolytes before, and not doing so in a race like this was suicidal. Previously, I had relied on salty snacks but on actually reading into it I realised these were giving me only one of the four salts in abundance and were lacking in the other three.

I was told that Mark was moving again and looking ok. I thought at this point he was unlikely to get the Buckle (sub 48 hours) since he had lost a lot of time, but really hoped he'd finish.

At the CP, I sat in a sun lounger in the shade of a gazebo. It was the first time that any shade was available, the sun was directly overhead and even the van could not provide any protection from the sun. I wondered what I would do if I was actually stuck out here? There was absolutely nothing to hide under. The only wildlife I saw in the whole race before Lone Pine were some little beetles and a scorpion. The wildlife here comes out at night, does whatever it does to get food and then spends dawn digging a hole to bury itself in for the duration of the day. Every mile I was getting sprayed with water and drinking half a litre. How many miles would I last if there was no support van within a mile of me at all points? 2 miles? 5 miles? Not long that's for sure. Humans don't belong here. They certainly should not be running here.

Laurie was keen to look at my blisters, she was well prepared for doing so. However they were not blisters but painful callouses and hence she was unable to remove them. There was one blister which took several attempts to lance before it squirted. It was a little relief but I knew I'd have to suffer the others for the remainder of the race. It suddenly occurred to me that I had not taken any painkillers during the race. This was out of forgetfulness rather than deliberate. In other races such as the Spartathlon I was swallowing them like Smarties. I didn't really feel the need to take them and then I decided not to for the duration of the race – I was curious to see just how much this would hurt.

I now had 45 miles of downhill/flat to run starting off with a few miles downhill. I was looking forward to it.

I got back into a jog along a very long straight road that headed into the mountains that I would be climbing later. I could see the snow of the mountain tops, which looked like a postcard. The road was so straight and still very difficult to tell whether it was going up or down. I managed to run most of the downhill and as it flattened out I was really struggling with the heat. I suffered more strange hallucinations, thinking that the white line in the road was a man in the distance rolling toilet roll at me. The postcard view of the mountains looked like a billboard about to collapse on top of me. These were the worst ones I have had and even when I tried to focus I could not rid my head of them, the guy rolling the toilet paper was still there. I could not run or even walk in a straight line and my speech was garbled. I had overheated and had to stop again.

I stopped at the van and said I needed a lie down because I was seeing things. They all stood around holding sheets over me to keep the sun off and covering me with ice cold towels and flannels. I lay there for about 20 minutes and tried to sleep again to get the demons out of my head. Soon after, Debra made a sign to say that we had passed the 100 mile mark, this pleased me lots.

The road didn't seem to get any shorter as I plodded down it (or up it?). This road ended up being very hard to get out of my head, for days afterwards I would struggle to sleep thinking I was still trying to get along this stretch. Some vast stretch of nondescript road cutting right through walls of rock and Joshua trees. Someone should write a song about this. There was a town called Keeler which looked completely out of place here, as it was set back off the main road. There was a lot more activity on the road now; more cars, more support people and even some road works. It felt just like London. Several times I saw Tim Welsh's van speed up and down the road. All I could think of was Tim demanding an ice cream.

Lone Pine marks the "half marathon to go" point of the race and it took ages coming. I could see in the distance a small town but the road didn't go straight there, it cut back to the left and then onto a main road. I started getting grumpy again about how far it was to Lone Pine. Was it 2 miles or 4? I promised myself I would not bother about this as in the big scheme of things it did not matter, but all of a sudden a timetable popped into my head. If I could get to Lone Pine at 6 pm I could rest and cool down a little, leave at 6.30 pm and then have 5 and a half hours for the long steep ascent to the finish at the Mt Whitney Portal. 2 miles turned into 3, then into 2 then into 4. There was no way I was going to make it for 6 pm. I got quite upset and moaned a bit at the crew but they knew exactly how to appease me; by reminding me that there was a McDonald's in Lone Pine and taking my order of a fries and a strawberry milkshake. Way to a man's heart and all that.

The 2 mile section into Lone Pine felt quite difficult, and for the first time felt like I was running/walking through civilisation. It was still incredibly hot and I was on the side without shade, not even thinking about crossing the highway to get out of the sun – there was no way I could make it that fast. It also felt a bit like cheating. I got to lone pine with my McDonald's waiting and lay down again to cool and put my feet up and enjoy the fries and milkshake. The webcam seemed to enjoy them too, broadcasting out to whoever was watching that I was eating McDonald's during a race. They also seemed keen on following me into the bathroom, though I closed the door. I did remark that it was so nice to be able to use a proper toilet after all this time, something that feels like a guilty pleasure in an ultramarathon.

When washing my hands, I looked into the mirror and could not see myself in the reflection. It was me alright but I didn't recognise it as me. Instead I felt a bug-eyed stranger looking back at me. It was like I was an empty shell, nothing was behind those eyes anymore. I didn't know what to say to this stranger except "you are about to finish Badwater".

I started the climb just before 7pm, heading across the busy road and onto Whitney Portal road. I was right up close against the rocky mountain range that I'd been looking at for the past day. This climb goes from 4,000-9,000 ft and was the steepest climb of the whole route. I was always going to walk this part, as do all but the elites. I passed another runner right at the start of the climb and then did not see anyone for ages. The crew were going to stop every mile up the hill on the dot, so I knew how far I was going. The sun was still up but as it was after 7 pm we had to wear our hi-vis jackets and lights again. The rocks here were amazing, and the mountains themselves were covered in sharp edges. As night fell these sharp edges came to life, like Rorschach ink blots. These are used to stare into your soul and gauge your emotional state. All I was seeing were really aggressive spider like animals all glaring at me as if defending their mountain. No beautiful butterflies or cute little sheep at this stage, everything was a beast trying to eat me. There were odd looking rock formations alongside me too that almost look sculpted, like masses of human bodies piled on top of each other. These were playing havoc later on.

I found the first few miles really hard; it was still very warm and I was getting out of breath too quickly. I had to use my inhaler for the first time and used it a lot. I still had the heartburn of the dry winds of 24 hours ago and water still tasted like ash. Counting down the miles did not happen as quickly as I hoped and I was doing each in around 25 minutes. It was pretty steep and my power march slowed as I tried to get my breathing under control. Laurie and Debra were going to crew me till about 5 miles to go and then Debra and Dave were going to see me through to the end. For the end game I gave 3 instructions; keep my inhaler at hand at all times, don't let me sit in the chair and on mile 134 have my Serpentine club top ready with the spare number on it.

The higher it got the cooler it got, it was very noticeable. The sun was setting and I knew then that there was nothing else it could do to me. All that stood between me and the Badwater Buckle I'd been craving for 4 years was a dark road up to the mountain. I still didn't bother with a head torch but the light was so poor I did use a hand torch occasionally. I was hallucinating again but this time it was a feeling of claustrophobia rather than the wide open space of the previous night. The twists and turns of the road and the walls of rock either side looked like I was in a tunnel. There were huge cacti on the sides of the roads that looked like animations, like people and animals poised to jump out at me. This would not worry me except that on getting onto this path there was a "beware of the bears" sign and Smokey the Bear seems to be the fire service mascot of Lone Pine. One of these cacti could be a bear, for real.

I started to move faster up the hill, getting each mile done in less than 20 minutes now. My breathing got better and for the first time I felt like it was cool enough to make the effort. It was so dark that often I thought I might have taken a wrong turn, but I was not turning back. The walls felt like they were closing in, I could see the lights of the switchbacks up ahead in the distance and then again behind me, it was amazing and this time I knew that the glow was not leading to the halfway point but to the end of the Badwater Ultramarathon, the thing that I had been obsessed with for 4 years.

I gave myself 5 years from seeing this race to complete it. Here I was in 4 years about to finish. I applied this year with no real hope of getting in. Since I took up ultra-running 4 years previously it had become harder and harder to get into the "classic" ultramarathons because of the competition. This year the Spartathlon had sold out for the first time. The GUCR and the UTMB were lotteries for the first time, Comrades sold 15,000 spaces in 5 hours this time and the MdS now had a 3 year waiting list. It's fantastic that there is such huge interest in the sport now. When I first started it was hard to find events and there were only a few in the UK. Now we are tripping over them, there is something to do every weekend.

But there is something about the classic events. I want to do them all. I had applied to get into the Western States 100 this year again with no real hope of getting in (lottery chances are about 1 in 10. I watched the lottery online and watched 350 names get pulled out and none of them were mine. This hurt more than I thought it would, like a personal rejection. If I had gotten into WS100 I would not have even considered applying for Badwater this year, but the WS100 rejection brought it home to me; I don't have much time to do these events before they become impossible to get into. "Do what you can while you can" as Jack Denness would say. So I put in my application for Badwater including my essay on why I should be allowed to run. What's the worst they could say? Yes?

Just over a mile to go and I was winding through the switchbacks looking for the red blinking lights of my next and final mile marker. This is where I was going to take off the sun baked white top I'd been wearing all day and put on my nice cool fresh Serpie top. I was looking forward to doing this, it meant the end.

I saw the car in the distance and yelled, "Pull the ice chest down, I'm going to sit for a minute". They responded, "Would you not prefer the chair?" and I snapped, "No – the ice chest, I won't get out of the chair". I had told my crew clearly that if I needed to sit they were to get the ice chest so that I did not get too comfortable. They struggled to pull the ice chest out of the back of the car and I sat myself down and thrust my water bottle at them. They filled it as I said it's only a mile to go. "Yes, just over a mile" they responded. I was a little annoyed at the "just over" bit but didn't let on, I just asked for my Serpie top. This was not forthcoming, I was tired and wanted to hurry up. I looked up and said;

"You're not my crew".

I was staring into the face of a complete stranger. I had sat down and barked orders at the crew of another runner. I apologised profusely and they were just in hysterics about the whole thing. They had done everything I asked of them (apart from the Serpie top). It was the crew of Keith Straw (the fairy) who was just ahead of me. I made my excuses and sheepishly left their van and staggered on where I could see *my* support crew. The other guys stopped and chatted for a minute and all I heard was laughing. I slowed as I made sure they were indeed my support crew. They had everything for me, the ice chest to sit on, another water and most importantly the vest with the number 30 on it. It was time to get it done.

It is traditional in Badwater to cross the line with your support team; it only seems right. More so than any race I can think of this really is a team effort. I had the simple (though not easy task) of just moving forward until I got to the end. I managed to do that (with the exception of those

20 meters which I never told anyone about). My crew had to do so much more. I was quite difficult and vague when saying what I would need during this race and I would not have been as prepared if it were not for Laurie knowing exactly how to do this. The night before the race she and the others were sorting out ice chests and food boxes while I stood and stared into space. I could not watch and I was no use at all. Debra suggested I just go to bed and get some rest, which is what I did.

Debra and Dave were friends of Laurie and were incredibly enthusiastic for helping a British stranger complete his dream. They bought along a truckload of food and other treats. I destroyed their collection of sweets towards the end of the race, they were just what I needed. They were brilliant at hosing me down with water, making my greasy noodle snacks when I wanted, and always being a welcome sight particularly in the night when I thought the car would never come at all.

I had met Debra H on the forums. She was enthusiastic from the start and coped well with my hesitation about the race. I was not easy to deal with before as I was pretending the whole thing wasn't happening. The closer it got the more I'd zone out of it. Debra helped with the organisation and had most of the gear. She ran with me while I was unable to talk or walk straight. She made the sign that showed I had run 100 miles which made me feel great. She would have suffered the same lack of sleep that I did and still managed to smile every time she saw me.

Laurie was the one who held everything together. I had met her in London a couple of weeks before and as soon as I did meet her my mind was at rest that I was in good hands. She got talking to all the others and made sure that everything I needed was there. She came and met me in Vegas and helped me shop for supplies before driving into Death Valley. She made sure all the forms were in order and did so much before the race had even started. Then when it did start she was amazing, tending to my blisters, making sure I ate and drank, and finding new ways to keep the sun off me while I was lying down. Laurie wants to run this race next year. She'll be fine.

I waited for my crew to line up as I prepared one last burst of speed to get to the end. It was an honour and a privilege to cross the line with these guys.

I had watched lots and lots of videos of people finishing Badwater and thought I'd know exactly what the finish would look like. But I had not seen it from this side before, from the side of someone running through it. I ran through it, 39 hours 24 minutes and 4 years after I started.

During the race I looked forward to the moment where I could lie down and not have to get back up again. It was hard getting up each time that I did to carry on. I decided long ago that I was going to wait at the finish for Tim and Mark to complete it. My crew were worried about leaving me here but I insisted they go back to the hotel as I was sleeping under the stars tonight to wait for the others to get in. Laurie made sure that one of the organisers knew I was there and he gave me a load of blankets and I lay down on the mat glad in the knowledge that when I got up again I'd only have to clap.

James Elson was next in. 1:55 after me but having started 2 hours later meant that he did it 5 minutes quicker. We had a quick chat that resembled 2 very drunk people trying to figure out where they are going to meet tomorrow. He said, "See you at the UTMB". Not long later I saw Caroline who was part of Tim's crew, who was only an hour away. I took a nap before hearing the noise of his arrival, finishing comfortably under the buckle time. Tim hung around a bit before he was escorted back down to the car park to be driven back down to Lone Pine where everyone was staying. It was gone 2am, so I figured it would be sunrise before Mark got in and braced myself for a few more hours sleeping on the rocks. But as Tim left Mark arrived, I was astonished. Somehow he had picked himself up from near catastrophe to record a very decent time well under the buckle time. From what I heard, it was touch and go as to whether he was going to finish, so he must have smashed the second half.

I got a lift back down with Mark and his crew and slept on his floor. It must have been 4 am when we went to bed and by 7 am I was wide awake again. I struggled to sleep and even eat for the next week; in fact I was still struggling as I wrote my race report 7 days after I had finished. I kept waking up thinking that I was still running that long straight road into Lone Pine. Some nights I thought I was swimming it.

The End?

Well, there it is; 4 years of running obsession cumulating in a buckle. I really didn't see much past the finish line in terms of what I wanted to do next like I had been able to for every other race. It's funny how my life had changed so much in the past 4 years and all because of my decision to run this, all because of a random email I got at work one day.

When I first thought of this I didn't know of anyone who did this kind of thing. I didn't know of any events. I knew that most big cities had road marathons and other shorter road races, but I had no idea about this world that I had now become so deeply involved with.

In those four years I met so many people who just love running as I do, just doing it for the hell of it and not caring what a guy with a stop-watch says. I had become part of a growing scene in the UK, people who seek these kinds of adventures every week. I love that. I loved turning up to events and being able to chat to friends rather than being caged in a pen with other anonymous bib-numbers. I loved writing my blog which documents everything I have gone through.

Four years previously, I thought that getting the buckle at Badwater would be it, proof that I could handle the toughest race in the world. That was never going to be the case though.

Watching Jack Denness finish his 12th Badwater aged 75 and then head straight to the pub; hearing about a guy who, having finished the race, was running back to Badwater; hearing all the stories from all the characters I had met along the way of how there is so much more out there. I was still only 30 and I had just finished Badwater, and that was just the beginning.

Finishing Badwater was amazing for me and for the first time in my life I felt like something I had made a long term commitment to achieve actually came together and happened. I set out to finish this impossible race 4 years ago and did it ahead of schedule.

However I felt a little pang of disappointment about it. From the start line, there was no doubt in my mind that I would finish. Baring an accident or real bad luck, I knew at the start line that I had what it takes to finish Badwater. That feeling was absent in my first marathon and on my first GUCR, the feeling that I may not have enough to complete this. The feeling of finishing something that you are not sure you can finish is exhilarating. I got that in my first marathon and my first long ultra. There is something much less satisfying about doing an event that you know you can do.

There is something incredibly satisfying about finishing something that is not a given. My first marathon was not a given; my fastest marathon was. My first ultra was not a given; the Marathon des Sables was. My first Grand Union Canal Race was not a given; my second GUCR I thought was a given but taught me a brutal lesson in over-confidence. My first Spartathlon I thought was a given at the start, but during that race I discovered it was harder than anything I could ever imagine and I was made to pay again for my over-confidence.

But I never thought there was a chance that I wouldn't finish Badwater. By the time I got to the start line it was less scary than I hoped it would be four years previously. I was not worried though, I had plenty more to look forward to. A month later I started the Ultra Tour Du Mont Blanc, a 100 mile circut of Mt Blanc passing through France, Italy and Switzerland. It got cut short because of the weather and we only ended up completing about 60 miles of it. It was a disappointment but I knew that this year was about one race, not Badwater but a reunion with an old friend.

13

SPARTATHLON 2010

I thought about the streets of Sparta every day since I finished Badwater. I had made Badwater my four year obsession and finishing that was something that I had to do, however along the journey to Death Valley I came across a race that just blows everything else out of the water. I did not see this coming when I set out to complete Badwater all that time ago but I am very glad of the discovery. I don't want to say that Badwater didn't mean anything because it meant the world to me, but even while ascending those long passes and struggling through the heat I knew I was going to finish and hence the fear of failure was not there. Deep down I knew that this was another step on the way to the main event of the year.

It's quite hard to say what it is about the Spartathlon that has me (and hundreds of hard-core ultramarathon veterans) flocking to Athens late September every year. Maybe it's the history? Or the international field. Or the welcoming nature of the organisers and helpers of the race. Or perhaps it's the severe cut-off times that eliminate more than half the field each year. Whatever it is the Spartathlon is a fixture in the calendar of so many runners, for most including myself it is the last "big" race of the year. I had unfinished business here; though I had finished the year previously I did not feel like I had beaten the race. My body was so broken I could not run to the statue of Leonidas as I had dreamed of before. This time I was back to live that dream.

The Start – Getting to Corinth

The race starts as soon as the sun starts to shine on the Acropolis of Athens, high up in the capital on a Friday morning. It really is an inspiring yet intimidating sight to see such a huge formation of rock that was present 2,500 years ago when the pioneer of ultra-running Pheidippides ran the distance we were all about to start. I tried not to think too much about what was up ahead because I knew how hard it was.

It all felt very familiar as we descended the cobbles of the Acropolis and down into the city, as if I had never left this race. Perhaps I never had? I had been thinking about it so much; the concrete paths with random bollards sticking up, the police halting the rush hour traffic of Athens and then the long uphill road out of the city. I even found myself running with some of the same people as last year; a girl with a pink skort, a very large Norwegian guy with a very impressive moustache and a Korean guy who seemed to run with a load of pots and pans who jangled along like a brass band. After a couple of miles a tram crossing closed to allow a tram by but some runners just ignored and ran straight across. For the sake of 20 seconds is it worth getting hit by a tram? Well, actually sometimes those 20 seconds...

I had become separated from the other Brits and was not too sure where everyone was. I figured Mark and Peter were up ahead. I was intending to take the first 50 miles slower than last year as I felt like I burnt out a bit doing the first 50 miles in 7:37. It was not as hot as last year (it was going to be about 28 rather than 33) but it was quite humid as it had been raining quite a lot. That combined with the traffic and the oil refineries made breathing quite hard work for everyone. My achilles, calves and groin were already complaining just as they were this time last year. I stopped to stretch a few times but knew I didn't really have too much to worry about, just like last year I just need about 30 miles in the legs before things loosen up a bit.

The first marathon came in around 4:15, half an hour slower than last year. It was perfect in terms of time but I was worried that I didn't really feel any fresher for it, I was warm and uncomfortable and sweating profusely. I had made a decision (a good one I think) to carry a water bottle with me and the electrolyte solution which may help me avoid the kidney problems I had last year. The next 24 miles were tough too, it was getting warm and the sweat was blinding me. Miles 30-50 were along a road next to the Aegean Sea. It was a beautiful blue colour and in the heat of the day the temptation to wander down and jump in was huge. There was a slight breeze sometimes but not enough to dry my face. I spent this section running close to Neil who was here despite a foot injury which had not yet caused any bother. We talked about how bloody tough the race was even though we knew we were only a quarter of the way in. The sea looked so blue and there were moments when we were only a few feet away from it. The temptation to dive in was incredible.

Checkpoints became less and less busy, it became much easier to grab things and move on. I decided to take no personal food with me at all this year as last year I took lots and ate none of it. I was relying on the supplies on the tables which were very basic; crisps, biscuits, fruit and drinks. There was plenty of coke which was diluted with water. I heard a girl rush up and ask for "just coke" from one of the helpers. They looked back a little concerned and said "you know it's not good for you don't you?" I nearly spat mine out.

The last few miles into Corinth are on a busy highway in the heat of the day. It goes up slightly and felt like more of an effort than it should have done. I was looking forward to the first major checkpoint of the race, 50 miles with a 9:30 cut-off. I got there in 8:35, almost exactly an hour slower than last time, which was fine as that was the intention. However I felt shattered and out of energy. I felt great at this point last year, and I was an hour ahead.

Getting to the mountain

Now the route was becoming quite nice. The roads were much quieter and most of the traffic was that of the support crews for the race who were only allowed to start supporting after the 50 mile point. I had broken this race down into 4 parts; getting to Corinth, getting to the mountain, getting over the mountain and then getting to the statue. I was 9 hours in, a quarter in absolute time and a third in absolute distance, but these meant little. I remembered that later in the race every mile can feel like 5 and minutes feel like hours. I ran with Neil for a few more miles but decided to push on as I really started to feel much better.

A support car was driving slowly and asking everyone where they were from. I heard "Korea", "Italia" and "Brasil" behind me. The car caught up to me and without even asking they just pointed at me and yelled "GREEK". I would have protested but I was sporting a beard and a tan so could easily see the confusion. If you are going to run this race I have a little gem of advice – if you run near the Brazilian team you get followed by a car full of hotties, helps to distract.

Not long after I upped the pace I spotted Mark, he looked like he was struggling. Gemma had been texting me with updates on how the Brits were doing and told me that Mark had gone through Corinth nearly an hour before me along with Emily Gelder. I chatted to him for a few minutes and walked up a short hill. I said "see you later" and carried on, expecting him and Neil to catch up with me again at some stage.

Around 60 miles in I started chatting to an American who

seemed in really good spirits except he told me that he was shitting blood and asked me for advice on what to do. I really didn't know what to say as I didn't know how serious that is (apparently it IS serious). I told him about my experience of pissing blood and suggested that if nothing was really hurting then it probably was not too bad. I could not tell him that everything was fine but nor could I tell him that he should pull out of the race. I said as much and headed off again.

Soon after I passed the village where the kids run up to you and ask for autographs. I signed a few and they seemed to really go crazy for it. Martin told me after the race that he likes to sign "David Beckham" when he does them. It's quite nice though you can't do them all and I felt guilty when I ran past a child with a pad and pen held out. Still, not as guilty as I would feel if that American died.

100 km came in around 11 hours and I was still feeling really good. The field was really spacing out now and sometimes I had no one in view, ahead or behind. The roads are permanently marked so well that it is almost impossible to get lost. Not long after I caught up with Kevin, whom I had met the previous day. He looked to be going through a rough patch just as Mark had and I told him that it would pass. Such a huge race you are going to go through several low points and I had had some of mine in the first 50 miles, but now I was making good progress and had to run my own race and press on. I said bye again, fully expecting to bump into him later on.

I remembered from last year that the big rolling hills started here, they are a bit steeper than the ones we had faced so far. The sun set suddenly and I realised that I had stupidly left my night gear at CP35, and I was only on 30. I had a good 10 miles to go in the dark with no lights. The clouds had covered the moon so natural light was minimal. I used the light on my phone when needed to keep on the road and followed any other light I could find.

This year I had gone really easy on drop bags, leaving only 4: Sun cream at CP15, night clothes and Torch at CP35, a change of shoes and socks at CP49 just after the mountain, and then daytime clothes at CP60A. I took absolutely no food and was going to rely on what was at the checkpoints. Last year I had 20 drop bags with food but ended up not touching most of them. I just kept it simple this time although I messed up the timing of the sunset.

Not long after I got my night gear, which was nothing more than a long sleeve top, a reflective gillet and a torch, just as it started to rain. It just started with drizzle but slowly got worse until you could describe it as proper rain. On the plus side the water gushing down was acting like ice on my legs and easing the pain a little, but worryingly I was starting to feel cold. It was nowhere near the coldest part of the night yet and I still had the mountain to climb, which is cool at the best of times. One of the guys in the checkpoint commented on my running attire; I was wearing a shirt with collars and a silly hat. He said he saw me at the start and just assumed I was a tourist following the race. He said I looked like the smartest runner out there which was funny as I was recently called the second scruffiest man in the Serpentine Running Club.

I worried a bit about the mountain. I didn't do a good job of it last year and if I was freezing and slipping about all over the place that would only make it worse. Almost on that thought the heavens really did open and turned the roads into streams and mud baths. I was amazed again how muddy it got as the rain coincided with the off-road section of the run at about 90 miles. It got so bad that I cowered under the gazebo of the next checkpoint and stole a black bag to use as shelter from the pouring rain – it was horrendous. I stayed there for about 10 minutes waiting for the rain to abate as slowly more and more runners came and did the same. The cover was small and others complained of being cold.

We joked at the start about me being cursed in races and them ending up being cut short. It happened in the Marathon des Sables and again in the UTMB. Ultra-runners (well the ones I know anyway) don't want anything to be cut short or even for other circumstances to make it easier. No one wants to do Badwater on a "cool" year or Rotherham on a dry year. I looked at the weather reports before the race and was actually a little disappointed to see that was only about 28°C rather than the 30's we had last year (though the humidity more than compensated). Many of us have this perverse desire for the conditions to be really bad just to make it even tougher, like 40°C or a tropical storm or hurricanes. The rain sure was making it hard and I was thinking about how difficult it would be to get up the mountain, but I was more concerned that they might not even let anyone try. I completely missed this last year.

It finally calmed down and I started to run on again, faster for some reason as if I could outrun the next down pour. Runners covered their reflective tops with black bags and became ghosts on the road, and you could not see them even while shining a light near them. It was a strange sensation not knowing whether it was a person in front of you or just a blip in your vision. I was getting tired, still a bit cold and some of the road turned into river. I was ankle deep running through some times and the darkness make me paranoid about twisting my ankles. Still the cold water on my legs was very welcome.

Before long I could see the point of the race that smashed my legs last year, the long switchbacks on the roads leading up to the rocky climb of Sangras Pass.

It looked a lot like the climbs I had seen in the UTMB the previous month with headlamps heading off up into the stars, except this one had a long stretch of highway building up to it. I was starting to feel sleepy and remembered that I had a Red Bull shot in my belt and was thinking of the opportune moment to take it. I had managed to sleep quite well the previous night, I don't panic about not sleeping nowadays which helps and I tried to lay off the caffeine the week before. There was a CP just before the 2 km climb up to "Base Camp" – CP47. I had a cup of coffee and took a leisurely walk up the road, the first time in the race I felt like I was taking it easy. I could see for miles behind me at the villages that I had been through and the small glowing lights making their way towards the mountain. It really is an astonishing sight and one that I'd like to keep on seeing every year.

Base Camp – I got there around 3 am, a little behind last year but I was certainly catching up with my former self. There was a different feel to this checkpoint, as there were a lot more people there and several places to lie down and have a massage. I took this opportunity and felt great afterwards. While drinking a coffee I took some time to chat to the mainly British staff. They commented on how young I was and what I was doing such races for at that age. I didn't know what to say really; what was the alternative? I've just spent 20 hours running and now I have to climb a mountain. Would I trade this for being caged up in a pen to run some road marathon somewhere?

Getting over the mountain

As soon as you walk out of the checkpoint you start the ascent; very steep, lose rocks and lit up with glow sticks and bike lights. It was sometimes hard to tell whether a light up ahead was one of the markers or another runner. The previous year, my scramble up this seemed to take forever and I was passed by at least 15 people on the way up. This time no one passed me at all which must have meant I got up there a lot quicker. It certainly felt much easier and shorter this time, although I had no way of knowing as I hadn't timed it last time and I was not wearing a watch now anyway. I had decided against this as I remembered how crazy it had driven me last time. In what seemed like no time at all I was back at the checkpoint where last year I was bundled into a chair and wrapped in a blanket. No need for bundling this time, I just walked over and sat down.

A lot of people get the chop here. If you arrive just short of the cut-off you then have 40 minutes to get to the top of the mountain and then 35 to get back down. Fail that and you'll be picked up by the "Death Bus". I heard lots of stories about the Death Bus.

The Death Bus hangs back from the race and crawls along at the pace of the cut-offs. Though I had never been that close to the cut-offs I had visions of this thing snapping at your ankles and trying to run you over. Once you are on the bus you join all those who fell before you. In all likeliness they are going to be an unhealthy bunch. They may have had to pull out with sickness, stomach problems, dehydration, exhaustion or injury. Sat on this bus are living (just about) examples of some of the bad things that ultras do to you. If you happen to not be in such a state you soon will be on smelling and inhaling the terrible things that slosh around the place. You will be hoping the bus arrives in Sparta quickly, except it will only start the journey to Sparta when it is full. They joked about trying to knobble runners who were flagging just to fill the bus so everyone can get out of there. I don't want to get on that bus. I don't want to be anywhere near it.

It did not rain at all on the mountain, I was amazed it was bone dry. The downpour that seemed to follow us for a few miles only got a few of the runners, some missed it entirely and wondered what the fuss was. I jogged carefully down the other side. It's not nearly as steep as the up and the path is generally good but I didn't want to put a foot wrong. I broke here last time and around 20 people passed me. The previous year I had felt so lame as everyone else seemed to trot down the other side with some new found energy. I was terrible at downs and I now knew that I was a bit less terrible. Only 2 people passed me this time. I felt good about this, as it meant I was not so lame anymore. I had one fall on my arse but got to the bottom without incident and went further down the roads into Siagas, Checkpoint 49, where I had a fresh pair of shoes waiting.

Getting to the statue

I was glowing having gotten up and down the mountain without any bother at all. I continued to run and for the first time I didn't recognise any of the roads ahead, it was like I was running here for the first time. It's strange how a race with so many miles, so many twists and turns, checkpoints, signs, bridges and other furniture that you run with a constant sense of deja-vu, but for the next 15 miles or so I did not remember any of this. I was running in a valley with some roads by my side and much higher up. There were lots of buildings, bridges and a nice uphill section, all quite memorable but for this bit I had amnesia. Why didn't I know any of this? Perhaps I was going the wrong way? Funny how my memory wiped this whole bit out.

I remembered the sun rising last year and it was while I was running through a park. I ran through this park in darkness this time which meant that I had overtaken my previous run. 40 miles to go.

I could still run, uphill and downhill. The aches and pains that started so early went away for a while but were back now including a soreness in the sole of my foot. This was a new injury and hence a little concerning and I thought about what could have brought this on. Not long after I remembered that I had just run about 120 miles – that'll be it.

I remembered the last 50 miles as being mostly downhill but I was wrong; it still rolls up and down. The roads were deceptive like in Badwater and I couldn't tell whether I was going up or down. The "50k to go" then the "only a marathon to go" points should have lifted me but I was having a low spell. I guess I should be thankful, I suffered in the first 50 but had a great 80 miles, it was time to feel bad again.

Gemma had texted me to say that Peter, Neil and Kevin were out which did not help matters. It would be a dream to finish this race and for everyone I know to do the same so that we could sit down at the end and reflect on a job well done. I felt a bit awkward last year talking to those who didn't make it about my experience. I was still having a great race and it would have been great to clap the other guys in.

It was getting warm, it was still humid and every now and then it would rain a little but not much. The weather conditions were enough to make me feel really warm sometimes and cold at others. Hitherto I had done a good job of not sitting down too much but I was faltering now, sitting down far too easily with excuses that did not exist: "I have something in my shoe"; "I need a coffee"; "I need to check my phone". My momentum had gone. I had left the quiet roads and was on the highway that headed into Sparta and it was much harder than I remembered.

A guy passed me while I was sat down at a checkpoint who was running like I had been 2 hours ago and he climbed into the distance with great speed. He was the first person to pass me since the mountain 30 miles ago. I watched him get smaller and smaller and felt bad because that is exactly what I was doing earlier. The roads are lethal, cars whizzing around blind corners and without much respect for the walking lane. I zigzagged along to avoid death and would walk around corners to be safer. It was much lonelier this year, not many people around at all whereas last year there was a whole chain of us. I thought this was possibly the most dangerous conditions I have run in. I've done deserts and mountains and they have their risks but this was something else. At any other time it would be stupid to run against this traffic. There I said it, this race is pretty stupid.

I got another text to say that Mark was out. This was a shock, as he had not DNF'ed anything since this race in 2004. I had already been told that more than half of the starters had dropped out and this was normal. I didn't want to get complacent and say I was definitely going to finish but with a half marathon to do in 5 hours I was still in good shape. I had no excuse to mope around really, I just had to get it done. I didn't have a finish time in mind, just a finish and a better finish than last time. I just wanted to run to the statue instead of crawling to it. A finish would still do but I really wanted to leave here loving this race, whether that was done slower than last time or faster I didn't care. I was currently ahead of where I was last year and looking strong. My legs still allowed me to run up hills and down hills, I just couldn't be arsed. I just don't remember the road being this busy or going up as much as it did. With about 20 km to go there was one last big push up hill and then it was down, all the way to Sparta.

You can see Sparta from miles away. It looks busy and confusing as roads stick out everywhere and there seems to be 2 cities in the distance. I can't imagine what Pheidippides must have seen when stood on top of this hill looking down. I guess it would have looked even more spectacular, a large warrior city surrounded by green. In fact it was on fire, there was smoke billowing out of somewhere. I can remember what all the next 4 checkpoints looked like; the one next to the petrol station, the one just before the small town, the one in the middle of a traffic island. A few people passed me again at great speed as if they had just started running, or "doing a Woolley" as I like to call it. I was able to run again but was not going to try to pace these guys, there was still 10 km to go. Something could still go wrong. In fact something did.

(You don't have to read this bit). I was having a few chaffing issues, nothing major and probably unavoidable completely when doing such a long race. It gets worse after going to the toilet though after wiping. I went one final time in some trees and obviously wiped off what remained of the Vaseline I had on. When I got back onto the road I felt like someone was scratching my arse with a rusty spanner, it was agony. I yelled a few times (no one was around) and almost wept as I contemplated finishing with a long walk again. Luckily I had some lube on me and while I would not normally use my hands in this way to avoid germs I had no choice. With complete disregard for hygiene and a completely new use for my water bottle I sorted myself out. Mental note for next time – take some wet wipes and hand sanitiser. Mental note for the rest of the race – don't drink out of this bottle anymore.

Now I was ready to run, down, down, down, until I hit a very busy road with a checkpoint at the start. Along this road I passed a couple of people finishing in the same way I did last year, with a slow limp. I shook hands with a Hungarian guy who was over a mile from the end but I knew from experience he was a good hour from the finishing, the race had smashed him but he was going to make it, he had loads of time.

The last checkpoint, on that island in the middle of a busy intersection. It was a glorious sight. All I had to do now was head up into the main street in Sparta, turn right after about a mile, turn right again and then I'd see the end. I had no idea where these right turns were but on the other side of the road was a kid on a bike and he was there to guide me to the end. "Are you here to get me to the finish?" I said. He did not speak English but it did not matter, I just followed him as he braved the busy traffic through the town.

The last mile is slightly uphill but I was getting faster. All the pain went away. After around a mile I did the right turn and my cyclist was replaced by a Policeman on a motorbike. He would stop traffic to let me run through, the drivers stopping to clap and cheers as I ran past. Another right turn and that was it, the end.

I could see the end of the road but the statue was obscured by trees. The crowd of people got denser and denser and then I spotted Lawrence, the first person I recognised since I saw Kevin about a day ago. Then I saw Mark and Peter and high-fived everyone and started to run even faster. This was the dream finish; running. There was the statue and the steps, I leapt up them and then onto the pedestal of Leonidas and let out a scream. It was done and done so much better than last time.

I stepped down and went through the ceremony. Wreath, water from the river, perspex thingy, handshake, photo. I looked over to my friends at the left and at the bar they were drinking in. They reassured me that I had a beer waiting and I was just about to head over when the medics apprehended me, like they do with everyone. I sat down and had my one blister popped and treated and she asked me if anything hurt. I had to think about it for a while before responding that nothing hurt at all. All the soreness for a few moments had disappeared, until I stood up. Hard to get lost in this one

James: 2 – Spartathlon: 0

Finish time 33:24

Emily Gelder had come 1st in the women's race with an amazing time of just over 30:17. Heather in 32:43. Martin came in 34:19 and Colin finished in 35:10.

Why come back?

Miles and miles of choking through the hot and noxious industrial lands of Greece made me realise just how ugly this race is. Playing chicken with fast cars on a winding highway having run 5 marathons without sleep made me realise that this race is pretty stupid too. There has to be something that draws people back?

What about the history? Well, having read so many different versions of the heroic tale of Phiedippides the one that sounds the most likely is that he ran to Sparta to summon an army. He ran the 246 km in 36 hours, a deed that would have been unthinkable at the time and even unthinkable until recently when this race was born. On arriving into Sparta Pheidippides pleaded with the Spartans to send an army to save Athens.

By the time he got back to Athens the Athenian army had won the battle anyway. Epic though the run was, it was in fact pointless. I can't imagine what he must have felt like in Sparta on hearing that he was not going to get any help or how much that played on his mind on his return journey. What reaction did he get on his return to Athens when the battle was already won?

I can imagine them all in the pub that evening celebrating the victory over the barbarians and laughing at some guy who ran 300 miles for nothing and then missed everything. "How many savages did you kill Pheidippides? Oh no wait I remember, you were scrambling over some mountain in the dark and even then God told you to turn back as it was pointless. Ha ha ha ha ha". I suspect that to protect the man's dignity they made up the story of him running 26.2 miles and telling of victory and then dying. "Even though it's a lie at least you won't go down in history as some pointless ultra-running idiot". I'm sure he did not care about the mocking though. Whatever message he was delivering at least he had his dream job. I reckon he did not even care for the messages he had to deliver, he just wanted to run from place to place and probably ran all over Greece. It's the journey and all that. I doubt he would think people 2500 years from now would be re-creating one of his many runs every year but he would surely know that people will be doing exactly the same thing, in different places and different times. Even after cars had been invented.

So, to summarise the Spartathlon is ugly, stupid and ultimately pointless. See you next year.

13A

WHY? VERSION 6

I loved that moment in the Spartathlon where I overtook myself from last year. I don't think I was in better shape overall but I had run a more sensible race, more conservative and I could reap the benefits later on of my smarter running.

Since taking up ultra-running I have derived an enormous amount of pleasure from looking back at myself in the past and seeing someone less experienced and less capable than I am now. Keeping all my thoughts in a blog has helped with this. There is a real sense of satisfaction in growing as a person in this way. Knowing that I am capable now of things that I thought were beyond me a few years ago.

I thought about my first marathon and how I was so nervous that my nose bled, and now I can run six of those back to back without getting nervous. It made me think that anything that makes me nervous now will be looked back upon in years to come with a satisfying nostalgia.

The feeling of personal growth and development is such a powerful motivator in running and in life and it was so easy to measure in this way.

That is why I ran.

14

A FATEFUL ONLINE CONVERSATION

Rewind about four months. Shortly before I was preparing to run Badwater I had an online conversation with Mark Cockbain about what was next for him. The conversation went something like this:

Me – So what's next for you then?

Mark – I have a race planned but right now it's a secret.

Me – Really? What is it? I promise I won't tell anyone J

Mark – You better not tell anyone, there are not many places and it will sell out fast.

Me – Sounds interesting…

Mark – Honestly if I tell you, you CAN'T tell anyone else, not until it's finalised.

Me – OK I won't. I'd sooner become a triathlete than tell anyone J

Mark – OK then. [sends a link]

I then look at the link Mark has just sent. It is for a race across America. 3220 miles in 70 days, Los Angeles to New York averaging 45 miles a day. Passing through 13 states next summer. Looked insane but from Mark I'd expect nothing less

Me – Blimey, that looks ridiculous, FORTY FIVE MILES A DAY FOR NEARLY THREE MONTHS?

Mark – I know. Don't tell anyone.

Me – I won't.

I look at the site a bit more and see that there is a shorter race too, 300 miles from LA to Las Vegas in 7 days. That sounded pretty cool. I've never run that far in a week before and reckon I could do that. I wasn't sure what could be next for me after Badwater but this seemed like a good thing. I would run with Mark for that week then perhaps stick around for another week and help crew him and be part of this amazing race somehow. I thought Mark would be pleased to have me come along. I replied;

Me – Cool they have a 300 mile race from LA to Las Vegas. I might come along and do that.

[I waited for his reply, expecting him to be really pleased that I'd come over and run the first week with him I expected a "cool" or "that'll be awesome" or something similar. Then after a few minutes I got…]

Mark – Don't be such a pussy. Do the whole thing.

And from that moment, like with the Badwater email four years ago, I wasn't going to put it down. One way or the other I was going to attempt to run across the United States of America.

The odd thing about this was that when Mark first sent me the link to that race it did not even enter into my head to do it. It's not like I appraised the difficulty, 45 miles, 70 days and then said that it was impossible. It just never even went into my mind at first that I could try such a thing. It was only when Mark came out with the pussy comment that I started to think about how I could do this race.

Later that year while running in Badwater and in the Spartathlon all I thought about was running into New York next year. I was going to make this happen.

Around four years ago, well four years ago exactly I was preparing my body and mind for a 45 mile ultra along a canal in England. 45 miles in one go? Sounds ridiculous. I thought that humans were designed to explode soon after breaking through the 26.2 mile mark but apparently not. I remember being quite anal about it at the time. I was looking at the wind speed before the race to see whether it was favourable or not, wondering what shoes to wear, the terrain, the food, the daylight. After all, 45 miles is a long way. There is a lot to panic about.

I didn't really talk about it too much as I was not really believing that it would happen. There is so much that could go wrong between now and the start; I could get injured, I may not get time off work, I may not have the money. The biggest risk I thought was that the race wouldn't happen.

I took a day off work in November when the entries for the race came out. I wanted to be the first to reply to the email that gave details on where we were supposed to send $6000. The race was organised by a French organisation and Serge Girard, a legendary runner who has run all over the world. I sent off the money minutes after the email came and ended up being the first entry into the race and hence given the number 1. Mark was number 2.

There were a few little details to sort out before I went out there to run. Little things such as;

Getting 3 months off work

Finding a support crew for the first two weeks (as required by the organisers due to the intense heat)

Getting the money to pay for 70 days of eating like an elephant, 70 nights in motels, flights to the USA and about a dozen pairs of trainers.

Oh – and getting my body ready to hammer out 45 miles a day without a rest for 70 days

Very lucky for me my work was going through a downsizing exercise and I was happy to be part of that. It was time for me to move on from there anyway, I'd been there for seven years from graduation and got a great deal of experience but needed a change. A lot of others said they were happy to "take the money and run". I literally did that.

So with the money and time bit sorted I only had to organise a support crew and do some training. Easy.

Soon after being made redundant I had great plans of how I was going to run around the UK in lots of different places, discovering what I might not have the chance to do when I started to work again. I bought maps of trails in the UK and was all set to run all over the place.

Before all that I entered an event called the Quadzilla, a 4 marathons in 4 days race around a lake near Milton Keynes. It was organised by David "Foxy" Bailey who organises loads of races, raises loads of money for charity, has run more than 100 marathons and still finds the time to produce naked calendars of runners (of which I was Mr May in 2010).

I was on day two of the four days and felt something bulging in my groin. I remember this feeling vividly from about 8 years ago; it was a hernia. It was sore and I pulled out of the race at around 8 miles and immediately made an appointment to see a doctor.

I saw the doctor and then had an appointment with a surgeon, all very quickly and it was confirmed that I had a hernia. Luckily I was still covered by the medical insurance of my previous employers and managed to get an operation pretty quickly. In fact the surgeon just pulled out his diary and said, "When are you free, I can do two weeks on Saturday?" I said I was "busy" on that Saturday and would it be possible to do it the following week.

"Sure" he said and then booked me in, it was almost like booking a haircut. The actually reason I was "busy" in a couple of weeks was because I was running the Trans Gran Canaria race, 123 km of spectacular rocks and volcanoes on the small island of Gran Canaria. It was on my birthday and I wanted to spend my birthday doing the two things I love most, running a long way and having a beer. The race started at midnight and in the end took 23:45 hours, leaving just 15 minutes for me to neck just the one birthday beer. It was totally worth it though.

The hernia operation went fine. It was the middle of March and I could not run for a month. It was frustrating but it was unlike being injured. I felt like I had been punched in the stomach for about a week and for a few weeks I had no desire to run, just to rest.

I told my surgeon that I "do a lot of running" and that I am training for a race in America in the summer. I said it "starts in June", implying that it does not "finish in June" and hence might be quite long but I think the subtlety was lost on him. I think he assumed I was running a marathon and said quite confidently "you'll be fine by mid-April, plenty of time to train". Yes that gives me two months to train for a race that is more than two months.

Don't panic.

I managed to get a bit of running done in May but I realised long before the start line that there was no way I was ever going to feel "ready" for this race, I would have to make myself ready as I went along.

There were a few things I still needed to sort out before heading out, one such thing was a support crew for the first two weeks of the race. The reason for this was that the first two weeks would be the hottest, through the deserts of California and Arizona. I sent a speculative email to Laurie asking if she knew anyone who would be interested in doing such a thing. I really wanted her to say that she wanted to crew but for some reason I was too embarrassed to ask. She said yes that she could do the first 6 days with me and would ask her friends Deb and Dave if they could do the second week. They said they could do the last 5 days, leaving me with a three day gap.

I was so happy about this. As soon as these guys were on board I felt more at ease with the whole thing. There was still that three day gap but I was sure that would be easy to fill by tagging on to someone else in the race or finding someone free that weekend.

I booked flights, one way to LA and then one way return from New York. The person on the phone taking my booking reminded me that I'd "have to make my own way from LA to New York". It's ok, I've got that covered.

I was so excited about doing this race, I wanted to tell everyone and talk about it all the time but was holding back a bit. I was holding back because there were doubts as to whether Mark was going to be able to run. He had been having problems with his feet and had spent a long time off running. He saw various specialists who told him he had to rest and about a month before the start he confirmed the worst possible news, he was going to pull out of the race.

I was truly gutted by this. It was Mark who had gotten me into this in the first place and I was really looking forward to running the summer with him. I knew just how excited I was and to understand how he must have felt I turned that on its head and imagined the same amount of disappointment, anger and frustration. That must have been huge. Absolutely devastating. There was nothing I or anyone else could say or do that would make him feel any better. I was gutted that I was not going to have the pleasure of his company while out there doing the challenge of a lifetime. But that was insignificant to how much I felt for his own loss.

June came along suddenly. It's strange how I have been thinking about this for a year now but somehow I can't remember a time when I was not thinking about this. It felt like I had been building up to this all my life, even though I only knew it existed a year ago.

One by one I was saying goodbye to friends and family before I was due to head out. Shaking hands with people in pubs and at running events as they told me "good luck" and "next time I see you you'll be dead" and such things made me think that what I was about to do was even more significant than my own experience. People were looking forward to tracking my progress.

Thursday 16th June, it was raining heavily in London as Gemma and I got a taxi to Heathrow Airport in the morning. It was going to be the last time I would see Gemma until about a week from the end of the race where she was due to fly out and see me.

I didn't want Gemma involved in this, even though she wanted to be. I was adamant that I would do this on my own and did not even consider her an option for crewing me for those first two weeks, I wanted this to be *my* race. I was really excited about leaving and going to the USA to spend the summer there and thought 10 weeks away from her would be easy. I held back the emotion as we hugged at the airport as I was about to go through security. She was very upset and after separating she walked off and down an escalator. I looked at her expecting her to glance back and smile or something but she didn't. The last thing I saw was the back of her head disappearing down the escalator. I was hit by a dull and sickening feeling as watched her go. I realised that I'd just made my first mistake.

I sat by the window on the plane looking out over the continent I was about to run across. It takes 5 hours to fly from one end to the other. Friends would often joke that some of the runs I have been on are long train journeys, such as from Birmingham to London. Now the run I was going to do was not a train journey but a flight.

Towards the end of the flight I was amazed by just how big Los Angeles was. I thought it would be about the size of London as the population is around the same but it is much bigger than that, spanning an area the size of southern England. This one place was going to take two days to run out of.

On arriving in LA I was met by Ruth Jackson who was a Serpie who had just recently moved out there. I was staying at hers for the first night and then over to the Ramada hotel for the race briefings.

We were in a small room and at first I did not really know who was running, who was organising and who was in charge of laying out the sandwiches. Trans-continental runners could fit in anywhere, they look totally average. However what is going on inside their heads and the experiences they have had is far from average.

I remember going to the Spartathlon two years ago and being made to feel like a baby, in a good way. I had done the Grand Union Canal Race twice at that stage and in normal circumstances I'd be considered one of the more experienced ultra-runners, but when I went out there everyone had run what I'd done ten times over.

Now that I had done two GUCRs, two Spartathlons, a Badwater, a UTMB and some others I would certainly consider myself amongst the most experienced ultra-runners in any group. However I have never felt so inexperienced as when during the race briefing we were asked to say who we were, why we were here and what we had done.

Serge Girard had run across all 5 continents before, breaking the Trans-USA record and still holding the Trans-Australia record. Markus had run across Australia too and had done more 100 milers than I had done marathons. Several runners had run from Paris to Tokyo, others across Japan, Rainer Koch was only 30 and had won the Trans-Europe race the year before. The only person with a similar amount of running to me was Alex Bellini, who had rowed across several oceans.

But Laure the race director (and wife of Serge) put me at ease, mainly by saying, "the race briefing will be long and boring but afterwards we'll have a beer". Laure said that she wanted everyone to ask any questions now before they get really tired and grumpy which usually happens after day 2.

There was then some talk about the rules. Some things were cleared up which was good. Highlights were:

There will be no water stations but the organisers guarantee to see every runner at least every hour and give them water and food as required.

Cut-offs stand at 3.5 mph pace which means the first day is 13 hours.

From now they will talk in Kilometers only as there were no Americans and only one Brit in the race.

You are not allowed to drink beer outdoors in the States, which means you can't drink at the finish line. This was a disappointment as she really wanted everyone to have a beer at the end of each stage.

It's going to get really hot. Next 8 days the temps are 21°C, 26°C, 31°C, 41°C, 40°C, 41°C, 40°C

There are snakes.

There is a 140 km section along a straight road with no life whatsoever.

The overall leader will run each day with a yellow number. She held up my yellow number as an example.

We need a tent. I forgot a tent.

Laurie came to join me the day before the start. We went to Walmart to fill the car with highly caffeinated and sugary foods that I thought I'd be eating constantly over the next few months. I had my last meal before the race, a steak and a couple of pints of IPA (too fizzy, I feared that everything was going to be fizzy in the USA). I sat and savoured this moment of not having to rush to eat my food, getting a good nights' sleep and generally feeling ok. I was going to miss this feeling.

THE LOS ANGELES TO NEW YORK FOOTRACE

- June 19th - August 27th 2011

15

HUNTINGTON BEACH – LOS ANGELES – JUNE 19TH 2011

It was a perfect day for a run. Cool, cloudy, slight chance of rain. It was dark next to the beach on the Pacific Highway. The roads all have 6 lanes here, like motorways cutting straight through busy city centres. However it was just the 30 or so of us assembling by a sign for the beach. There was no fanfare at all for the start, in fact to this day I can't even remember the race starting. Surely Laure must have said "go" or something; I don't know, we just started running.

We could have just been a bunch of guys going out on a Saturday morning run, the pace was sedate and the chatter between us didn't reflect the enormity of what we were setting out to do. All we were setting out to do was to run down some dark streets of LA in the morning.

It seemed to get light pretty quickly along some deserted big residential road. There was a lot of stopping at lights and lots of chatting with other runners who right now did not really know each other. I quickly found out those who could speak English and who couldn't. Rainer and Markus, both German, spoke it very well and I chatted to them as well as Alex.

"Treat it like a job" I was advised by many people who had done this kind of thing before. This is the first day, just settle in, get to know everyone and don't make an idiot of yourself. The first day at work is supposed to be easy. This wasn't.

I had had a groin strain for the previous two weeks and hoped that it would clear for the start of the race. I didn't think it was serious and I could still run but would rather it would go away and let me enjoy the first few weeks but it bothered me for the entire day. I kept having to sit down and stretch, getting concerned looks from other runners that I really had bitten off more than I could chew here. It was a worry, I wasn't going to stop because of it but thought about how all 70 days were going to be painful. The thought of carrying this little strain all the way across the USA with me was a little depressing. I wanted for some other ache to come along to take my mind off it.

After a few miles of chatting to Rainer he set off ahead and demonstrated clearly that he was several leagues above everyone else here. I settled into a group including Jenni from Holland who was the only woman in the race and was being supported by her partner Anneke who was cycling, and Alex who had a large crew of people via his sponsorship with Jeep. The streets of LA started to wake at 7 am and no one there really gave us a second look. I think LA is a fairly sporty place and so people running up and down the streets is probably normal there. There were a few comments made asking us what race we were doing.

I would delight in telling others what we were doing, just because it sounded so stupid when saying it out loud. In the months before I was almost embarrassed to tell people "I'm going to run across the USA, from LA to New York". It sounded silly. Now I got to say "I AM running from LA to New York". We were still in LA though, a long way to go. The responses we got ranged from "That's awesome man!" to "Fuck!".

The first day was 45.7 miles or as I like to consider it an "average" day. This is the average number of miles I'd have to do each day though there was no way I was going to be as fresh as I was here.

The first marathon or so was through residential, then industrial, then residential areas. It was like we were running between lots of different cities whereas we were always in the same one. Laurie would stop in the car every few miles or if there was a turning, though there were not many. All the roads here are so straight, you can see for miles and miles. At least here there are some buildings to distract you. Towards the end of the first day we entered a town called "Norco". The climate seemed to change as we entered it, from drizzle to sunshine, quite warm sunshine. A lot of the runners were concerned about the impending heat, it was only in the 20s just now, but soon it would be in the 30s and then higher as we headed into the desert.

On arriving into the small town I caught my first glimpse of two little yellow flags that were to become part of the fabric of this race. The two yellow flags that signal that the days running is over, time for rest and eating.

I finished the first day in 9:38, a bit quicker than I had planned but hurting a lot more than I had hoped to be at this early stage. One day down, 69 to go.

It was quite a surreal atmosphere in Norco, an old horse town near the edge of LA. Laurie and I went to a small diner and saw another few of the other runners there. I fell in love with this kind of life; a 10 hour run, a beer at the end and loads of food in a diner while chatting to runners about today's run. I could get used to this. However if this were a job I'd say that I had bitten off more than I could chew, I was quite achy and felt hard done by for just the first day.

I slept quite well on the first night. This was really good, sleeping was going to be important in this race. 5:30 AM again we started running from the motel we finished in the afternoon before and out the opposite way we had come in. We were headed out into the great Mojave Desert of California.

On the second day I woke feeling pretty good, I could come down the stairs very well and the groin strain seemed to have disappeared. After all those weeks of worrying about it, all it took was a mere 45 miles of running. Up at 4, some faffing around until the race briefing at 5:15 and then starting all over again at 5:30.

There was a frustrating 15 miles on busy roads on a Monday morning where commuters and trucks would speed down the huge highways with little thought of pedestrians. Why should they look out for pedestrians? They are almost non-existent. The USA struck me as a funny place, it seems that a pedestrian is allowed to wander anywhere so long as they are willing to share the road with tonnes of speeding metal. There are no pavements. Sometimes you have to cross three roads to get on the other side of the one you want to be on.

We were told that the second day was going to be much harder. It was, but because I was feeling so much better I found it easier. At some point while going over a mountain pass we left LA and headed towards the desert.

On hitting Route 66 Laurie and Ruth soaked me with a water pistol which I was very grateful for as it was getting incredibly hot. As soon as I got onto Route 66 I thought about the original bunioneers in the 1928 race across the USA. The road is quite barren now, with weeds growing through the cracks where cars don't seem to drive anymore. 80 years ago this was a new road built for cars that were to take over America and was used quite perilously by runners going for a $25,000 prize. Now all the cars are on much busier highways, leaving this one behind for tourists and the occasional transcontinental race.

On the first day I got a small blister on my left little toe and it didn't bother me until the second day when it started to burn. At least the groin strain had gone. There were a lot of hills today that seemed to coincide with when the temperature went up.

The highest today was about 30°C. It was going to get hotter. The off-road section up hill was amazing but really hard. There were LANY flour signs in many places but the heat getting to my head made me paranoid about whether I was still on the right track. That's when you start doing the doomsday calculations. If I go 2 miles out into nothing and then have to go back will I still make the cut offs? Or more trivially if I go out for miles and can't find my way back then will I die? If I lie down in a bush will I get bitten by a rattlesnake?

After much doom-mongering I saw Ruth at the head of the pass and was very relieved that was all over. A small descent and then a 10 minute lay down to sort the blister out. In doing so Laurie poked at a part of my foot and said "Is this not bothering you?" There was no feeling at all. "Okay then, let's pretend I didn't mention it".

So all in all the second day felt much better. New York was only 49 miles closer but in my head it felt twice as achievable compared to the first day.

Two days in, with the miles barely dented, and we were almost still in LA. However we were all a little shocked in the morning to discover that the race had claimed its first casualty. Phillipe had dropped out with bad cramp and blisters caused by the heat. Yoshiaki Bando had complained of the heat too. I sure felt it but didn't dare complain. It was going to get a lot worse.

16

CALIFORNIA – IT'S THE HEAT THAT'LL KILL YER

I'd never been anywhere like this. Once into day three we were well out in the desert though, still on a road and usually with the occasional car or truck driving past. I felt like a traveller and the gas stations around 30 miles apart were like outposts. I can't imagine what it must have been like for those who came here in the 1850's with no gas stations to get ice and shade.

Each day from 5:30 AM we got a limited amount of time to run before the sun came up from behind the mountains into the valley it likes to scorch every day. The sun really owns this place. The sun is ultimately responsible for the life and death of everything on this planet and if it should choose it could mess up the personal adventures of 14 fragile humans as they tried to pass a scrap of land on a planet 100 million miles away. It had already claimed one of us. How many more would it let pass?

At least the route descriptions were easy; leave motel, run 43.2 miles then finish at motel. The straightness of the roads was astounding. The Romans would have been proud. There was the occasional billboard – usually advertising opportunities to sue people; had an accident? Used a drug that had side effects? Got sunburn on a ridiculous race? Answer yes to any of these questions then someone owes you money.

The white line in the road burned onto my retinas. I had to look down at it because looking upwards I could feel the sun burning into my skull. Within a few days it was well into the mid-forties, hotter than I had in the Sahara and nearly as hot as Badwater. There were times when I'd have to stop and take refuge in artificial shade provided by Laurie and some towels.

Strange though it seemed I performed much better in the heat than most of the others. At the start of one day after a pretty decent 51 mile run into Ludlow I was greeted by Alex who said "James, you are from London, you should run like a penguin yet you run like a Kenyan". I think it was the first and last time I have ever been compared to a Kenyan and was just as confident that it would not be the last time I'd be compared to a penguin.

Every now and then there was an abandoned gas station, you could guess how long it had been abandoned for by the price of gas displayed. One had only $1 a gallon, must have closed decades ago. These became picnic points because they offered shade from the sun. They were so easy to stagger into, but so hard to get back out of again. Most animals bury themselves in the days like this, humans stay indoors yet every day we were out in it slowly getting sapped by the sun's power.

Those ten minutes spent in the shade were wonderful though but always nagging at me was the fact that I had to leave. On a normal day I might stay there till the sun had finished and then move, maybe having a nap and eating. This summer was going to be about overcoming these inertia moments, whether in the shade of a tree, lying in bed or slumped at the back of a car. It was all very nice but none of it was getting us to New York.

The fourth day into Ludlow caused more damage; Jenni, Mr Tanaka and Mr Ishiara had to drop out, the heat being the reason once more. Girard came in after the cut off using walking sticks, he had bad shin splits and those extra hours in the sun had taken their toll. Four days, four runners out. Were the remaining 10 going to make it to the end of the second week?

But despite the sad news of others falling behind I was feeling quite good. I don't feel like I deserved it. I did no heat training whatsoever. I did one session of Bikram yoga, promising to return every day for a month but never did. I found the heat quite liberating though, I'd read a few books beforehand on how humans took over the open plains as their bodies became capable of tolerating the heat. I felt like what I was doing was part of the human design. It was a knife-edge between feeling great and exploding in sweat and dizziness. It was frustrating to stop sometimes but often it was necessary. For this stretch I tried to remember the greatest ultra-running quote from Winston Churchill "When going through hell KEEP GOING". I don't think he had desert running in mind when he said that though.

Staying in the small towns of Barstow and Ludlow was an incredible experience. Ludlow is basically a gas station and a motel, which only had a phone line installed in 1988. Barstow is a much bigger town, still not sure why it's there. On approaching the finish on that day I had to stop at a crossing so I leaned against a lamp post to stretch and burned the palms of my hands, it was like grabbing hold of a hot baking tray.

Laurie was amazing throughout the first six days. She'd drive up the straight road and I'd wonder why she only parked a few yards up and then after 10 minutes of running when I still had not got near the car I realised that she was much further away than first thought, and that the road was tormenting me.

I stopped sleeping well after a few days, dreaming of the white line in the road, which still burned on my eyes. I just could not put it down. I was tired after every day and the pressure of having to sleep enough for the next day was getting to me. I'd usually sleep for a few hours from 9 till midnight and then stay half-awake until it was time to get up. This time would be spent in a semi-conscious daze where I'd think I was on the road, running or just sliding along the white line. I knew that it wasn't real but just could not get it out of my head.

I'd wake up thinking that I'd already run 10 miles but only in my head and they were to count for nothing. This was frustrating.

At the end of day five, as I ran into a place called "Fenner" which is basically an overpriced gas station I had to say goodbye to Laurie, she was headed home after her amazing five day job supporting me through the hellish heat of California. It was so hard to say goodbye. I would have liked it to last longer but Laurie had to get on the road, and she was now 250 miles away from home. We only started five days ago.

But tomorrow I had a new crew. A couple of guys who I only knew through "fetcheveryone.com" – an internet forum had volunteered (via Gemma's request) to come out and crew for days 6 and 7. I was so pleased and humbled by the unbelievable kindness of strangers. Lesley and Dave from Fetcheveryone.com were currently driving all the way up to Needles from Pheonix (about 400 miles, I still can't get my head around the fact that every city in the USA is as far away from the next city as London is from Edinburgh). I didn't know them, know what to expect from them and didn't even know why they would come out and support me. They didn't know me. Why would anyone drive 400 miles to be barked at by a grumpy heat exhausted runner they didn't know? I was really pleased that they decided to come along.

We didn't stay in Fenner, we had a 45 mile drive to Needles, a large town on the border of California and Arizona where we would stay for two days. I was looking forward to this, a biggish city where maybe I'd have a choice of eating place. We drove down the highway and could see it in the distance. It looked wonderful. From a distance Needles looks like an oasis, a beautiful fertile area on a river punctuating the end of a hostile desert with trees and water and life. From a distance it looked like we were driving into heaven.

Close up it looked like that toilet from Trainspotting. It was not a nice place. I got into my room which was hellishly hot and the air con did little other than spew fishy air. It was suffocating and to add to that the smoke alarm kept beeping intermittently, every minute or so. I went down to the reception where the owner suggested a novel fix. "Just smash it off the wall". He said. I wasn't going to do this and eventually he came up and replaced the battery. The Wi-Fi didn't work and I didn't dare complain about the air-con. I figured that was just how it was going to be here.

I didn't sleep well at all that night and had to get up early in the morning to drive back to Fenner and then start the 51 mile stage to Needles. Lesley and Dave were still on their way and said they were not going to get here until after midnight and would just stay in their own room and meet me in the morning at 3:45.

3:45??? I would get no sleep tonight.

I woke up about 2 minutes before there was a bang at the door, as promised Lesley and Dave were there ready to cart my stuff into the car. I'd never seen them before, they'd never seen me. I didn't really know what to say or do. Do I shake hands? Hug? Kiss? Ask "are you here to read the gas meter"? I settled on a low key handshake.

I got in the back of their car with all my clutter and Italo's too who was going to tag along with my crew. He didn't have any crew on turning up to the race and think he played the "I don't speak English" card very well. I wasn't too sure what he was asking when he asked Lesley and Dave to carry his water.

The day didn't start too well. I had had the worst night's sleep since being here and in the 12 hours or so that I was left to organise myself I managed to mess it up completely. I left my two large bags in the truck that the organisers would take to the finish each day and gave Lesley and Dave a plastic box full of my stuff for the day such as food, clothes and drinks. After two miles of running and expecting my usual 500 ml of Gatorade I was told that there was no Gatorade in the box, only some vitamin drink that I had accidentally placed there instead. Doh. This is what happens when I am left to fend for myself. Their first job was to drive back to Fenner and buy some Gatorade at what were apparently highway robbery prices.

Today was going to be tough, a long hot descent into Needles where we had just driven from.

Lesley and Dave had picked up the crewing brilliantly today. Lesley is from Newcastle originally and has a licence plate that says "WHYIMAN" which made me laugh every time they drove past me. When they would stop they'd erect a parasol and a British flag which was a welcome sight to run to each time.

This day was a funny one though and one I'd have to get used to. There was nothing specifically wrong with me I just didn't feel like moving too much today. My legs were obviously tired and I think I was not eating as much as I should have been, and that took its toll on my energy levels. I tried to keep in a constant motion and given that I was not really going any slower I should not consider this a "bad" day but in my mind the extrapolation started. If I felt this sluggish now what about in ten days? Twenty days? Fifty days??

The last six miles into Needles were on a busy highway where the sound of a truck hitting rumble strips just 3 meters from you felt like a plane about to crash into you. It sure was a pant-messing experience. I was keen to get off this road as soon as possible and at least twice some people pulled up alongside me and asked if I wanted a ride into town. I must have looked quite distressed staggering around at the side of a busy road.

And speaking of pant-messing experiences, for the first time in the race I got some chaffing, something I was keen to avoid. Another 62 days of rubbing skin was not something I was willing to endure – I don't think I had enough skin down there in the first place to endure 62 days of grating.

I felt like I had got off lightly though, Markus was suffering badly and came into Needles after the cut-off time but would be allowed to continue. He had been having bad stomach problems caused by the heat. It was taking its toll and there was a long way to go.

Finishing today was sort of a milestone though. I had run about 320 miles now and was at the end of the seventh day. About a year ago when first alerted to this event that was the finish line. I would have just completed the Los Angeles to Las Vegas race, 320 miles in a hot desert over 7 days, pretty epic by my standards. In the end there was no Los Angeles to Las Vegas race and the route went through Needles instead about 50 miles south of LV. Still if it weren't for Mark Cockbain and his pussy comment I would have been finishing here. Instead I was only 10% into a challenge that had barely even started.

I thought about getting the first week out of the way all week long, this was what I originally wanted to sign up for, not the whole lot. I felt a year ago that running across the USA was beyond me, perhaps something to do in ten years' time when I have more experience of running ultramarathons. I had no reason for believing that I could run across the USA.

But now after a week, with 320 miles and California almost complete, I had no reason to believe that I couldn't.

17

ARIZONA – IT'S THE ALTITUDE THAT'LL KILL YER

"Sleep don't visit, so I choke on sun and the days burn in to one" – Radical Face

By this stage, I couldn't remember the last time I had slept and thought about something that didn't involve following a white line or making sure I had enough ice. Sometimes I would nod off and then wake thinking that someone had left my beef jerky in the sunshine and then panic. It was hard to know what was real and what was just made up in my head.

I had hideous chaffing after the run yesterday. The 200 m walk to the pizza place made me look like I was from Needles and so did not really look out of place, but it was bad. I spent the night covering every square millimetre of my moving parts with Sudacrem, thoughtfully brought by Lesley.

The sunrise was a joy to behold every morning and today we were going to see it as we crossed the Colorado River and left California into the State of Arizona. One down.

Arizona looked different as soon as we set foot in there, there was a line of trees along the road we ran as we headed into the Martian red rocks up ahead. California was white and yellow, flat and straight, scorched and desolate. Arizona was beautifully red and brown, three dimensional and scenic, still hot and wild but a different place entirely.

Lesley and Dave were on form again and blasted "Born to Run" from the car as I crossed into their state. I absolutely love the welcoming treatment you get from Americans when you are in "their" state. Lesley and Dave lived in Phoenix and were really looking forward to me running in their home state. I was really looking forward to letting them show me around.

Italo was running with me today and was being supported by Lesley and Dave too. He was having lots of injuries but was dealing with them without any complaint. He was the MacGuyver of ultra-running, he had bad shin splints but with a balloon, some ice, a scarf and a safety pin he could invent some contraption that would fix it.

This was the first day of the proper climbing, not those little wobbles we had on leaving LA but some proper climbs up to altitude. The first climb lasted about 10 miles and near the end we ran into a town called Oatman. This was a proper wild west town with donkeys strolling in the streets and full of saloons and shops. I wished I could have stayed to enjoy this, a perfect place to stop on a drive through. We were bought ice-creams which we ate as we headed up to an even steeper climb out the other side towards the gold mine (yes it was very wild, wild west). Dave was joking around with a huge water gun and soaked Serge, Italo and me as we headed up to the top of the pass. Alex was suffering up here but I was bounding along having more fun than I recalled having so far.

There were curves in the road, there was something to look forward to after each turn and after each turn a new landscape unfurled. It was magnificent. After a week of running along a white line on a grey road along the straightest line I had ever travelled down I was winding up and down in the Arizona mountains, with other runners who were enjoying the ride. Whatever your mode of transport, bike, motorbike, car, RV or on foot these roads were amazing.

I was relieved the chaffing problem never really materialised though I felt a shin split while making the long descent. It was a little sore but I was having so much fun in the mountains I just let it go. It took a long time to get to the bottom of the climb we had been making all day and when we did we were hit by the monotony again.

A long straight road, going slightly upwards was what greeted us having spent most of the day in such beautiful surroundings. It felt like a punishment for enjoying ourselves too much earlier. It was like I was in prison and was returning back to my cell having been allowed to wander around for a few hours. I was back on the hell of the straight white line and to make things worse I had a shin splint.

With nothing else to look at, the pain in my shin occupied a larger area of my brain than before. I was being tormented again by the road and now by my own body. There were still 14 miles to go and they were all horrible.

Was this how the whole summer was going to be?

Lesley and Dave were doing their best to keep my spirits up but I was so deflated having been so high earlier in the day and in the back of my mind I knew they were leaving after today's stage. I'd known them for about 36 hours but they felt like an integral part of my race now. However they had to return to their real lives in Phoenix and leave me to mine here.

Goodbyes are so hard. Dave bought me a McDonald's meal to the end in Kingman and said they had to get on the road soon. I couldn't really think of much to say. What could I say? I owe them so much and can never repay them for what they did at such short notice for a complete stranger. Lesley later admitted that she was worried about crewing me, that I might be demanding and they might screw it up. It seems silly that someone who is willing to drive 400 miles to support a stranger would be worried about not being up to scratch. They were both brilliant.

This was my second goodbye in as many days and they always feel like a kick in the stomach.

Thank you Lesley and Dave.

The next day I was unsupported and then Debbra and Dave were driving up from San Diego to support me through to the end of Arizona. I was looking forward to seeing them again.

That night I ate in the restaurant near the motel. I got there just before last orders and had a burger and fries. The food was good and the waitress was lovely, always filling up my lemonade. I just wasn't that hungry. I actually felt a bit sick but not from any stomach problem and instead an emotional problem. It was all starting to get on top of me.

I was using some of the ice from my lemonade to rub down my shin to make it feel better, I expected it to feel better right away but it didn't. I asked for the cheque and she would not have taken longer than 30 seconds to get it but in those 30 seconds I just started to burn up inside, my head about to burst into flames and my eyes were welling up. I just threw my money onto the table and ran out, leg still stinging and on getting outside I very nearly burst into tears.

For the first time in the race the whole thing just felt too big. I was not really thinking about just how far there was to go until now and I had such a great feeling getting through the first week that this came as a shock. I thought I had bitten off more than I could manage. New York was too far away for me. I was alone now.

I didn't cry in the end, I just about held it together. I looked up at the stars in the clear sky and that helped me calm down a bit. I looked across the car park to see that Laure and the others were still there waiting for someone to finish. I went over to ask and it was Markus again who was finishing late. Markus was going to sit the next few days out of the race and hence was out of the rankings. I also heard that Girard Bavato had pulled out earlier that day with infected blisters. The 14 runners who started eight days ago were now just eight. Who was next?

I slept better that night, it was a relief to get some sleep especially after my episode in the restaurant and now the additional worry of being "next" to pull out from the race. This day though I was to be without crew, the organisers had insisted upon it for the first two weeks but I said this to them at the start and they were fine with it. Actually Laure said it was a good test to see how the organisers support crew would work for the last eight weeks where they'd be supporting me, Italo, Jenni and Anneke.

Day 9 was a simple 42 miles on a straight road into Truxton though there were going to be climbs. At the finish I'd meet up with Deb and Dave who would be supporting me for the next six days.

I was elated that the shin that had nearly caused me to cry the previous night did not seem to hurt in the morning. However, around ten miles in my right shin started to hurt instead. It wasn't too bad but the extrapolation on the other leg had started again. What if both of my legs snap?

It was noticeably cooler with a breeze today, "only" 38°C. I was loving the weather and the scenery opened out into another spectacular Arizonian landscape. It seems I had to "earn" aesthetic treats like this by plodding up miles of straight road.

The shins got sorer as the day went on and in a rare moment of mobile phone reception I called Gemma to let her know how I was doing and that I was likely to end up today in a place without phone reception. It was only around four miles from the end, I spoke to her a little and then just said to her "I'm going now, my bones are hurting".

That last four miles were the hardest I could remember so far, I ached a bit but had no bad injuries I just felt all over pain. I walked much of it and headed into Truxton in a fairly grumpy mood.

Later that night the café was opening specially to feed us which was great. Debbra and Dave were due to join me later on after a 5 hour drive from San Diego. I had completely lost all concept of distances by this point. 5 hour drive? You can get from the top of England to the bottom in that time.

After lying down for an hour I headed over to the café where all the other runners were seated and awaiting the food. This was really nice and what I imagined the whole race would be like – a day's run then a gathering at the end to eat and talk. However my shin was worse, I could barely walk on it. My limp was obvious to everyone and I'll never forget the sympathetic and wincing look I got off Patrick as I walked through the café and took my seat.

I could be next.

I only got through half the meal before the pain in my leg made my head burn. I broke out in a sweat, I don't know what it was. It was like some terrible realisation where you have made a terrible mistake like forgetting your passport when you are at the airport. The heart starts pumping hard, sweat drips from every pore and the whole body feels like burning. I got this just sitting down eating pasta. I was not in a good place.

I made my excuses and left, limping back out of the café into my room and onto my bed. Now every extra minute I could get lying down might be enough to heal the injuries. Might be enough to put me back in the race.

I had very little phone reception and was worried that Deb and Dave would not be able to find where I was but they managed OK. It was really great to see them again but I felt like I could not greet them as enthusiastically as I would have liked. I can't really remember what I said but I was in a grumpy mood. I hoped that it didn't show too much. It was really great to see them I just thought that it was not great to see me right now.

Having others along for the ride made me conscious that

some of the places we were staying in were a bit grotty. Not that I would complain as these motels were in the middle of nowhere, I think only used by low paid construction workers when they are fixing the roads. It does not strike me as the sort of place people come to very often.

That night I didn't sleep very well, I was in a little pain but the worst thing was feeling like it could not get better. In the morning I'd lie in bed nervously awaiting the moment of truth, when I put my foot on the ground for the first time of the day. Would I feel nothing or a sharp stab up through my tibia? Today it was the latter, and another day of pain awaited.

Today was going to be a long slog uphill for the first 20 miles, which might work in my favour as there would be less impact in my right leg as I climbed. It was cold at the start, it was the first time since I had been here that I shivered. Bando looked a mess on the start line, he had another bad day yesterday and looked mummified on the start line.

It was hard to keep my mind off the shin today and Deb and Dave certainly helped, but with long slow climbs up straight roads it's hard not to indulge your own suffering. The race instructions today were simple, "go straight, after 37.9 miles follow curve in road". Wow there was a curve. Exciting stuff.

I was incredibly annoyed by the least likely of sources today; grasshoppers. They would all jump right in front of my feet as I ran and I was getting exhausted with trying to step out of their way constantly. Each extra unexpected movement caused more pain and I cursed these little insects with a suicide mission. Should I even bother stepping around them when they choose to leap under my feet? I said to myself that I would not bother avoiding them but I could not help it, every time one leapt for its death I would jump out of the way and hurt myself.

It felt a little less painful to run than to walk which was somewhat comforting except that it was hard to run up the steeper hills especially when there was a strong headwind. The wind seemed to be conspiring against me, every time I broke into a run it would step up and blow me back. I just felt like yelling "FUCK YOU" at it but its ability to sweep the air out of my throat would have made it sound pathetic. The 39.7 mile curve could be seen for miles and miles but I just could not get anywhere near it.

I tried to make myself feel better about the shin. I said to myself, "If I'd known I'd only feel this sore after 10, 20, 40 miles at the beginning of the day then I would have settled for that. It wasn't getting any worse, not physically anyway just in my mind, and that's what I had to worry about. When the mind quits it's over.

I finished the stage in just over 11 hours and Deb and Dave were fantastic throughout but there was little that would improve my mood. While they went out to buy me a Subway from Seligman I sat in bed and blogged about the day. I tried always just to write what I was feeling, In addition to finishing this race I really wanted to keep a record of exactly what this kind of thing does to a person.

I didn't want to take any pain killers on this run. There are too many stories of runners causing more damage by doping themselves silly. Masking injuries can be dangerous, especially over a long race and they can cause kidney problems too. I needed my kidneys to be in good shape for all the fluid I was putting through my body. However at the end of today Italo gave me something he gestured which I assumed was the international gesture for "reduces inflammation".

I wrote a paragraph at the end of the entry which upon reading many months later made my skin turn cold. It reminded me just how low I was feeling at this stage. I had forgotten about it until I did re-read it in order to write this book. I wrote:

To put a positive spin on everything, my shin hurts no more now than at the end of yesterday, I am still in the race. Tomorrow and the next day are "short", only 30 miles which gives me much more time to recover, Deb and Dave are here (gone out to get me a Subway as we speak) and they are such fantastic company, I have a lot of friends at home saying nice things and following my race. 10 days is sort of a milestone.

On the negative side, this has now stopped being fun.

60 more days was a long time to go without any more fun.

The next day just felt different. I still hurt but the road now cut through some great scenery. It had trees and flowers, the barren beige rock had been replaced by shades of green, gold and brown. Even the sound was different, the chainsaw buzzing of bugs in the desert had been replaced by birds singing. And what were those white things in the sky? Clouds? I had not seen any of those for over a week. I might as well be running in England again.

Italo was going to use my support crew again today, he was hurting too and we would go through the same ice routine at the end of each stage. Early on the pain seemed to fall through my shin and down into my ankle such that it swelled quite a lot during the day. I am not sure whether this was a consequence of running awkwardly that transferred the injury. I liked to think that if I ran enough the pain would just get lower and lower until it was at the soles of my feet and then I could just leave it in the road somewhere.

For the first time in a few days I felt pretty good running and through wonderful tree-scapes it made it better. Deb and Dave were on hand every two miles where I'd neck a bottle of Gatorade or Monster energy drink and perhaps have one of Deb's amazing turkey sandwiches which went down so well in Furnace Creek in Badwater nearly a year ago.

Italo was great to run with. His English was not fluent but he said to me very clearly today "your job for today is to finish without the leg hurting anymore so that you have time to fix the leg". This was exactly what I had to do. Today and tomorrow were "only" 30 miles each which meant I could have 16+ hours each day off my feet and trying to recover.

There were a few off road sections today which were hard work and the occasional territorial dog would run out barking and nose us along. They seemed aggressive but I am sure it was just their way of saying "well done, keep going".

Today was a Wednesday. For the last 6 years every Wednesday I go to the running club, run "three parks" a seven mile loop around the parks of central London then head to the pub to drink and talk. Today was also the "last Wednesday of the month" where we'd also have a spread of cheese and wine in the club room to enjoy after our run. Wednesday nights had become such a huge part of my life since I moved to London 6 years ago. I think the only reason I miss them was if I was out of the country running. This was the third Wednesday in a row that I had missed. I don't think I had missed that many in a row before.

I was told by a friend, Andy DuBois, that to get through severe pain I am to mentally retire to someplace I feel happy, far away from where I am right now. It's done by prisoners of war so it should be able to work for me. Whenever I felt misery at my current circumstances I would take myself away to a place that made me the happiest, and today my happy place was where I should be right now. In the basement of a London leisure centre in a small room full of sweaty runners and cheese. That felt wonderful.

Thoughts like that helped me through the day and the 30 miles felt much easier. I continued with the ice routine and then drove 30 mile to Williams where we'd be running to tomorrow. Williams was a fairly big town which is the gateway to the Grand Canyon. I didn't go to visit, some did but I just wanted to rest as best I could.

We went to a restaurant called the "Singing Pig" in Williams which was a fantastic experience. Deb proudly told the owner that I was running across the USA and they went crazy for it, saying "we must get you on our Facebook page".

It was great having a "going out" meal and having Deb and Dave around. I felt like I was back in it again.

I had a strange dream that night that after finishing one of the stages in a small town in the middle of nowhere I was told by the hotel to find somewhere else for my horse and cow. I found a stable nearby for $6 per night (is that a good price? Was I ripped off?). Anyway on getting up the next day I panicked as I wondered what on earth I was going to do with my cow and horse during today's run. It took a little while for me to realise that I had no horse and cow.

Apparently dreaming of a cow signifies some kind of rebirth and a horse is meant to represent power. I reckon they are just silly characters I gave my shins over the past few days.

Probably the strangest dream I have had to do with running was when I was in a hotel in Toronto after the Moose ultra. I woke up in pitch dark and thought I was still in the race and lost. I could not see a thing. I decided to stay calm, people know I am out here, just stay where you are and someone will come and rescue me.

A few moments passed when I realised something quite embarrassing, I was just wearing my pants. Oh no, this is dreadful. Not only am I out in the forest on my own in the dark, lost and cold but now I am going to appear on CNN as a guy who had to be rescued from a race in his pants. What would my mother say?

It took a little while longer for the penny to finally drop, I finished the race yesterday and I was in a hotel room. Phew, I just put the covers back on and went back to sleep, relieved that no one will ever find out about this.

I felt much better the next day but still failed the "foot on the floor test". As I place my foot on the floor to get out of bed that sharp sensation drove up my leg to tell me that today, once more, it was going to be painful.

I was in better spirits though and on driving back to the start in the morning I saw a sign that said LOS ANGELES 464 miles. It brought home quite sharply just what I had already done. I'd run more in 11 days than I would normally do in two months. That was about an 8 hour drive.

This was the second of the two "recovery" days where I'd hope to finish in good time to relax and put my feet up. It was great to see Bando running well again after looking mummified days earlier. It certainly gave me a lift to think that you can come back from the brink like that.

The nagging pain was still there but because I was mentally better it went unnoticed sometimes. The route helped, lovely trails and trees like I could be running in the New Forest back in England, though it was a hell of a lot hotter.

My ankle was now quite swollen, very noticeable when I took the compression guard off. It always felt hot to touch, even hotter than my skin generally. That said, the second of the "easy" days went really well, we started running into green stuff again with the view of wonderful lakes and nice trails. This would have been perfect for a horse. I couldn't believe I had left him in the stable.

As I approached the finish line I pointed out the sign to the McDonald's, almost missing the yellow flags. I placed my order with Dave, a Big Mac, large fries and strawberry milkshake.

The final day in Arizona was cold, for the first time at a start line people were shivering. We were high up and at 5:30 am there was a chilling breeze. Deb and Dave had said that they felt the altitude on their runs in the evening, I didn't really notice but it was probably one of a number of things that were depleting me. Exhaustion, injury, loneliness, hunger, heat exhaustion and altitude – it was impossible to isolate one thing that was getting to me.

The day had once again started with the disappointment of feeling a sting as my foot hit the floor when getting out of bed. The last day was more trail and I physically felt the same as I had done in the previous days, sore but getting on with it. I did today have a constant sick feeling, nothing to do with food but a nervous sickness. Today was the day that Deb and Dave would have to leave at the end of this stage and return home, from then on I'd be alone.

This occupied my mind all day. Up until now I have had great support from amazing friends helping me with the challenge. When Laurie, Lesley and Dave had to leave it was sad but I knew that I was soon to be joined by someone else. This was the end though, there was no more help after today. The race organisation was superb but the thought of not having a personal support crew was quite daunting. After today there would be no personal support crew until Gemma arrived a week before New York. That was 50 days of running away, about 2400 miles – most of a continent.

Shit, I had still barely dented this race.

Italo and I ran together as we had done for a number of days and every time I stopped and was handed a drink or food by Deb and Dave there was a sadness that this would not happen again tomorrow or for a long time.

The end of day 13 was at Flagstaff. It was the biggest town we had been to since LA and we stopped on the outskirts. I sat down in the chair at the end of the stage, enjoying the beer and another day done but dreading the moment when Deb and Dave said they were going to hit the road.

It was another kick in the stomach, it really hurt. I can't even remember saying goodbye this time, just watching them head off.

My first day as a solo runner was going to be hard already, 53 miles was another long day.

It's so easy to get distracted by numbers early on. 53 miles is a long day's work and too often I would get to 5 and say "well that's 10% done in 1 hour which means 10 hours if I keep up this pace which I won't", then you get to 11 miles and say "well that's a fifth of it done in much less than a fifth of 12 hours therefore I am doing ok". This stuff buzzes through your head like an uninvited guest. It gets worse, then you find that you have done a third of the race in less than 4 hours and calculate the pace you need to finish under cut-off. For me it was about 4 mph which is not a lot less than the overall cut-off pace and therefore I must be doing shit. You go from doing well to doing shit based on a different calculation of the same thing.

And if you don't stop it, that kind of shit just messes with your head for the whole race and never makes you feel any better. I was reading a book called "Adventures in Numberland" by Alex Bellos who spoke about isolated tribes. Some of them don't really have a concept of "53" or even numbers above 5 or 6. Many have 1,2,3,4 then more than 4 or "many". There is no use in having a number 53 as it's not that different from 52 or even 27, it's just "many". Some of them don't even know how many kids they have, they just have "many". I wish I could think like that. I don't have 53 miles to do I just have "many" miles to do.

But my head was in a better place today and I was thinking about happier things and being nearer other runners today was quite motivating. When I got to 16 miles I thought, "Shit I still have 37 to go, this is never going to end". By staying more positive and ignoring my watch as much as possible the miles just went and all of a sudden I had done a marathon.

I felt like a runner again, looking down at my shadow in front of me watching the rhythmic swinging of my arms and legs. My shin was hardly making a noise at all. It's a good job that there were no dolphin in the desert because they would have been deafened by the sonic booming of my pace. I must have been running 10 minute miles at some stage.

Today was the first day of my proper "unsupported" time, something that I would have to get used to. It was much better than I expected. The guys were awesome in catching me every hour and giving me a spray, drinks and food. Laure came up to me at the end of the day and gave me a list of all the times that I had been given support and what I took. She was a little concerned that I only ate 2 cliff bars during the whole run. Most of my calories were liquid. Today and for the rest of it I think I switched my camelpack from water to Gatorade.

I finished in 11:05, an hour better than my best expectations and with no injuries. I was really chuffed with that. The sleeping quarters tonight were some sort of town hall (in an igloo) with sleeping mats and a solar shower. It was nice as we all got to hang out with each other and eat together, something I thought we'd do lots of while we were there but the bone aching and tiredness just got in the way of all that.

We were now deep in the Navajo desert which is a Native American area in Northern Arizona. There are some impressive rock formations and what look like volcanoes. Each one is isolated and looks great on its own, some are really cubic and from a distance you could think it was part of a city skyline. It's not as hot as the Mojave desert but it's more beautiful. It didn't matter to me that the roads were straight as there was always a wonderful panorama to enjoy.

The clocks went forward last night meaning we had less rest after a long day yesterday. I woke up long before the new 4:30 am feeling more awake than usual though. The pain had subsided further and the 41 miles today felt like it was going to be comfortable.

My mind was in a really good place again today and I let it wander off as usual. I was determined not to clock watch or calculate as I did yesterday and just appreciate every mile as they passed. Early on when I was near everyone I thought about the very different styles each support team has with their runner. I never see June who crews for Rainer as they are always too far ahead. I imagine she takes about a million photos of every stage though.

Patrick's wife sticks quite close to him in the car, he manages to keep on running when she comes to him with refreshments and it's obviously working as he's having a great time here. Serge's support guy makes me laugh. He walks like a butler and holds out a tray in an outstretched palm at a perfect 90°C. I really want him to wear a bow-tie on one of the stages.

Alex's team are like a Ferrari pit-stop. He walks along, has his bottles changed, pictures taken, beard trimmed and anything else all within about 10 seconds. They are very slick. Dan who supports Markus is very laid back and parks the car and sits down for a while and watches the world go by. He has become my preferred supplier of toilet roll in recent days. The Japanese crews will take lots of photos and when not tending to their runner they can be seen washing their hire cars.

Philippe's guy is quite funny too. He gets out of the car, runs half a mile to meet Philippe, jogs along and past the car for about another half mile then back to the car to meet him in 2 miles. Now correct me if I am wrong but this guy seems to be covering the same distance as Philippe?

I finished the day feeling quite strong and knowing that I didn't have to push it too hard to get to the finish each day well under the cut off times. Could it be getting easy?

After a glorious 41 miles on day I woke up in a funny mood. I had slept fairly well but something just didn't feel right. I gathered all my stuff together and got myself to the start line just outside the igloo shaped building we were staying in. The rocks looked formidable again and there was plenty of up and down today, it seemed there was plenty of up and down with my emotional state too.

My injury was getting better, I was still going strong and I was surrounded by spectacular scenery, great new friends and a fantastic organisation. Why did I feel so depressed?

We started in darkness again setting out and I immediately realised that I had forgotten my running number. There would be a penalty, but I did not care too much about that – I just got angry at my own stupidity. I felt fine running but after about 5 miles it all just became "too big" again.

I had spoken to Gemma (on IM) the previous night about how much we were missing each other. This was the longest I had ever been out of the UK and probably the longest I had been from her. It did not help that there had been no phone coverage for 2 days. We spoke about the possibility of her coming over in the middle of the run, but I wasn't too sure. It would be great to have her there, but then her having to leave would be too hard. It hurt each time a support team left me and it would be many times worse with her. I didn't know what the answer was.

I missed home a lot too, the early morning start with the faffing and trying to find something to eat and clothes to wear and drinks to fill the camelpack with and then cramming everything into 2 bags and taking it to the truck. It was so much harder and more frustrating than I thought it would be. When the sun rose above the mountains I went to put on my sun glasses and realised I had forgotten them too. I felt so fucking useless and then the tears came again.

I was near the back at this point and let the others go past and disappear into the sun. For a good mile or so I just sobbed at where I was and what I had to do. Sometimes it just felt too big. Even 48 miles today which I had run many times before felt like a job that could not be done. 54 more days of this didn't bear thinking about.

I've known ultra-running take you to the extreme of your emotions. Euphoria, depression, anger, pride etc. Within a race you may hit several peaks of various emotions. I was in for 2 more months of these euphoric highs and crippling lows and I was not entirely looking forward to it.

I tried to kick myself out of it. Just watch the miles go past and the days would take care of themselves. I actually thought more about my leg today than normal, trying to get a feeling out of it and trying to take comfort out of the fact that it was rock solid, like I could kick down these telegraph poles with it. Yeah.

I think a lot about what others think about this and that helps me through. I know people think I am "crazy" for doing such a thing but I know deep down they all want to be doing it too. I have a chance to do something everyone wants to do which is pretty special.

And so I broke out of it. I could use the "suncream in my eyes" excuse for anyone who saw me. Without much thought 12 miles had gone already, that's a quarter of the day gone without even thinking about it. I might be able to get through today after all.

After around 15 miles I had a massive breakthrough. I actually got a photo of a lizard. I see loads of them just jumping out of the bushes, scuttling along the road a bit then jumping back in. This one was just sat there. Long enough for me to get the camera out to take the picture. I was really pleased with that, this could be an awesome day.

Around 20 miles in there was a guy with a table selling trainers. It was the weirdest thing I had seen that day, how many people would want to buy new trainers in the middle of the desert. Well, if he did not sell any today he should just give up.

On the subject of shoes most runners now had cut the toes

off theirs. Some runners were getting blisters and swelling and performing surgery on shoes seems to fix it. I have yet to suffer with blisters (aside from that one little one on the first day). Another reason to be cheerful?

After 30 miles we headed onto a dirt track which was quite nice to run on and there were loads of little buildings around. I passed Dan and he held up the toilet roll but I did not need it today, my bowels felt fine. I wished him a happy Independence Day, he was the only American in the whole event.

It was warm as usual and every hour or so I'd get sprayed with cold water by Anne and Rene (whose birthday it was today). They were brilliant as usual, I can't believe I felt so alone earlier when the support here was so fantastic.

While on the trail there were spots of water falling out of the sky. I would not call it rain but when every single one hit my skin it was beautiful. Thunder boomed in the distance and I yelled at it to come over and soak me. There was a short lived shower but it was wonderful.

It was a great day in all despite the early morning sobs. Music was playing at the finish, Laure was dancing, and everyone seemed to be having a great time. Tomorrow we would be saying goodbye to the beautiful Arizona and entering New Mexico. I was looking forward to it.

18

NEW MEXICO – IT'S THE FOOD THAT'LL KILL YER

In two weeks I had lost 4 kg from my original weight, down from 84 to 80. This felt manageable, losing 2 kg a week might take me down to a normal skinny runner's weight by the time I get to New York. I was trying to eat as much as I could but I just don't feel hungry in the mornings.

We entered New Mexico around noon on day 17, quite close to a McDonald's that I stopped in. I don't recall exactly when we entered but I do remember losing mobile phone signal and not getting it back for four days. This was frustrating as the radio silence made Gemma worry. Hopefully she'd have nothing to worry about.

Other than that the first half a day in New Mexico was nothing out of the ordinary. I was pleased to be in a third state, only about 11 more to go. At the end David in the crew gave me a lunch which he had not eaten earlier, a steak and potato rosti takeaway. It looked lovely, exactly the kind of thing I would normally eat and took it on the drive back to the motel, "El Rancho", which was about 30 miles away. New Mexico was going to involve even more wilderness and staying in very small buildings in the middle of nowhere or having to drive at the end of each stage, cutting precious hours from my relaxation time.

I got back to the motel, had a shower then napped, leaving the steak on the side. On waking a few hours later ravenously hungry I wolfed it down and then headed to the bar downstairs to get wireless signal so I could write my blog of the day.

I wrote that the day had been a bit frustrating, but not the worst and it does not mean that I would have a bad day tomorrow. I got half way through my day's report when I had to run to the bathroom to be sick. I felt like someone had just knifed me in the stomach. All of my bones ached like I had bad flu and I was sweating profusely. I just quit typing then and headed back to bed, trying to drink as much fluid as possible and hoping that whatever poison had just entered my body could be flushed out overnight. I lay in bed, hoping.

The night's sleep was probably the worst since I had been there. I just lay there and watched miles of tarmac road and white line unroll in my head over and over. In a semi daze I'd snap out of it and say, "Stop it, don't do the miles in your head, they don't count. Do them on the road tomorrow. Think of something else". I just could not seem to think of anything else except of course when I got punched in the stomach again.

On leaving the motel room and waiting in the car park I spewed all over the ground, in full view of the other runners and crew. Rene didn't really know what to do except give me a bag to take in the car with me for the drive to the start. Anne (who normally gets all the runners to sign in each morning) asked if I was okay to run. Whether I was okay or not was of little consequence – I would run.

There was some confusion at the start about the distance. 41.2 miles was the advertised distance but a mistake in an instruction meant it could be 2 miles less. Alas no, normally those 2 miles are nothing, but today they would be at least half an hour of sleep, or rest, or eating or anything but running.

The first 2 miles went okay – I only had one shit. I ran very slowly and watched everyone else pull away. Very soon it occurred to me that I was not going to be doing much running today at all. I was pretty much walking from the start.

The cut off was 3.5 miles an hour, which is a brisk walk. It's easy to say that you can walk that fast when doing a couple of miles at home, but for 41 miles when you have to stop and eat and shit and with hills and heat, it definitely does not feel comfortable.

I was timing the miles from the start, pleased when I'd do one in 14 minutes (there were mile markers on the roads, not from the organisation but as part of the road), and then beating myself up when one came up as 17. I'd say to myself that maybe it was because I stopped to have a shit, but I knew that this now only took 5 seconds at a time and that this would be a feature of most miles today.

Within 5 miles everyone was out of sight. There was a long waving section of road which must have stretched 10 miles and, though I could not see anyone on it, I imagined everyone dotted along there somewhere.

My knees were weak and wobbling, a combination of the tiredness and lack of energy. Sometimes I just could not pick my legs up to even walk, I was all over the place and I had not even done a quarter of the stage yet. Several times I just felt like falling into the sand and lying there. I needed to sleep.

This was the first time so far I had pictured myself getting carried out of the race and to the finish. If I fell down now I would be done, the car would come, pick me up, take me to the end, I'd rest a few days then start again. But then I would become a "stage runner", put in a separate list from those still in with a chance of getting a ranking for getting to New York.

Half way took a lifetime to get to. No amount of coke or energy drink would kick me awake. Rene and Anne were doing an amazing job of crewing for me, right out at the back when they also had to attend to Italo (near the front) and Jenni who was near the back too but not nearly as far back as me. At 23 miles they put out a chair and a parasol and asked me to sleep. I sat down in the chair, covered from the sun by Anne and the parasol while Rene drove on to deliver another aid stop for the others.

It was beautiful. I just sat there, cool, relaxed and for a while I had no care in the world. The breeze and my own rhythmic breathing calmed me not quite to sleep but into a meditative state. I thought I would only take 10 minutes but I took half an hour. I was not asleep but I was somewhere else.

From then on it got better. I woke up. I was still crapping a lot (up to twice a mile now) but I felt I had a little more energy to get the job done. Rene and Anne said not to worry about the cut-offs as today would be my "bad day" and tomorrow would be better. With about 12 miles to go I threw my watch into the van and Rene and Anne laughed. Time did not matter anymore. I would get to the end when I got to the end; not before, not after.

With about 10 miles to go I started counting the hours until I could go to sleep, like a little kid waiting for Christmas or something. Rene had to leave with the jeep and Bertrand replaced him in the Toyota as Rene had to drive those who had already finished back to El Rancho which was now an hour's drive away. I felt a bit bad for being the slow one who was messing up the plan, but Bertrand and Anne would have none of it.

"COURAGE JAMES. COURAGE".

It got quite hilly in the end as Anne walked with me and I pointed at things and asked what they were in French. I was getting into a manageable distance from the finish now, not long from sleep.

The finish was again in the middle of nowhere, a place called Crownpoint where there just seemed to be a few warehouses. I walked over the line, my legs aching from all that walking about

25 minutes over the cut-off of 11:45 but that did not matter here. I sat and had a Sprite, the first I kept down all day as David took down the finish flags. I got into the van and slept for the entire journey home.

Laure said to me on my arrival at El Rancho to not do any blogging tonight, just sleep. That was fine by me. I had a shower, had some rice that Laure bought for me then hit the sack. Today was by far the worst day. So far.

I slept much better that night, not thinking of the road as I really was that exhausted. On making it to the start line again in the morning Laure said that I had a "much better face this morning". This pleased me though I was still feeling ill. I had not eaten anything since yesterday and my saliva glands had just packed in. My mouth was rejecting food as well as my body.

The day started with the optimistic feeling that I could at least run the first few miles and stick with everyone and not get behind. I was still tired and weak but moving, slow but steady. I was feeling good given the circumstances. I could still run, I remember when I was panicking about the shin splints and how I got over that by just remembering that I can indeed still put one foot in front of the other, without too much bother.

But then after only a few miles that became difficult. It was like my legs were not responding properly to the instructions given by my brain, they wobbled again after about an hour of running and one by one the runners behind me just passed and disappeared into the distance. I wasn't sleepy today, just weak.

Today was "only" 41 miles which was very welcome, if I could go at the same pace as the previous day without the sleep, I would finish under the cut off and have time to recover. These things surely don't last more than 48 hours?

My plan was simple, try to run and get as far ahead of the cut offs as I could so that I would have more crawling space at the end. It's a strategy that I tell people not to do in the

Spartathlon every year but here I thought it was the only way. My legs giving out were a ticking time bomb. I wanted to be as close to the finish as possible when it went off.

After around half of the stage the same things happened again, I walked, crapped, tried desperately to drink fluids, juice, coke, whatever but just could not keep anything down. I drank everything too fast like I'd been deprived of drink for days, the sugary sensation felt ecstatic as it rushed down my throat and I willed it to just stay in there. I imagined the molecules of sugar somehow entering my bloodstream, being welcomed by my body in its war against this disease. It was losing though, every time I got up off the back of the support car having taken on the sugar it would get thrown right back out. I tasted every drink twice, it still felt pleasant in my mouth as this ice cold liquid sugar raced out of my stomach. I just looked at the puddle on the ground in despair. At some point I would run out of energy completely. That's the point where I would leave the race.

I finished just under the cut off time and tried to eat something before going straight to bed. The next two days were going to be very hard; 54 miles then 52 miles over hills. Hard enough to do on a full tank.

What made this even more difficult was that there was still no mobile phone reception. I could not call or text Gemma to tell her how I was doing. She had an inkling that I was not in the best of states.

I didn't record much of what happened in this period, I tried to make the effort of blogging every day and responding to messages on email, text and Facebook but with no reception and in a complete state of exhaustion I just lay down at the end of each day. My blog had gained a fairly large following in the UK and many were worried that I was not doing well. There was no communication from me, and the results of each day that somehow got posted showed me right at the back of the pack now. There was a general feeling that I was next out.

Day 20 I was told was beautiful scenery. I don't remember, all I remember was doing the same thing as the last two days, trying to run as far as I could before my knees locked in exhaustion. It happened sooner and sooner each day. I vaguely remember some roadworks after about 10 miles of this stage and feeling really put out by having to walk around barriers in the road.

I worried about the race crew having to spend so much time with me. Jenni, Anneke and Italo were also unsupported and they needed time with the crew too but right now I was monopolising it. Italo was so far ahead that often they would have a 20 mile drive from him to me. I didn't feel fair on anybody. I wasn't going to drop out though. I was just waiting to drop.

The sickness got a little better and the Japanese support team were wonderful in giving me fruit drinks along the way. I was at the back with Mr Koshita and Bando. I was still getting inside the cut-offs but not by much. I was down to 72 kg in weight after starting three weeks previously at 84 kg. 4 kg a week is not sustainable. I was wasting away, starving my body and if it did not reverse I was just going to grind to a halt. There was nothing mental about this anymore, it was purely physical. No matter how strong I might feel in the head I could not disobey the laws of thermodynamics. I couldn't create energy from nothing. I couldn't run another 2000 miles without holding on to something that goes down my mouth.

That's not to say I was even mentally strong at this point. On finishing the stage in a small town called Cuba I misread the instructions and crossed a road that I should not have done then moaned when I got to the end and had to cross it again, rueing the extra few minutes that it had cost me. Then I moaned about my motel room being a bit further from the organisers van than some of the other runners who got there before I did. I was resentful of those who finished a lot quicker than me as they got so much more time to rest.

There were lots of restaurants in town and usually I'd have loved this. Eating options had been limited in New Mexico though I was not in a position to take advantage. I went to the gas station across the road and tried to buy something inoffensive but such products do not exist in US gas stations. Everything is super carbonated, super caffeinated, high sugar, high salt. I just wanted an apple juice or some nuts. I could have nuts so long as they were covered in honey and sugar and caffeine.

Sleep got worse. Before I was dreaming about running in the road and waking to disappointment that it was not real, now I was lying awake and just thinking about running along the road. I could not switch off. It was like I was stressing about an exam where I'd have some equation looping through my head. I was exhausting myself thinking about it as much as I was running it.

By day 21 I stopped being sociable. I grunted at people if they were to pat me on the back and say "well done" or "good luck" or "sorry to hear you are still ill". It was like it wasn't really me here anymore, just some ghost of me remained after something horrible had pillaged my body. I just didn't want to be here anymore.

It was going to be another hard day, 51.4 miles of hills and ending at Abiqiui Lake. It was a stunning day to run again but I just could not enjoy it.

The day started the same as the other three, I hit the wall after about 10 miles, only 42 more to wobble along. I started to have a long hard think about what the hell I was doing out here.

Being starving and sick and exhausted makes you paranoid about everything. I thought the race crew and the other runners wanted me out. I thought the people back at home who had not heard from me for days were laughing at me and would revel in my failure when I returned home. I thought about what I'd actually do when I dropped out; would I continue after spending a few days resting and recovering? No I decided I was going to get the first possible flight out there.

I felt like the clouds were against me, mocking me with temporary shelter and then disappearing to allow the sun to beat upon me again. It was nowhere near as hot as in the first two weeks but without taking enough liquid it was hurting. The wind was laughing at me too, blowing sand into my face.

Trucks were only there to screw up my race too, driving down the highway and blowing off my hat or drenching me in the smell of animals, live or dead I could not tell. Whenever I wanted to use the outdoors the trees and bushes seemed to have disappeared as if they too were in on the joke.

In retrospect this all sounds ridiculous, I've had moments like this in all big races I have done. It never lasted four days though and I never felt so sure. The world hates me.

There is a feeling I sometimes get which always seems ridiculous. I think that no one in the world is suffering or has ever suffered as much as I am right now. That despite all the bad things in the world people have to suffer they can't possibly understand what I am going through right now. It's stupid, selfish and delusional but very real.

It is usually short lived, only a few minutes or hours and then later I can laugh about it. What was I thinking? How silly of me. However I'd been feeling this way for days now. I felt like I was suffering more than any human has suffered before but yet logically I knew that this wasn't true, not by a long way. This contradiction then leads to another set of emotions; feelings of patheticness, hopelessness and weakness.

I really am the most pathetic person in the world if illness has reduced me to this. I don't deserve to be here. Others could be out here running this instead of me and doing a much better job of it. The great fortune that landed on me to allow me to take part in this great event should have landed on someone else. It should have been Mark Cockbain here or any one of a number of brilliant and resilient runners I know instead. This is wasted on me.

I am going to have to return to the UK and tell my friends that I never made it, that my body rejected doing such a thing and I am no way near strong enough to run across the USA. They would agree and laugh and say "what were you thinking?"

I just wanted for someone to come along and say that this was as bad as it was going to get. That this was rock bottom and from now it was only going to get better. I felt like I could deal with it if I knew this was the lowest, if someone were to just reach out to me and say it would not get any worse. Even if it just stayed this bad I could probably accept that and struggle on. I decided to draw a line under it. It's NOT going to get any worse, I can still do this if I stay like this. I was comforted by this feeling that I had hit the bottom and the only way was up. For a moment there was a new feeling of optimism that I was going to be OK.

From here on things were not going to get any worse.

And then that dog ran at me.

All books like this one start off with some sort of "warzone" scene from a run where there was a turning point in the author's life or race. I have had many such moments before that I have already described that would make a good start to a book. Before heading over to Los Angeles I knew that something would come up that would have to make the first few pages of my story but in all honesty I thought I would have to exaggerate their significance to make the book read better.

I speculated about what it might be before I got on the plane. What I'd have to fill the first few pages of the book with and then write at length about the significance. There is no way in a million years I would have predicted this.

The crying stopped after a few minutes, mainly because my

head ran out of water. It was just that awful dry choking sound which no one could hear apart from maybe that dog who decided that he didn't want to stick around to hear me. Around 20 miles in now there was a turning onto a winding road through beautiful trees. I think there is skiing here in the winter, it looked fabulous.

I found a place to clean myself up a little and carried on, resigned to the fact that this was going to be another long walk to finish and potentially an even longer walk to New York. I wanted to get better or collapse, neither were happening. I accepted that this was how my summer was going to be, walking in my own filth every day until I collapsed or I entered New York. The problem was I just wasn't collapsing; I was still standing and moving forward. I just wanted this to be over but could not take myself out of it.

I was a walking corpse. I had forgotten why I was here. I was not fulfilling a dream I was just slowly wasting away. I was mentally spent now too. There was nothing left, not even enough to think about how to quit.

As I shuffled along I was caught by Bando. He had been suffering every day with injuries that had on some occasions reduced him to tears. I didn't know what was going through his mind every day for him to come out here and limp along with the rest of us and always with a smile on his face.

He started spraying me with a water spray he kept with him, an ingenious device that I had come to expect from the Japanese team. He just kept spraying me and saying, "Come on, we'll get there. Let's go to New York together". I didn't really want to play along but he was persistent.

I ran just behind him for a little as he spoke. I wasn't really listening and English was not his first language. It was nice just hearing someone chattering away even if I couldn't hear them. He started singing "The long and winding road" by the Beatles, assuming I'd be a fan as I am from England. He then asked if I had any requests of Beatles songs, I suggested "I get by with a little help from my friends". Bando said he did not know this and I tried to mumble the words and tune but didn't do a great job of it. Then he just picked it up, singing the words to a song he did not know, with a tune he did not know, in a language he barely knew.

Listening to him trying to cheer me up by singing bought the first rush of positive emotion I'd had in four days. I was overwhelmed and let out a noise that was a combination of laughing and weeping. I really didn't know what to do or say except that now I knew that New York was more reachable than a few minutes ago. I felt like I was not alone anymore.

From that moment I can't really explain but *I just got better*. Better in every way. My bowels were still a mess but I stopped thinking about it too much, I was sick less and my mind started to clear the evil fog that had obscured my memory of why I was here. I was here to have the adventure of a lifetime, to make new friends and to have some memories that would stick with me forever.

Right now in this moment I was having one of those and it burned brighter than any I had ever experienced before. Just moments after the most traumatic memory had carved itself into my brain I then had this, an experience so intense that it would burn alongside what had happened an hour ago. I will always remember both. I had to dig deep into hell to get this feeling. It was worth it.

The road did indeed wind on and up and down. It was a beautiful road through the forests of New Mexico and I felt like I could look around and enjoy them again. I still had to stop a lot but I knew I was going to get to the end of the day and I was even more optimistic that tomorrow was going to be better.

Bando insisted that I ran downhill wherever I could, his quads were hurting so he couldn't. I did not want to leave him behind and slowed to wait for him sometimes but he would tell me to go on. The Japanese crew were wonderful to me, giving me orange juice, coke, fruit and all sorts to help me.

There was a long slog uphill to the finish at a large lake where we were supposed to be camping but the plan had changed and we were going to be driving to a motel instead. I broke into a bit of a run and finished the day at the lake to see a buffet meal at the end put on by Laure. I sat down and for the first time in four days I felt hungry, and I ate.

It was hard holding myself back from eating, I felt like a starved dog who had just stumbled upon some fresh steak. I was ravenous, my mouth was actually working, producing the saliva to allow me to eat and I shovelled it down like I had not eaten properly for 100 hours. I knew every mouthful would make tomorrow easier, David told me to slow down in case I made myself sick. I wasn't sick anymore though, my body wasn't rejecting it anymore. I'd lost 4 kg in the last 4 days and was doing my best to take it back.

Laure came up to me while I was eating and said, "James I am glad you are feeling better but I need to talk to you about something, don't worry". I did worry though. I feared I'd be pulled out of the race as I was becoming a burden on the organisation or that they felt I was too ill. In fact later Laure said that she was going to take me to hospital that night. Four days with diarrhoea is too long and she feared it might be bacterial rather than a virus. I really didn't like this news, I felt better and worried most about not getting any sleep that night. I didn't want some doctors to tell me that I was not allowed to continue.

We drove to the motel, I showered (lucky for the doctors) and then Laure took me to the hospital in the town of Española. I was tired and confused and had to fill in some forms to be seen by a doctor and the fact that I had no US address made it difficult. The person on reception also couldn't understand my accent and it was Laure who had to translate my English into English for the American on reception. I was tempted to say,

"For fuck sake, I am from England, this is what English sounds like when it's spoken properly". I figured they could make me wait for a long time though and so didn't.

I went to the toilet and looked in the mirror. I did not recognise what was looking back. I wish I had taken a photo of it. Staring back was an insect looking man, gaunt and pale, eyeballs sticking out the side of the head, pupils dilated. That was a very sick man.

I was only waiting for an hour and then I got to lie down in a bed. I had my blood taken, it squirted across the room as the needle went in. I was told I had very high blood pressure. I was also told my resting heart rate was very high, around 85. Last time I had that measured it was about 43. I was also badly dehydrated and given some potassium tablets and a couple of IV drips. While waiting for this fluid to enter by body I tried to chat to Laure. She would have been in this position before with Serge, probably in much worse conditions and hospitals. She told me to just go to sleep.

For the next hour I just lay there, still awake but dozing and resting. It was like a few days ago when Rene and Anne had me sat in the chair with the parasol. I was miles away again, I could check out of the race for a while and forget about everything that was bothering me. I felt at ease with the idea that the race could be out of my hands now. That the doctor could come back and say I had some nasty bacterial disease and that I was going to be kept in for longer. That would be okay, I had given this everything and more. There is no way I could have put in any more effort than I had done in the past four days and if that was not enough then so be it.

The doctor came back and gave me the all clear. There was nothing majorly wrong, just bad dehydration which I could resolve. Now I felt like eating and drinking again, it was definitely going to get better. Starting now.

18A

WHY? VERSION 7

When I broke out of that funk in the Grand Union Canal run four years ago I didn't expect the moments that happened to have quite a long term impact. When I broke down crying after 27 hours of non-stop running I thought it was a moment for that race only. I thought it was the point where I realised that I had completed this race in every way except for the little task of just getting my body over the line.

In actual fact it was much more than that. It was to become a reference point for me to hold onto for any time in the future when I was struggling, with running or with anything. It was a reminder that even in times of crippling lows there was always going to be some joy around the corner. It was a gem, a precious stone owned only by me.

I collected more of these in the next few years. The three hours of effortless running in Canada, the Brazilian guy who finished the Spartathlon, the feeling of falling off the end of the world in Badwater. It's hard to say exactly what it is that makes these moments so special but suffice to say that I made it my intention to collect as many of them as I could, and running seemed as good a way as any to do that.

At times in my life that I feel sad or lost I can look back on these moments when I have overcome hardships and had something magical happen afterwards. It always gives me hope that whatever I am going through there is going to me light at the end of the tunnel. Whenever I feel like I am digging I know that at some point I will find a gem. I was making my life all about finding these gems.

Not only that but merely by thinking about these moments sometimes just makes my skin glow, like I have embedded in my brain a network of connections which I can use as a drug. During a hard run or a bad day at work I can think back to the times when I was digging through the earth and found something magical. I can think back to the time when I dug right into hell in New Mexico and found the world's biggest pink diamond. That diamond belongs to me and me only, I worked hard for it. I deserved it.

I am not really into material possessions or owning things. I am not bothered about owning a house or a car or fancy gadgets. I am not career focused, trying to earn more money to buy more things. I just want to fill my head with these experiences that I have so frequently got by running long distances. I don't own much or have money in the bank but my head is full of gems. I consider myself a very rich man.

And I want to make myself even richer.

That is why I run.

18B

NEW MEXICO CONTINUED

As I got back into the car I thought a bit about the events of the last few days. I was feeling much better but still a bit shocked about what had just happened. This was the first time I'd had to go to hospital like this. The race was taking its toll, it was much harder than I ever imagined it could be. In a rare bubble of having mobile phone reception I used it to send a couple of distress flares. The first one to Gemma. I send a text message saying "Can you come out here?"

I realise in retrospect that it's quite selfish to ask someone to just drop everything and fly out from London to the USA. I had tried to keep her away from this race, thinking it would be boring for her and that I didn't need her here. I realised that was wrong when I left her at the airport.

I slept well in the 4 hours I had left that night and got up the next morning for the next stage.

We lined up back at the beautiful lake that we'd arrived at yesterday and everyone was patting me on the back and telling me how great I was doing. It was really nice to see everyone, it felt like a long time since I had chatted to people. Serge then came up to me and hugged me. I think it meant more coming from Serge because he probably knows better than anyone what I had just been through. He had similar days in South America with diarrhoea, and told me about a run where he'd had really bad toothache for days and had to go and see a vet to pull them out. He had suffered before and was acknowledging that I too had suffered. That meant a lot.

It was now day 22, we still had barely dented the mileage of this race but I was feeling a million times better than this time yesterday and really felt like getting the race started again.

David and Bertrand were my crew today and they looked really pleased that I was doing much better. I was really grateful for their help and that of Rene and Anne over the past few days and I really wanted to make it up to them by running faster so that they could relax more. We joked that Bertrand was "mon Pere" and David "ma Mere" who would look after me at each stop, giving me milkshakes and fruit and ensuring that I didn't drink anything that was too cold as it's bad for the stomach.

Yesterday we were warned about today being "very difficult" and I can understand why, the mileage was just over average at 46.9 but the whole lot was uphill. Our weary legs were going to make slow work of this, mine too. The cut off times only reflected the distance and not the terrain or heat and so it would be possible that I'd be sailing close to the 13:30 hours that were given

It was uphill from the get go, just slightly so you think you could be running on the flat but just enough to trick you into thinking that you are a lot more tired than you are. I did not feel tired at all, I had a reasonable sleep, managed to do a bit of justice to the all you can eat buffet last night and this morning I produced my first solid for 5 days. Today could be glorious.

The first 10 miles or so were along a river, gently

trickling down. The sound was so very soothing though it was interrupted by the morning traffic.

Since I had been coming in each day near the back I stopped wearing my watch. I didn't really want to know how fast I was going any more. The green mile markers on every major US road were too tempting to do all the calculations with. Now I didn't look at the time and was just thankful when I saw one, when I would know a little more had been done. When going through the bad times the minutes feel like hours, but in the good times the hours can feel like minutes. It didn't matter to me what the exact time was now, just so long as it felt fast.

I loved to look at the river. The first time we saw water a couple of days before I just had to stop and look down at it for a few moments. There are a number of things I want to do more when I am done with this. One is to just sit by a river and listen to it. Another is to just lie down under the shade of a tree on a sunny day and not have to worry about going anywhere.

Around half way we were promised a spectacular view and we sure did get one; a massive open panorama of a gorge and mountains. Things like that were what I wanted to see out here. It was awesome.

I invented a new drink too. I had lost craving for really sweet drinks and really loved the taste of sprite mixed with water. It always went down a treat. I gave this cocktail a name. I called this slightly fizzy watery drink "Budweiser".

I got a text from Gemma to say that she managed to get the time off work and had booked a flight and was going to be with me in five days. That was brilliant news. I'd been thinking a lot about the "47 days to New York" but more about the "42 days till I see Gemma". For some reason the latter felt longer. I can't believe I didn't involve her more in this from the start. 5 more days.

I managed to stick quite close to Jenni for the first 30 miles until we turned up onto a mountain road that would contain most of the elevation of the day. She shot off like a natural hill runner whereas I plodded, but ran nonetheless and was really pleased that I could do that.

The scenery changed dramatically. I was surrounded by trees, the sun was behind clouds and the whole place just felt very oxygenated. I have suffered in altitude and hills before (I was climbing up to the highest point of the race (2900 m)) but having breathed nothing but dry air and rock for 3 weeks this felt like a shot of oxygen. It was tricky with the cars on the narrow road and no shoulder but I loved it, it was so green, birds singing, groundhogs scuttling around, and lots of little houses that looked like they had been built by the owners. I said hello to everyone I saw and they said hello back, it was quite an idyllic 16 mile street.

I could still run up hills, I considered walking to save energy but preferred to run. It rained for about half an hour (like the dogs here the clouds bark a lot but rarely bite). It was cool and breezy and I loved it, I was no longer in the dust. I was where life was.

I reflected on a job well done in many respects. I ran most of the day albeit slowly, I did not stop in the van too much (except to eat when ma Mere told me too) and I was full of positive thoughts all day. No injuries either, except that near the end I had an unbelievable itch on my left foot. Is an itchy left foot a good enough reason to pull out from the race?

That was indeed a tough day and it's hard to imagine how I would have got through it two days before, but I did and did it well. I was back on track in the race and now at the highest point. All downhill to New York.

We went back to a gym in Angel Fire, a beautiful skiing town, and I took some time to catch up with my blogging and all the messages I had got through the blog and Facebook. I was astonished, there were so many wonderful messages from people who I knew and others that I didn't. I'd picked up a large following of runners in the UK and abroad who were reading my blog every day and living the journey with me. It was amazing and humbling to feel like so many people were interested in what I was doing and how I was doing it.

I made a priority of blogging every day, which I did apart from when I was ill. Arguably the time could have been better spent sleeping or eating but I wanted a record of everything that happened along the way and how I felt. I wanted a record of what running across America did to me. It would be unlike anything I have written before as I was writing when still in emotional states. It would come out in the writing if I was angry or upset or exhausted or happy. In everything else that I had written about previous races the experience has had time to settle in and can get edited in my mind. This summer I was just gushing out everything I had in my head onto the blog. It was fantastic to see others following it.

I also had my second distress flare answered. When leaving the hospital a few days ago I contacted Bob Brown who ran and won the Trans America 2004 race. I had met him a couple of times earlier in the year and was amazed at what a nice and unassuming guy he was. He didn't look much like an elite runner but his CV was impressive. He won this race 7 years ago, getting faster and faster as the days went on. He had won the GUCR 145 mile race and had countless other achievements including running across Australia. It was great having him to contact and I avoided asking him questions about "how" I should run across the States myself as I knew I'd have to find that out myself. I told him about how ill I had been and how upsetting it had been and asked him one question; "Did it ever just feel too big?"

I had been feeling paralysed by the weight of the task, the sheer size of it hanging right in front of me so I couldn't see past. Having only done one quarter of the distance and without knowing how I would make it to the end of another day let alone 50, I was desperate for some reassurance.

Bob replied that he was in pieces all the time, that it always felt too big but that you just have to concentrate on the now, forget about New York and put one foot in front of the other. It comforted me to know that even a great runner like Bob felt the same way as I did, that I am not weak or pathetic but that this feeling is normal for someone running across the USA. On being able to draw upon Bob's same experience I felt a lot better about myself; that although I felt like I was drowning in hardship, self-doubt and fear, these feelings were normal. This is what running across America does to a person.

From then on I had a new resolve to maintain the blog, to record everything I could exactly how it happened. All the fear, the panic, the joy, the love, the hate. I wanted everyone to know what happens to a person when they do such a thing.

The next few days out of New Mexico were really nice, the place is beautiful and it's a shame I missed half of it. There was a short day out of Angel Fire downhill through the ski slopes and through some other small towns. Then there were two long days of over 50 miles each which were going to take their toll physically but I was now getting into the mental state of just doing what was there each day, treat it like a job. I couldn't control how many miles I had to run and all I could do was run them.

I threw away a lot of clothes from the first few weeks and felt much fresher. I wore a top that a friend had given to me with Badgers on in and ended up having a strange conversation with David about what a badger was. Do they not get them in France? How do you describe a badger to someone who does not know what it is? It's like a big black and white rabbit?

Since being ill I stopped wearing a watch. I had my phone with me so could look at the time but was not checking it mile by mile, that was driving me crazy. Sometimes I'd look at my phone and see that three hours had passed and be quite pleased that it seemed to go by in a flash. There was a point where I thought I'd run 16 miles then immediately got to a highway which was the 19 mile marker. I was thrilled, I was running faster and wasn't even noticing. It felt like someone had just given me three miles. Then I got some mobile phone signal again and could call Gemma. I wandered down the highway chatting to Gemma for the first time in a week. It was great to hear from her and in only a few days I was going to see her again. The whole thing felt much easier.

It had been so hard over the past few days not to be able to tell Gemma whether I had finished a stage or not. Just a simple text each day to say I had finished and was feeling OK was important to her. I don't know what I would have said to her during the times I was ill, it could have been a good thing that we were out of contact with each other.

We were running through a few towns again which were great places to get ice cream. I stopped everywhere I could to get one, it was still very hot at about 35°C. I was running close to Serge, Alex and Markus again which meant I was back to where I normally was. It was great being out running well again. I was thrilled when my quads and calves started to hurt from the ups and downs of the road. I even put in my blog that my legs were hurting and I was liking it. Proper running pains, I missed you.

We had a few days of having to get up earlier because we were staying in motels 30 miles from the start/finish area. This was frustrating as it meant an hour less to sleep/eat each day and with the mileage ramping up that gave us even less time. It was now not unusual for the distance to be over 50 miles for two consecutive days. Say that's 12 hours of running, an hour each side for driving to and from the start/finish does not give long to rest.

But I was still in great spirits and soon we were heading into a new state, Oklahoma. This was going to be the longest state, about 9 days running across a straight 500 mile road along the pan handle. I was looking forward to leaving New Mexico behind, it was a lovely state and I'd dearly love to go back there but I felt like I could draw a line under all that suffering by leaving the it.

19

OKLAHOMA – IT'S THE WIND THAT'LL KILL YER

Oddly just as I arrived at the border I got a rumbling in my guts once more. I was still not fully recovered, I announced on my blog when I passed my first solid for a week and this was a cause for huge celebration back home. That made me laugh, people feeling joy at the products of my bowels. I felt like this rumbling was just my body wanted to do something for old time's sake and sure enough I found a bush by the side of the road just before leaving New Mexico. I hoped that was the last time I'd need to use a bush in such a way and I was almost right. There was not another bush for 500 miles.

As soon as I entered Oklahoma I was greeted by Russell and Claire Secker. I didn't know either of them but Russell last year ran the Trans-Europe and knew Rainer and Jenni and some of the Japanese crew. I had a vague awareness from Russell posting on my blog that they were coming out and were organising some things for Gemma when she got here but didn't recall the detail. I felt comfortable immediately in their presence and knew it was going to be great having them around.

Russell said he originally had his name down to do this race. I asked him why he didn't and he said it was because it was going to be too hot. Doh.

Laure had said that of all the states we run through we'd

remember Oklahoma the most. It sure was going to be a tough one, it was suffering its worst heat wave in living memory and was forecast to be over 100 F (40°C) for the duration of our run. These were not quite the temperatures we got in California early on but their effects would be more devastating. In California we were fresh and rested and quick. Now having been depleted by nearly 4 weeks of hard running we had the sun on our backs for 12 hours a day. Oklahoma was going to be brutal.

Oklahoma was mentally tortuous. The roads were very straight; you could probably see the end of the stage just by looking up the road. There were no trees or wildlife, just fields of corn and scarred grasslands. In the distance I could see a corn silo and I made that my next reference point, my next thing to run towards to break up the monotony. After an hour of running the silo was still no closer, like it was moving away at the same speed.

The landscape was very different which I thought was very interesting at first. The crops here are engineered with precision. This is the place that feeds America and who can deny it does a world class job in doing so? The rolling fields of corn were almost intimidating to look at, everything here is done on a much bigger scale than I have ever seen before.

The novelty soon wore off though as I craved the simple things like trees. The mile markers on the roads were no longer here, passing these always felt like punctuating progress but now they were gone. Perhaps they look too much like trees? After miles and miles I just wanted to see a tree, but there were none, it was incredible. There was more life in the desert.

I could cope with the boredom though as this was going to be my last day alone, tomorrow Gemma was going to arrive. She was flying into Tulsa which is at the far end of Oklahoma and then she'd drive 400 miles out to meet me. That was going to be a great moment.

Today was a sad day though as David, Bertrand and Anne

were leaving us to head back to France. They were coming back for the final days of the race which was great to hear but they were going to be a huge loss for me. They had all been such amazing support particularly during my bad times. I was going to miss them.

Day 28 was the longest day so far, 56.6 miles and we were going to lose an hour with the clocks going forward. In a way the clocks moving forward was a good thing, it meant I was moving closer to the end and closer to home. Practically it meant having less time to recover. However I felt like the miles and the hours were all just circumstantial today. Today was all about seeing Gemma for the first time since I watched the back of her head disappear down the escalator at Heathrow Airport. The first time since I realised that I screwed this up before I even started.

Russ and Claire were out again today and it was fantastic running with them. I was treated to a brief history of Oklahoma from Russell who told me about how the displaced natives were moved to this wasteland from the more fertile areas such as New Mexico, Florida and Texas, forced to walk long distances with many not making it alive. Brings my own efforts into perspective when you hear stories like this, proper hardship and suffering. In comparison I am crossing the USA like J-lo would.

I was not entirely sure what time Gemma was going to get here, I figured it was going to be towards the end of the stage. I was looking out for her all the time, every car that approached I thought might be her, every person I saw (or thought I saw) at the side of the road could be her. Usually it was just my mind playing tricks and it was a road sign.

Russ and Claire took Jenni to the finish in the car as she was suffering from the heat and I had no company for a while. The sun was taking its toll as I staggered on in the heat always looking out for Gemma. I got a bit distracted by it all and didn't drink or eat properly, I just wanted to see her. Then I saw a white car move slowly into view, it wasn't just passing. It stopped about 100 meters away and I saw a figure emerge. It started walking towards me. It must be her. I sped up as did she and a few moments later I saw that it was her. Within no time we collided and hugged. I'd been waiting for that for ever it felt, I needed that more than anything. We'd later describe it and always will as a "suncream in our eyes" moment.

I thought about how this story has everything so far. I could make it into a film later. Love and hate, conflict, suffering, succeeding against all odds, action, comedy and diarrhoea. I'm sure the wizards and aliens were going to come along later to make it into a proper Hollywood blockbuster. I said Colin Farrell should play the part of me though I would have to test his beard growing capabilities beforehand. Alex would have to be played by Brian Blessed.

Despite all the distractions today the day did drag a little, at the 23 mile point I screamed, "Is that all"? 56 miles today was a long drag in the heat we just were not expecting. Gemma came out to run with me for the last few miles into Guymon which was a fairly big town with lots of stuff and a pool in the motel at the end which I was looking forward to all day. In the end it was a bit grotty but it was nice to be able to cool my legs again.

Every day in Oklahoma was really tough. There were a lot of variables at play which could make the difference between a tough day and a hellish day. Firstly there was the temperature in the morning, sometimes it felt like an oven before we even started and we could not get an advantage of a couple of hours of running in cool conditions. Then there was the roads, the big long wide roads were great because they had wide shoulders and the trucks were great in giving plenty of space. You could just put your head down and run. Sometimes if we were on a narrow road with no shoulder you always had to be on your guard, ready to jump out of the way at any point, staring up into the sun. It was mentally exhausting.

Then there was the wind, sometimes there was none but other times there was a vicious hot wind that dried eyes and mouths. Then there were the clouds, never present in the first three quarters of the day but then sometimes you'd just see them in the distance and they'd come floating over you providing a temporary parasol against the sun. It was wonderful when it happened and I felt like I was chasing clouds across the road but they were always rare.

The monotony was a factor too. Long straight roads of wilderness were so demotivating. I could see for miles and miles, a truck might overtake and then I could still see it for miles into the distance and I regretted that I could not cover this distance that fast. This was all farmland, some of it scorched by the heat but there was no doubt about it this was the place that feeds the USA. Everything looked so precise and straight, all of the farms were divided into mile square chunks of land separated by little roads. The farm machinery here looked like it was inspired by the transformers movies, I'd never seen vehicles that looked so big and powerful and robotic. I marvelled at the sheer scale of farming here though running through it mile by mile was quite boring.

There were very few trees. There were very few bushes. I had to take my toilet stops whenever there was a good hiding opportunity. I thought it would be a good idea to put signs on the bushes such as "next bush not for 15 miles". Then I'd know to take advantage of that pit stop.

Gemma was fantastic at supporting and was stopping every 3 miles to fill my hat with ice, spray me with water and give me whatever I wanted to drink. My choice of drinks had changed over the past 4 weeks. At first I was drinking heavily caffeinated energy drinks, now I was drinking lots more regular sodas, fruit juices and my home made Budweisers.

I was running close to Alex, Serge and Jenni again and it was great being around them. Having spent most of the last week on my own I had three other runners and their support teams around me which was great for taking my mind off the pain and monotony. The heat was taking its toll on everyone though. I think Alex suffered more than I did and his running history was in the arctic rather than the deserts. Jenni too was suffering and several days she had to stop and get driven to the end. She was already officially out of the race but was determined to carry on and run as much of it as possible. There was one time where I saw her legs were massively swollen, a result of water retention which is likely to be the effect of a kidney problem. I don't think she was taking electrolytes properly and Russell and Claire were helping her out in this.

Electrolytes were the one thing I think I managed quite successfully in this race. There were obviously times when I was dehydrated, particularly when I was very ill but on the whole I was dealing with them well. I used a solution called Elete Water, which is basically a small bottle of salty liquid which can be put into anything. I informed Gemma and all my previous crew members to squirt some of this into everything I drank. It was simple and it worked a treat.

The ends of the days could be hard though. After I ran through those yellow flags, high fived everyone around, kissed Gemma and then sat down for a beer the intensity of the heat seemed to rise. I would always try to sit in the shade and then getting up and moving into the sun to get to our motel or the car felt like walking through an oven. It was amazing to think that I had just run 50 miles in this, but now I could barely stand in it. On the second night that Gemma was here we booked a motel about a 30 min drive away from the finish area where everyone else was camping, in a small town called Beaver. This place was grim.

We got to the motel which was not the nicest place but better than Needles and then headed out for some food. There appeared to be a steak bar, a Mexican place and a diner – all closed. The only place to eat was a Pizza Hut and a burger van. Normally Pizza Hut would be fine for me but Gemma is a coeliac and there is absolutely nothing in Pizza Hut she could eat so we sat outside near a burger van and had a burger and chips there. I got really grumpy about the coeliac thing and just wanted to get out of the heat. I would rather have stayed where the rest of the runners were staying in sleeping bags in a library so that we didn't have to spend all this time driving and trying to find food. The heat can really turn your head here.

Day 30 was another 52 miles, the 6th consecutive day of more than 45 miles. The following day was a "rest" of only 32 miles which we were all looking forward to. This was such a high mileage week and everyone was starting to show signs of suffering.

Every morning before the start the runners were presented with the rankings for the previous day and the race so far. By this stage they never really changed. Rainer was well in the lead, Patrick second, then Italo, then Serge, Alex, Me, Koshita and Bando. I never really looked at the sheet but this morning I could not help noticing that I had just passed 300 hours of running. 300+ hours in only 4 weeks? That is incredible, I had literally spent half my time running while I was here. A few years ago that was a year's worth of running for me and now I was doing it in a month.

Everyone seemed quite refreshed at the start of the "short" day, as if the thought of only running 32 miles had produced some sort of mental recovery. We all set off quite fast and all seemed to be doing pretty well until we entered the town of Buffalo. I was stopped by a photographer and had my picture taken for the local newspaper which was pretty nice and was the first time anything like that happened. When we were running through the town however it was like someone just cranked the heat right up again. The last 10 miles of that day were horrendous but at least we got to relax at a picnic table at the end.

Laure said to us before we entered this state that we would never forget Oklahoma, that it would be the hardest state we would run through. She was right. It wasn't just the heat and the distance, it was having no time to do anything else. This place was deserted, people were staying in their houses and the few that we saw outside asked what the hell we were doing. This was the worst heatwave in living memory for the state and for much of the USA, it was making international news. We were told by anyone who saw us not to worry as this heat was slowly moving east. WE WERE SLOWLY MOVING EAST. This oven was travelling with us at about 50 miles per day. The famous Sri Chimoy 3100 mile race around a block in New York was cancelled for one day because of the intense heat. Every church we'd pass had a sign saying "pray for rain" and it was even the official advice from the governor of Oklahoma to pray for rain. I am not a religious man but even if I was I'd expect the governor to come up with something a bit better than that.

A big regret of mine was that I never really had much time to spend with Gemma. Often at the side of the road there was a lovely picnic table or a tree and I just imagined being able to lie down under it and let the world go by for a few hours, not really worrying about the time. I craved being back in London in Hyde Park and just relaxing under a tree. I vowed that was going to be one of the first things I did when I got back.

The thought of another 6 weeks of this brutal exercise played on my mind a lot but the thought of Gemma leaving in a few days bothered me even more. All I could do was run and then when I stopped she would run around getting me food, clean clothes and sort out any admin. I did not have much time to just be with her which upset me greatly but I was too exhausted to do anything about it. We actually did once do something which was illegal for an unmarried couple to do in Oklahoma. If it's any consolation to the authorities there it didn't last long.

The last few days in Oklahoma were amongst the most memorable of the whole race. It finally got pretty, beautiful trees and hills and some nice towns. Gemma was getting on very well with the rest of the race group, particularly the Italians who she got to hang about with as I was running with Alex a lot. I loved that she seemed to be enjoying herself despite her complete devotion to me. I didn't really think about it at the time but I was being quite selfish in having her there practically as a slave, barking demands and being grumpy. I was treating her like a slave and at the same time drawing comfort at her presence and counting down the days till she was leaving. I hated that she was only going to be here for another two days, another 48 hours and all of those I was going to spend running, sleeping or eating.

I just wanted more time, I wanted there to be more hours in the day, 24 just wasn't enough to do what I wanted to do. Before I came out here I felt like I must have had all the time in the world and I just squandered it. Gemma became tearful as I said that I just wanted more hours in the day, I just wanted more time. Such a valuable thing when you have none, so easy to take for granted when you have it all.

The penultimate night of Gemma's stay was in the town of Pawhuska, nothing there apart from a couple of motels and diners. We stayed in the Economy Inn, I am not sure what economy it was based on but this place was awful. The sheets were dirty, the shower didn't work, the air con pumped out fish stinking air, the carpets were dirty, the toilets looked like the portaloos you'd expect to see at mile 18 in the London

Marathon. This is the kind of place I'd get dumped for taking a girl to.

But the town was actually lovely and in the diner we went to the locals were loving hearing about what we were doing as well as our accents. Gemma being a Kiwi was obviously pegged as an Australian and I was just a regular Brit. I had an all-day breakfast of 4 eggs, sausages, bacon, pancakes and potatoes. This is the kind of thing I'd love to be able to eat every morning, I didn't realise how hard it would be to have breakfast while out here but this was amazing. Then to cap it all the guys we were talking to paid for our meal. They had left already so we had no idea until we came to settle the bill and the waitress said it had already been paid for. Acts of kindness like that will just live with me forever. If the guy by the name of "RD" ever reads this book and remembers that, I'd like to thank you for that wonderful gesture.

Gemma's last day of crewing was day 36. In terms of days we were half way but it wouldn't be until halfway through day 37 that we'd have half the distance done. The start of today felt like half way though. It's not the miles that make this hard, it's the getting up in the morning, the trying to force carbs into a dry throat before the run starts, it's spending all day thinking about how much further it is to go and how many days it is till New York. It's the constant paranoia about twisting an ankle, fracturing a shin or eating something harmful. It's the nightmares of the road when lying in bed and then dreaming about the bed when on the road. It's missing my normal life in London, leisurely drinking a coffee with friends, having a few pints in the pub, missing other events that I'd love to do like beer festivals, comedy festivals, races, pub quizzes, birthdays and weddings. I only had to suffer this for another 35 days max. In my mind I was half way.

Day 36 was gorgeous, it seemed fitting that her last day

would be this nice. Still searing temperatures and now some humidity starting to rear its ugly head. 22 miles we turned into a lovely quiet road. It was a dream to look at. Surrounded on either side by trees, no traffic and a beautiful winding road with ups and downs that was a joy for anyone to travel down whatever their mode of transport. Running, Bike, Motorbike, Car, anyone could have enjoyed this stunning section of tarmac. But it was a trap.

The moment we descended into the valley that the road cut through it became apparent that we were in an oven. There was no wind, the humidity was high and the Sun was as mean as ever. I was choking on the heat, struggling at times to even walk without wobbling. Any slight distortion in the road would push me around like some annoying bully. I had no power to overcome little inconsistencies in the road and I was reduced to hobbling forward in a Brownian motion (different from my Brownian motion in New Mexico).

Alex and Jenni were close to me at this point and we'd take turns to collapse into our respective support cars. I would walk along and pass Jenni slumped on the back of the organisers support car then Alex sat down by his Jeep. Then when I saw Gemma I would lie down in the shade on some grass, drink lots, ice lots and watch Jenni and Alex stagger by again. No one seemed to manage more than 2 miles without having to keel over. I used my inhaler lots during this time.

Around 10 miles into this I was walking with Alex and noted the number of houses that were around. I said, "You know we have passed two towns and a load of houses today and not seen a single person outside. Why do you think that is?"

The valley only lasted those 10 miles and then we had a 5 mile section of interstate where we'd climb out of that low point. As soon as we hit it I felt the pressure drop massively. It got cooler, darker and to my right there were grey clouds making noise. The anticipation was incredible – something was going to happen here.

I put a Facebook update to say that this would be a contender for the hardest day so far but there were rain clouds close by. I yelled at them to come.

I felt cooler possibly with the goose bumps of expectation of a rain shower and then I heard the distinct noise of water hitting the ground, and then again, and then a drop hit me in the face. It was going to happen, for the first time in a month we were going to get proper rain. And then the heavens opened, it properly pissed it down. For the first time in weeks I wasn't worrying about how much cold water or ice I had on me, I was getting rained on, getting soaked and it was wonderful. I pranced around like I was in a Westlife video.

I yelled at the Italians as I ran past at high speed "I AM IN LONDON NOW". It felt like the best 15 minutes of the race so far. It stopped abruptly and then the sun came back out to continue its evil work. I just looked at the ground and commanded the soil to absorb it all quickly before the sun takes it back. Simone said, "Yes the rain was good but now you must pay". The water was about to rise up and choke us. Yet it didn't. The rest of the day seemed to pass without any more hardship. A few more miles of lovely quiet roads and then onto the finish.

Today was a good day, tomorrow was short but there was the sickly feeling of the worst goodbye in the morning.

We had to drive again to the motel and then drive back in the morning, getting up at 3:45 to do so. This was not a normal Saturday morning where I might stir at about 6 am, have a cuddle with Gemma while we both dozed off with not much to do today. We had to leap out of bed at 3:45 and start packing the car to get to the start. I hated it.

Gemma was heading straight from the start to Tulsa to get her plane, meeting up with Russell and Claire as she did. I didn't want the day to start, I at least just wanted another hour. This was the hardest thing yet. I paid no attention to the race briefing as I contemplated a day without her and then another month without her while I was suffering in this way. The stage started, the runners shuffled along and I stood still embracing Gemma for what felt like the last time. Tears in my eyes and in hers she told me to get moving. I walked forward, this time not looking back in case I felt some sickly feeling like I did last time I said goodbye at the airport. I couldn't tell you whether it was hot that morning, whether my legs hurt or whether I was hungry, I really don't remember.

When Gemma was here this race became everything I dreamt about, even though she was not in the original dream. Even with the brutally hard job of covering 50 miles a day on foot in intense heat I imagined a "summer camp" atmosphere with the runners joking about, ice cream being delivered roadside, silly photos and funny street names. At the end of each day having a sit down and chatting about the day, going out for food and beer and all getting along. It was not quite like that but I felt that while Gemma was here it got as close as it could, similar to the first week in California. Now I felt alone again.

I walked perhaps the first mile, as many do, but for me it was just out of reflection. I don't think my legs wanted to run yet. I did eventually break into a jog only to find than everything seemed to hurt. I stuttered in and out of walking worried again about pains in shins and thighs and hips until the penny finally dropped, "Yes this is how it has felt for every one of the last 36 days, it goes away, just fucking get on with it".

16 miles in we passed the statue of Andy Payne, the winner of the original 1928 footrace across the USA.

If you have not read the book I highly recommend "The Bunion Derby", a brilliant account of all the runners in 1928. Route 66 had "just" been built, in fact half of it had and others were work in progress. However a showman called C.C. Pyle (people thought the C.C. stood for "Cash and Carry") decided to organise "the greatest show on earth" and stage a footrace across the States.

199 men entered with the hope of winning the $25,000 prize. Pyle did this to make money out of the towns they would pass through rather than any interest in running. The pace some of these guys ran at was astonishing, imagine the shoes they were wearing, complete lack of endurance nutrition and having to sleep in real bad conditions. Most of the runners were poor and without support, they were not provided with enough food or any medication, they could barely sleep. The black runners were threatened in some of the mid states and had to sleep separately from the white runners.

In comparison to those guys I had it easy. Andy Payne ran to earn money to pay off the mortgage on his father's farm but also to earn the respect of a lady back at home who he hoped to marry. The crazy things men will do for a women hey?

But I can hardly complain about my circumstances here. In comparison to them I was running across America like J-Lo would. Berangere and Emily (new additions to the crew) were supplying me today and were under strict instructions from Gemma to make sure I ate some fruit each day and didn't completely live off sugar and burgers. I thought it was funny how she still seemed to be here, having her way with my nutrition again.

The next day we were nearly out of Oklahoma, it was such an epic state. The heat was not so intense anymore but the difficulty was being replaced by humidity. It was only maxing out at about 35°C each day now and I think the heatwave was coming to an end. I was glad of this and glad to be leaving Oklahoma and enjoying some greenery.

My last night in Oklahoma I was met by Russell and Claire

again who just could not get enough of this race. Russell had kindly bought me a couple of pairs of trainers which I was very grateful for as my feet were nearly coming out of the bottom of the others. One mistake I made in the race was to not rotate the shoes I was wearing, I just wore each pair till they melted. It was really great seeing them again and it helped with missing Gemma for a couple of days. I was delighted to hear that they would be making regular trips to the UK so I knew I was going to be seeing them again.

Shortly before I left Oklahoma someone yelled out of their car at me, "RUN FAT BOY RUN". I thought that was a little harsh as I had lost 10 kg in only 5 weeks and they clearly were not shy of the donuts either. Then in another surreal moment I saw a chicken crossing a road. Why did it do that? I ran ahead to tell Alex but don't think he really understood why I was excited.

The next state was Missouri. Laure pronounced it "misery" which I thought was quite funny because that's the same way I pronounce "New Mexico".

20

MISSOURI – IT'S THE HUMIDITY THAT'LL KILL YER

I entered Missouri feeling pretty good. I was sleeping better. I let go of worrying about the things that I could not control, like the distance or the heat or the state of the motel or food at the end. I knew these were all minor details that would not stop me from completing this race.

I also figured that if I could survive 38 days of this intense heat and niggling injuries then I could survive another 32. I also got my medical bill sorted with the hospital but not without some difficult phone calls again. They still could not understand my English.

I felt better money wise too, this was an expensive trip but looking at my account for the first time in a 6 weeks I felt like I had some breathing space at the end so that I would not need be homeless when I returned to the UK. I got into a manageable routine. All I have to do is run and eat and if I get a chance to write a blog at the end of the day and talk to Gemma then that is a bonus.

And then a little thing that I never thought I'd get so excited about, a friendly dog. I feared dogs ever since the New Mexico incident. They seemed to only exist in America to intimidate, that was my experience so far anyway. However I saw some fuss up ahead and there was a dog who was loving the attention of the crews. I approached hesitantly (perhaps there is something about me that dogs hate) and joined in, stroking this lovely friendly dog. That was wonderful and put me in a great mood to carry on running.

Dare I say this was getting "normal"?

I can't remember the exact moment we crossed into Missouri, we did so via Kansas for about 8 miles and on that day I managed to eat a McDonald's in three different states. I can't say that I experienced Kansas enough to be able to say that there is "no place like it". Missouri had a much different character to Oklahoma though, it was a shame that our first major sight there was really quite horrible.

We were supposed to stay in Joplin in the original race, it is a fairly big city close to the border. I didn't really pay much attention to the changes to the route as the race was getting closer to the start but I do recall a news story a month before I came out to the USA that tornadoes had swept through the middle of the country and caused havoc.

Listening to stories of hurricanes, floods, earthquakes and fires from afar can be quite sterile. I listen to the news, feel sad when the images are screened but in all honesty I don't get too emotionally involved, it's always quite a sterile experience.

And so the same was true when I heard about the stories of the tornadoes in the USA, it was sad and I was glad I was not there. It didn't occur to me that in a couple of months I'd be running though the site of the wreckage.

We ran down a busy road and I saw some signs of destruction, a gas station with its large sign fallen down on the forecourt. Various walls ripped down and some houses missing roofs. It all looked like a bit of an inconvenience to the residents. It looked like there was a lot of damage and perhaps the insurance would take care of it all and everyone could quickly get back to their lives. I continued to run down to the end of the street and took a right turn. What I then saw was sickening.

The scene I saw I had only ever seen in images on news programmes of complete and utter destruction. Houses were absolutely flattened, schools, shops, churches and unrecognisable structures were just piles of rubble. I had never seen anything like this. I had never felt so sick.

I slowed to a walk because it didn't feel right running through all this and I didn't really want to look but could not help it. There were houses flattened with toasters, ironing boards, teddy bears and clothes just neatly piled up next to them. Personal possessions of people who were probably dead. The whole town was awash with mobile homes and temporary camp sites, I think mainly to house those who were lucky enough to not be crushed by their own home.

We were later to pass a lake where a boy was found dead after being picked up in his garden by a tornado and thrown into it. The destruction was devastating and this town may never recover from that.

I was walking with Alex as we left Joplin to see that the path of the tornado was long. Streets on the outskirts of the town had a much different pattern of destruction, completely flattened houses lay next to others that had not even been touched. I can't imagine what a person who lives in one of the houses that was unscathed thinks about knowing his next door neighbour or the guy who lived across the road has nothing now, assuming they are alive.

Alex said to me, pointing at the eerie contrast we were seeing, "Look at how your life can change". Over 200 people's lives ended the day that tornado hit.

All of a sudden all thoughts of leg pain and hunger faded like a distant memory.

I thought I was going to like Missouri though, it was so green though still hellishly warm. The humidity was something unlike I had ever experienced though. We'd sometimes all be running along without a care in the world and then all of a sudden feeling that someone was on our backs trying to force a rag with chloroform down our throats.

There were a lot more busy roads and they were winding too, not like the 500 miles straight though Oklahoma. Laure had started to give runners warnings about not following the correct procedure when on the road, including me. I was annoyed at first with this decision but in retrospect I was Facebooking while on a busy road. Fair cop.

My injuries were working on rotation. Each day I would start with a worry about whatever it was that was hurting me the previous night. So if it was my ankle then I'd gingerly take the first steps of the morning and obsess about every nerve ending. It always went one of two ways; it either hurt about as much as it did yesterday or it did not hurt at all. Either was fine though the latter was more concerning as that always led to something else hurting more. I am not sure whether injuries came and went as much as I thought they did or whether it was my head rotating them around. I think Rainer was right though; "Injuries that are caused by running can be fixed by running". Even if they are all in the head.

We usually had an hour of darkness in the morning now and got to see some interesting wildlife as we started each day. I had an altercation with a skunk one morning, as I approached on the road it looked at me, arched its back and hissed. I am not sure whether it realised that I could definitely out stink it though.

There were a lot more interesting building now too. At 7 am one morning I passed a building for Jehovah's Witnesses. I was tempted to bang on their door and ask them if they wanted to go for a run.

The weather was still making it very difficult though. We'd chat each day at the start about the weather, I was turning them all into Brits. We'd say things like, "Oohhhh, it's not as warm as it was this time yesterday", tempting fate. It was pointless because the weather can really turn on a sixpence. At 8 am I might feel like I was running through a breezy cool London street, at 9 am I might be suffocating again.

Since Gemma left I was sharing a room with Italo each night again. It was nice having company each day and as he was so much faster than me he normally had all the checking in done by the time I finished and so all I had to do was to finish and the room was ready. I still never really looked at the road book telling me how much there was to do next day except that Italo would normally tell me. Except that he'd get 70 and 80 the wrong way round. So when he said that tomorrow was 82 km I braced myself for another 51 miles of humidity. It was funny when I got to the start to find that it was only 72 km. That was a relief. It was not so funny the time he said, "Tomorrow is 74 km". Not funny at all.

Days 43-45 though added up to less than 100 miles which felt like a holiday. 41 miles then 29 then 30. It was great to have a few days where we'd all have a bit more time to not be running. I was resigned to the heat too now. We all hoped that it would ease off and cool down but now after 45 days of it and we are all still standing I figured that we could do 25 more days of it.

My body was getting weaker every day, but I felt my mind was getting stronger. I was now shuffling at a pace that was not much more than 5 miles an hour and with frequent stops that was more like 4 miles an hour. I was running like the Penguin that Alex expected me to in the first weeks, my legs could not stretch out to give a proper stride.

I was constantly amazed by the incredible work by the organisers in this race. Now that Gemma was gone I had no one specifically looking after me but the crew were fantastic. It seemed that a priority at the end of each day for Laure and the crew was to drive me to the nearest McDonald's and get me a Big Mac and smoothie. In total I stopped in 43 McDonald's in the race. It was not really a deliberate choice to stop in so many McDonald's but I figured it was a great way of getting 1000 calories in the space of a few minutes. I was subscribing to Marshall Ulrich's "Incinerator Theory" of nutrition in that by now fuel was fuel and my body would burn anything.

During the short days I thought a lot about considering two 30 mile days "easy". Ten years ago when training for my first marathon I was genuinely scared that running 26 miles in one go might kill me. I thought about that one race for months in advanced wondering how on earth I could go that distance. I laughed at the stress nose bleed I remember getting at the start and how scared I was.

I think it was not until my 6th marathon in Paris that I actually came to terms with the distance of a marathon. It was only at that stage that I was confident of being able to complete it. Having done 5 before I knew that I was capable of the distance and that something major would have to happen for me not to finish. Paris was not a great race for me, I was aiming for a time of 3:30 and got 3:39 and I was quite disappointed with that. However that race was possibly a watershed for me for another reason, that's when I started writing about my running.

Back in 2005 there was no Facebook or blogs (can you imagine that?) and so I just wrote my race experiences in a word document and sent it to about 4 people who might be interested in reading it. I actually made a spreadsheet for Paris detailing how every mile related to a song of how I was feeling at the time. I really enjoyed putting that together.

From then on the running and the writing became one and the same. My first ultramarathon was written up and put in our club magazine and soon after I started a running blog and uploaded reports of all the races I did. It felt a bit geeky at the time and only about 6 people were ever going to read them. I wanted a permanent record of all the running I had done, I wanted to go back in time and read what I had written about a race that scared me long ago and be able to compare that to now. I was writing it mostly for myself.

Over the years as ultra-running grew in the UK the blog got a small following. Not quite like Justin Bieber on Twitter but I'd often turn up to races and have people come up to me and say, "James I loved your blog on the Grand Union Canal Run" or "Well done in the Spartathlon – it sounded brutal". I'd spend a lot of time in races chatting to others about the races that I had done and I loved being able to share the experiences with others. I think the best thing I ever heard was when I was crewing at the Grand Union Canal Race and a guy in the race who looked like he was suffering pointed at me and said, "Your blog made me do this!"

I felt bad for him for about 5 seconds and then felt incredibly smug.

I was committed in this race to write as much as I could about each day for the same reasons I have blogged for the past 6 years; to preserve the memory for myself but also a large amount of attention seeking. I loved that others were reading it and wanted to give the audience more.

The comments I got on the blog were incredible, I was as open and honest as I could be about how each day went. There were times when I felt useless and weak, others when I felt on top of the world. I wanted to put all that out there for people to see. I consider myself a "normal" person; athletically, emotionally, socially. I wanted to document what this does to a person. I wanted everyone to see what running across America does to a regular guy.

I often thought that blogging each day was a risk, what if it all went wrong and I had to stop? Would everyone following me start laughing?

In deepest Missouri we stayed in some historic German settlements, one being Hermann. This place was great, they had an Irish bar who were told in advanced about our iron deficiency and that we'd be drinking lots of Guinness. We spent the evening in that bar, drinking more than I should have done and staying later than I should listening to the locals talk about the weather. Apparently it has not been this hot for so long in their lives here, the same stories that were coming out of Oklahoma.

After the three easy days we had a nice 55 miler for day 46. This was a lot to get our heads around, perhaps made a bit easier by my first hangover of the race. The temperature cooled down to a Baltic 35°C, we nearly had to get the jumpers out. It was a hard day though and it took me 13.5 hours to get to Bowling Green. I was so exhausted at the end I didn't get out of bed to have food.

The lack of food the previous day affected me a lot for day 47, from Bowling Green to Hannibal. It was only 45 miles today (yes even my first ultra-distance I now regard as an "easy" day). It got warm again and I felt weak from not eating enough and this made me grumpy and focus more on the injuries. Russ's words of wisdom resonated again, "If you are grumpy that means you are hungry, so just eat". That was fine except that there wasn't much to eat other than the energy bars and fruit which I didn't like the appeal of. I wanted a McDonald's or an ice cream. We went through the town of New London (not as good as the old London) and I could not find anywhere to buy an ice-cream. This place had five churches and no shop.

I got through the day mostly on sugar which was not ideal. The twisty roads were hurting my body, the steep camber of some of the roads was making my left side ache much more than the right. Today felt like such a mentally draining day even though it all looked so beautiful. The weather was kinder, there were people outside their houses mowing the lawn or having yard sales. It all just looked so normal and it reminded me of home. I missed home a lot, I wished I was there.

We stayed in an old armoury in Hannibal which provided lots of food which I took advantage of. This is the birth place of Mark Twain and was our last stop in Missouri. It tried its best to kill us but we survived again.

A few years ago I used to think that fear was a negative emotion to be banished at all costs. I thought the only way to approach challenges like this was without any fear whatsoever. I thought Yoda had it right with "fear is the path to the dark side". Those who are afraid are likely to suffer more.

But my opinion changed recently, I have been afraid so many times in the past but overcoming those fears has led to the most emotionally significant experiences of my life. Being afraid of my first marathon, the first GUCR and coming out here to run 45 miles a day for 70 days. There were times when it felt overwhelming and crippling such as in New Mexico but I knew that the fear was just a prelude to something special on the other side. Fear was a sign that I was going to do something that was going to be special.

Mark Twain had the same idea. "Courage is resistance to fear, mastery of fear, NOT absence of fear".

One mile into day 48 we crossed the mighty Mississippi. It was the biggest river I had ever seen and took a good ten minutes to cross it over a huge bridge. It was a shame to cross it in the dark and not be able to see much of it but this was a crossing that punctuated the trans-USA race. Every trans-USA crossing will cross this river somewhere, for us it was about two thirds of the way into the run. Only 22 days left and I was in Illinois. I wondered what would kill me here.

21

ILLINOIS/INDIANA – IT'S THE CARS THAT'LL KILL YER

It started to rain as soon as we arrived in Illinois and soon it really tipped it down. I welcomed the rain though all the others were worried about blisters. I still did not suffer a blister since that one little one on day two, it was incredible. There was a minor worry of getting too cold which the crew were concerned about too but I just explained that my skin is all the waterproofing I need. I was only paranoid that the rain would ruin my $10 bill that would make a McDonald's stop difficult.

The roads were yet more dangerous, a couple of times cars would not see us and not give us any space as they sped past. Illinois – it's the airhead drivers that'll kill yer.

Now that it was cooler there was a debate about a possible rule change. Until now we had to carry water with us at all times but now it was not necessary and some of the runners said they would prefer not to carry the weight. I didn't really care either way and I had to carry the water anyway as I had no support crew. Others were complaining about the chaffing of the packs and would rather not carry them.

This was the start of an uncomfortable period where some of the runners were accusing each other of not following the rules. Warnings had been given out for not obeying the rules such as myself for not paying attention to the road, Serge for not carrying water one day, Alex for his crew parking haphazardly on the road and Mr Tanaka was banned from running for a week because he was so unstable in the road he could well have fallen right into the middle and got killed. There was always talk about "well if I got this then he should get this too" and all sorts of bickering.

I really didn't care whether others followed the rules or not. I just wanted to run across America. If one of the others took a motorbike then that was their call. This is by far the hardest thing I have ever done and I just don't have the physical or mental space to start stressing about what others were doing.

The 50 days on the road were taking their toll on runners and crew alike. We were all more sensitive, more grumpy and more depressed than before. We had got so far, 50 days into 70 and yet there were times when I thought we were going to all fall apart. Laure was amazing throughout but it was clear that the disturbances in the camp were upsetting her and she felt this was a reflection on how she was organising the race. I stopped one day in a stage to tell her that I thought this was the most incredibly well organised event I had ever been part of and she and her team were doing an amazing job. I think she was pleased to hear it. I think we all missed our homes, our families and our normal lives. I certainly did. It was only another two weeks till Gemma was back out here. Then I knew it was just a case of getting my body to the end.

During Illinois I started to run out of things to think about, or rather things would not just pop into my head and consume my brain. So much of my time was spent worrying about my injuries and not getting enough sleep and whether people back at home were laughing at me or whether the weather would ever get better. Now I had learned to put all that aside and only think about things I could control. Now I had run out of things to think about.

It became quite mundane. We still passed some beautiful places but it was not quite like what we enjoyed earlier on. Not the scorching California desert or the Arizona Mountains. It was highways and cities that all look the same, long drags on boring roads and drivers who were now less accommodating than before. I went through a long period of wondering what I was doing here again and struggled to find anything interesting to write about at the end of each day.

The silver lining was that there were more eating options during and at the end of each day, and of course that we were getting closer to the end.

The humidity was still choking. It felt a bit depressing that a humble 30°C would slow us down in our tracks but humidity is a silent killer. You can't see it you just feel like you are being strangled all of a sudden.

My body was slowly falling apart. Sometimes I'd wake up in the middle of the night with pain in my legs. Each morning I'd get out of bed and hobble around the room, trying to minimise the few feet I would have to travel to put my clothes on or brush my teeth and other parts of my morning ritual which seemed to be more rushed each day, just because I was getting slower at it. I'd sometimes sit on the end of my bed and ask myself "do I really need to go to the bathroom?" or "shall I just wear the clothes that I slept in today?" It seemed I had become an expert in laziness.

I was not the only one suffering though. Bando looked even more of a mess each morning. I saw him coming down the stairs on day 51, strapped up and barely able to move. I was inspired by this. I knew that although I was hurting myself I was not hurting as much as him and yet he could still keep going. I had a lot more room for suffering before not finishing was a risk. This made me feel better, even though it was inspired by looking at someone's pain.

However I had the wind knocked out of my sails that day when early on in the run Bando said to me, "I think tomorrow will be my last day". I really did not know what to say. I was gutted that he was thinking that and had no idea he was so close to the edge. My view on just how far a person can smash themselves day after day after day had changed so much in the last 51 days yet there has to be a limit. Had Bando reached his?

I was very sad for him but then more selfishly I thought about myself. I could be closer to the end than I thought? I would definitely be next. I felt like my fate was attached to Bando somehow, that if he would finish then I would finish.

Bando didn't drop out that day and we all made it through the longer days that bunched together, 57 miles then 52. These days were long hard slogs and I listened to music for most of the days. I usually only had about an hour of the MP3 player each day just to help put my mind in a better place to now I was needing it. It no longer felt like a luxury but an essential. It was one of my "in emergency break glass" items that I was now using all the time.

I only had one "emergency" item left to use; the pain killers. I took two in Arizona for my shin splints but then no more for the entire trip. I used to take them all the time when I was running long distance but since my first Spartathlon when I had kidney problems I stopped taking them. I don't even think they would have worked in this case but it was a constant temptation to take something to ease the pain. I started putting them in my running pack each day, just in case.

We only spent 4 days crossing Illinois and then into Indiana. I was chatting to Gemma on the phone as I crossed the state line andhad to cut the call short because the humidity was choking me again. I could not walk, talk and inhale water at the same time.

With the clocks going forward we had another hour of darkness to run in the morning which would normally be great but today it was on a windy narrow road where cars were still driving.

I felt pretty rotten for much of the first part, the darkness made me grumpy as well as the lack of food. I was struggling to keep any sort of pace up and for the first time since I was ill I was right at the back. I was really pleased to see Bando survive yesterday and he seemed to be having a good one today.

Bando owns a publishing company in Japan. He started it as a one man band and now it employs 50 people. He told me (in much better English that I first gave him credit for) that he thinks about New York all the time and it often brings tears to his eyes. I also think about New York all the time and it too brings tears to my eyes.

It was really nice to hear that (for the first time) from someone and I can imagine why he does. He finishes last pretty much every day after running on his own. His legs are a mess, he said he takes his mind off it all by singing. He was doing amazingly well today as at this pace we'd beat the cut-off by nearly 2 hours.

10 miles from the end we went onto an interstate that led to Indianapolis. I was still running at this point but Bando was now walking, not something he usually did. A mile up a hill I saw another McDonald's and I bounded up the hill (remember all words here are relative) to get in there and buy me and Bando a smoothie before he caught up. He seemed surprised when I waited and handed him a smoothie on the interstate but enjoyed it a lot. We walked together for about another mile and chatted some more. It was great to see he was well and truly in this race still. And me too.

I ran on, no longer really worried about how fast or when I would arrive. On the interstate there was a lady and a guy whose car had stopped and they were pushing it. I asked if they wanted a hand and then started to push the car up the interstate with them. I assumed they were going to pull into the next corner which was only a few meters away, but they said they were going to the gas station which was ages away. Shit, how could I get out of this? Saying that I was running across America just seemed like a lame excuse. I just said, "I gotta go" and went.

Two days after heading into Indiana we ran through Indianapolis, the biggest city we were going to run through and home of a famous short distance car driving race. We passed early in the morning as people were going to work, it felt so strange to be in a place where normal people were just going about their lives.

There were more long days in Illinois and often there was driving in between. Add to that losing another hour with the clocks changing and it really digs into the time. That was the last time the clocks were going to go forward. We were now on Eastern Time, the same time zone as the finish.

22

OHIO

Two years ago at Las Vegas airport I met a chap called Luca who was crewing for Tim Welch. I think we had a five minute conversation at the airport before I returned to London and he headed back to Columbus. I didn't think anything more of it until he contacted me to say that the race was going to go through his home town and he was going to meet me and run with me for a bit.

This was great news and the first thing Gemma thought of was, "Get him to do your washing". I was probably starting to get pretty smelly again with the sulphuric hum of my constant running and not washing it. I could not smell it anymore.

I met up with him in a McDonald's on day 55. The others got a bit confused about his presence and thought he was just some guy who started following me after McDonald's. He'd drive a few miles up the road, run back then run alongside with me and head back to the car and repeat.

Something else significant happened on day 55 too. It was the first and only time in the race that someone yelled out "RUN FORREST RUN" at me. I was amazed that it took so long, though we did not see anyone for the first 40 days and those we did probably had not seen a film before.

He also bought some new shoes for me. For the next few days I got a "new shoe bounce" of feeling really good running in comfortable shoes.

The days spent running with Luca were really nice. We'd only spoken for 5 minutes beforehand but it was like we had been running buddies for years. His wife D'lyn came to join us too and I had a crew again.

The best bit was the running though. At first I didn't think I would appreciate the company but Luca was so easy to talk to and I found it quite relaxing. It made me laugh to think of Lou who ran with me towards the end of the Grand Union Canal run 4 years ago and how I was grumpy with her because she was asking too many questions.

I felt like I had three easy days of running with company, I was sad to see him leave after we ran through Columbus but at that point we were less than two weeks from the end.

Italo woke up one morning looking more confused than usual and then broke the silence by saying, "Oh no, I dreamt that I had run 40 kilometres of today already and now I have to run them again". Welcome to my world my friend, I had been doing that all race. If I could bag the miles I had run in my sleep then I would have got to New York ages ago and be half way back to LA by now.

Today was great too because David "ma Mere" was back. I interrupted his conversation with Serge to give him a great big hug. Things were looking up, Gemma was going to be here again in 5 days and the race organisation seemed to be bracing themselves for getting us to New York. Well getting our stuff to New York anyway, we had to get ourselves there.

I had a dream last night that I had missed one of the stages and got thrown out of the race. I was trying to convince Laure that I could just catch up and run two of the stages on the same day but she was not having it. For some reason this conversation took place in Leicester. Anyway, I woke up a little relieved to find that I was still in the race and now on day 60.

Today was an exciting one, 3 states. The milestones were 20

miles – West Virginia, 26 miles – McDonald's and 35 miles – Pennsylvania.

The miles were slow going but with the hills and intersections I was not too worried. It would be nice to get this finished under 12 to have a bit of time at the end. I ran together with Koshita for the first half and he slowed to take lots of pictures of everything. A game I liked to play sometimes is "what would Koshita take a photo of?" While I was running I imagined I had a camera and that I was Koshita taking millions of photos. I didn't know how he was going to make cut-offs now we were seeing much more stuff.

West Virginia looked interesting from the start, a town called Wheeling and some huge bridges over a river. It all looked very industrial age with steel bridges.

I saw my first live snake, quite a big black one that made me jump and he went the other way and slithered pretty quickly up an embankment. I was amazed at its speed and wondered whether I could have outrun it if it decided to go for me. This occupied my mind for a while after.

David and Rene were at the top to give me some much needed refreshment while David and I continued our "English people are stupid because…", "No French people are stupid because…" debate. I was clearly winning. Stupid Frenchman.

23

PENNSYLVANIA TO NEW YORK – IT'S THE CONSTANT REPETITION OF "NEARLY THERE" THAT'LL KILL YER

I loved Pennsylvania though my first steps in it were not pleasant.

I just hated it from the start. The evil camber of the road made me run lopsided and the rocks strewn into the road, the smashed up sections and truck after truck after truck just made it unbearable. Well for me anyway, I was right at the back already and thought I'd been running ok till then. My promise of staying positive was broken on this road.

I was thinking of things to be pissed off at and could not really come up with anything. These drivers were only doing their jobs. The organisation of the race was phenomenal, last night Emily drove back to the previous motel to retrieve my phone that I left there, a 2 hour trip. Seriously, how many race organisations would do that? My injuries were minimal. Somehow I managed to overlook all this and stay grumpy.

Well today went just as I kind of hoped for yesterday, the opposite of yesterday. I woke up in a good mood but that was shortly ended by the nature of the start of this run. The town of Uniontown was like most other towns we had crossed. Broken traffic lights and uneven sidewalks (usually with an injury lawyer practice beside them). It could be hard work in the dark trying to step over all the obstacles but within 3 miles we were on a highway that put me right off running.

I didn't really pay attention to the profile of the routes, didn't really see how it would help me. Peter had been talking about "stage 62" for a while now. I just got out of bed and got given the miles and then did them at my own slow pace.

I wish I had looked at this one though, the first climb was huge, on a busy road though the trucks were only doing 10 mph downhill. As the sun rose I grumpily trudged up this thing for about an hour and thought, "How many more of these will we have"?

I also got a bit annoyed at Girard who seemed to be able to walk as fast as I could run and he was doing it right in front of me, obviously not deliberately but I was close to asking him to at least look like he was making an effort because I was busting a gut here.

I had been told I had a significant limp, denied by me for a few days but now I could clearly feel my body rocking more to the right and my right foot curving in more as I staggered forward. I have become one of those old men you see at races who look like they are running sideways and I remark, "They should get that sorted out, it must be killing them".

I was getting annoyed at my beard too, everything I ate had hair in it and my beard got full of everything I ate. I couldn't wait to get rid of it. At the end of day 66, it was going to go (because that's a short day and this would be a big job).

Anyhoo, at the top of this first mountain pass was a lovely looking resort and then the rolling road from then on seemed to have nice resort after nice resort, much nicer looking places than we had stayed so far. I looked at my phone time when I knew I was at 11 miles to see how far behind the "4 mph" I was and it was only about 10 minutes, not as bad as I had thought.

But the grumpiness went away as soon as the highway got

less busy and the lovely trees and scenery came out, I looked back having made the first mountain climb and saw just how high we were. Earlier today we were way down there in the fog, now look at us. I think today will be a Cheryl Cole day, really pretty but really, really slow.

I was feeling a bit down about the whole race again, like I was just grinding out miles with no real point. I felt like once this was over I would forget all about it, that it would just fade into history. I felt like it was time to ask Bob Brown my second question, I emailed him and asked, "Does it ever wear off?"

I got a reply a few days later that confirmed my hopes, that it never wears off, that once this is finished it becomes an irremovable part of your life. This gave me a great lift when I heard it.

Now we were in the founding states there were a lot more interesting buildings. Ones made out of stone and brick and made to last. We had been following the "National Road" more or less from Indianapolis, one of the first national highways built about 200 years ago. It is not a very busy road but it is littered with relics from the past when the country was only 13 states. There are forts of previous battles and toll houses with prices on. To take a 2 horsed 6 wheeled carriage into Hancock would cost 6 cents I think. Not sure about a weary runner on two tired feet and a badger on his back,

Today I was excited about Gemma being at the finish though she got stuck in traffic. I had been counting the days since we said goodbye in a rushed way in Oklahoma at the start of stage 36. It seemed like such a long time ago, though I was having trouble discerning what had happened yesterday from the day before and from the day before that, like the days really were merging into one enormous tract of time. Los Angeles was two months ago (TWO MONTHS????) yet somehow it felt like that could have been years ago. My summer had been so crammed with excitement, despair, fear, hope, experience and all other emotions that my brain had probably spread it over more than a year just to stop me exploding.

Now I didn't feel like I could even measure time. I thought some days "I have about 8 hours left of running today". I didn't even know what that meant anymore. 8 hours used to be a working day, or a 50 mile race, or an after work pub session getting out of hand. I don't know why I even looked at the time anymore, I just plodded along and at some point during the day it finished.

Serge said to me, "From tomorrow we will be able to say this is the last Sunday, and then this is the last Monday etc.". It was true and it was going to be awesome. This time next week I'd be in New York. I preferred to think of it this way though.

Remember that thing I had to do ten times this summer? Well now I only had to do it once more.

This was the "last Sunday" of the race. No more running on Sundays after today. This time next week I wouldn't have to do any running. Etc.

It really lifted spirits to be able to say things like that, to say to a passer-by who asked, "Yeah we started 2 months ago in LA but this is the last week".

Gemma arrived later than expected while stuck in traffic in a place called "New York" and we did not get a huge amount of sleep. I felt quite tired but so happy that Gemma was here now. Things seem much easier when she is around. There was not the big hug in the middle of the road like in Oklahoma, she just came into the room and climbed into bed. For the few hours I did sleep I slept quite well, safe in the knowledge that this was almost done.

I also had a visit from John Price this morning. I had met John once at the Spartathlon two years ago and kept in touch with his crazy antics on Facebook. Earlier this year he ran across

America pushing a baby jogger on his own. It was great to see him and he brought along some good beer and cookies too. These were the best cookies I have ever had, they were perfect for running, melting in the mouth. Obviously designed by a runner.

Around half way a chap pulled over called Bennett who said he was a friend of Laurie and that he drove up from Baltimore to say hello. That was really kind and I said I was on my way to the McDonald's and that Gemma and John were there. I think they ate McDonald's together while my Big Mac and Smoothie were delivered on the road (this is the advantage of a support crew). I did not see him again but it was really nice meeting him and he even gave Gemma some beard trimmers (for me not her).

The second half of today felt a bit crap. The euphoria of "The last Sunday" wore off and the reality of "I still have 20 miles to go which is another 5 hours of slogging" set in. It's funny how I have been doing this now for 63 days, run nearly 3000 miles, and yet the thought of doing another 20 just made me feel crap. I had the blister on my little toe back that I got on the first day and it was burning a bit. I also seemed to have started creating electricity and every now and then got a shock in my balls or on my back. I think the humidity was quite high again and maybe my damp clothes were causing it.

Gemma's first day back – Waynesboro to York – 48.8 miles. This felt like a glorious day. There was a really nice stroll through Gettysburg around half way. I don't know too much about the battle of Gettysburg other than that it was a very important one in the American civil war, where the Union army defeated the Confederates somewhere near there.

There were a huge number of historical signposts with information on which I stopped to read but it was hard trying to put it all together. Taverns where armies gathered, roads that were marched on, profiles of generals and heroes and villains. This would be a great place to spend the day as it looks like such a proud historical town. I got the sense that I was marching along the same routes that the armies would have done nearly 200 years ago. Pennsylvania is full of history, the buildings look old but beautiful. Previous states where all the large scale farming happens have buildings that look like they are only built to last a few years before being pulled down and replaced. I liked this state.

New Oxford was lovely too and it had a McDonald's. Gemma asked, "Would you rather have this sandwich that I made rather than a Big Mac?" It was a loaded question like many of hers such as "would you like to eat some vegetables" or "would you like to shower before getting into the bed". It was a nice beef and cheese sandwich though.

Day 66 from York to Lancaster was one we were all looking forward to because it was "only" 26.2 miles. Seems quite fitting to have a marathon stage in the race. Today was going to be the day I'd get a haircut and shave and look much better for the finish line.

There was an announcement that Alex had had a baby girl that morning (back in Italy of course) and that mother and child were doing very well. He found out just before the finish, which probably explained his quick time and hasty exit. Today we had two guest runners of David (dressed as a cow) and Berangere.

We started on the same busy road that we finished on yesterday and in the pitch black 5:30 am morning it was still quite busy. I had the turn sheet and I normally just look for when the first turn is, today it was 16.9 miles which meant I could just put it away for a few hours and sleep run and follow everyone else.

We ran along and soon we were on an interstate, it felt a little strange but I could see a long line of runners ahead so stayed with it. After about half an hour on here Bando caught me and asked if this was the right way. I was sure it was not as Laure would have told us about this, there was no way a crew could access us on this road and she would have said something to us. There was debate, Phillippe said, "Yes, this is good way, good way" and sped off. I thought we should just walk in the same direction till someone told us otherwise (yeah stupid). I had no phone on me so could not call anyone.

Then we saw Fabien (Patrick's wife and support) drive past and honk at us and somehow she managed to turn around to tell us all to go back. Doh. We were now further from the finish than we were at the start. I blame David. Silly Frenchman

After about an hour and a half I met Gemma at the 1 mile point to have a drink and sandwich. I think we had probably added about 4-5 miles on with that detour. Still, 26 miles is a silly distance to run. We ran through a pretty town and I think we were reaching that critical point where I could no longer say hello to everyone I saw. In Oklahoma where you only see one person a day it's easy to do, in fact I would say hello to horses and cows too just because I was lonely. It was going to be harder now in all these busy towns. "Hello, hello, hello, hello, hello, hello, hello …" I would get out of breath quickly.

The quick and easy marathon day ended up being quite stressful for Laure because we all went the wrong way. I didn't see much of what went on behind the scenes anymore but it was clear that there was a lot to do for the organisers. Heading into the hugely populated areas brings about all sorts of challenges for 14 runners and 14 sets of support vehicles.

We arrived in a motel, just a regular motel like all the others we had stayed in so far and as I entered the room the ground shook. Was that an Earthquake? Apparently it was, centred in West Virginia a few hundred miles away.

The next hour or so in the motel were quite funny. It was

time for my tramp beard to come off. Gemma used the trimmers like a lawn mower on my face. It was so tough and mangled. I did not look after it properly, it got in my way when I was eating, drinking and even sleeping. Gemma said that kissing me was like kissing a hedgehog. Not sure how many hedgehogs she has kissed in her time though.

The following morning there were calls of, "Who is this new young good looking chap? And where is that smelly tramp who has been hanging around for the past 2 months?" Well no one actually said it but I am sure they all thought it. My new shaven face was certainly a discussion point this morning and during the stage. I still looked in the mirror and didn't quite recognise myself, I had lost so much weight and it really showed now in my naked face. I am not sure whether I should try to get fat again when I finish this, saves me having to buy new clothes.

The race briefing this morning was long. I think Laure was frustrated by people going wrong yesterday (or perhaps by people complaining about it) so she went through all the turns. I can't see how anyone could really complain about yesterday. It was basically one person going wrong and then lots of people sleep running, our own stupid fault.

The roads were getting much busier now and we were all aware of the dangers of getting run over. Drivers are just not expecting runners to be out there. In fact people are not expected to leave their car for any reason; they have drive-in restaurants, shops and even banks. I had survived shin splints, food poisoning and all sorts of injuries to get almost across America – I didn't want to end up in hospital because some guy swung out of the side road without looking.

In these last few days all eyes were on Patrick. He was in comfortable second place and now he was crippled, having to be held at the start line each day. Once he got going he seemed to be OK, quicker than me anyway, however today he was behind me and I did not see him at all. I stopped and asked Serge's crew how Patrick was doing as I was told he had gone to hospital to have some pain killing injections and then was going to be put back on the place he left and he would carry on. He had come so far.

It put all those "in the bag" feelings back on hold. With two weeks to go it was all too easy to say "only two weeks to go", but that was still 14 days of hard effort – still 700 miles. Even with "10 days to go" or "one week" it wasn't in the bag. We saw the dangers of the cars here and now we were all looking at Patrick thinking that this could happen to anyone of us. It wasn't in the bag yet.

24

NEW JERSEY

Near the end of day 68 we headed into New Jersey and it just all looked so British. We crossed bridges that could have been made by the same people as Hammersmith Bridge, it felt like running though a sunny British seaside town and it felt magical. New Jersey was only a little state, barely as big as Wales.

I loved New Jersey too, it felt almost like central London. I imagined Pennsylvania being like Surrey or Sussex, lots of interesting things to see and still only a few hours from the big city. New Jersey felt more like West London; busy and covered with construction activity but still not quite the big city. I could see myself living in either place one day.

It's funny, I was 3100 miles into a 3200 mile race and hence "near the end" but all I could think about was how it sucked to only be 17 miles into a 51 mile day. I couldn't get myself into New York mode for some reason, I found it easy to think about it before now but all I could focus on was the next horrible mile.

I finished in 13:30 and would not sleep much that night. The next day was to be about 49 miles and then the last day. Today was mine and Gemma's two year anniversary and she was treated to eating pizza in bed while I slowly dozed off into a coma.

I can barely remember the penultimate day apart from one thing. We were running up and down really hilly and windy roads heading towards New York.

There were plenty of hills and I was running close to Alex for the first 15 miles. Some of the corners were blind and we had to be careful. It felt mentally frustrating and I was not enjoying the penultimate days as much as I thought I would.

About half way through the day I saw Gemma's car parked at the bottom of a hill which marked the end of another 3 mile stretch. It was always good to see, and meant I could be rewarded with some food, like a treat a dog gets for fetching a stick. Funny how it was the feeling of being a dog fetching a stick that got me into this in the first place.

As I approached the car I saw another car parked alongside, it was a golden colour. Then from behind Laurie emerged with the "RUN FORREST RUN" licence plate that I had brought along. I really didn't know what to think or say as I was so overwhelmed. If I had that moment again I probably would have thought of something better to say than, "That's not your car".

Laurie said it was a hire car. I could not understand why she had a hire car, what's wrong with the black car she crewed me with in California? I left and ran on and it took a while for the penny to drop. She'd flown over here from LA, 3000 miles would be a ridiculous distance to drive.

That was another one of those gems that will be in my collection for ever. I walked and reflected a little on what had happened in the last 69 days. The amazing friends who had selflessly given their time to help me do this. Gemma had flown out, gone back home and come back again, Laurie was there at the start but I did not expect to see her again and here she was. The emotion took hold of me once more and I got suncream in my eyes again.

Today was meant to be the last of the "hard" days, tomorrow was just going to be a simple jaunt into New York. I had thought about these days lots over the previous year and when they finally arrived they were nothing like what I was expecting.

There was a dark cloud hanging over the whole race. It was in the news and official warnings were telling the people of New York to either get out of the city or stay in their homes. In a few days a hurricane was due to hit the city, around the same time we were due to arrive.

You couldn't have made it up any better. We had run for 69 days through deserts, over mountains, along the longest straightest roads I have ever known, through the worst heatwave in living memory and then we arrive near the finish to discover that we might not be allowed to finish. Washington Bridge, which connects New Jersey to New York, was a risk. If the hurricane was considered a threat they would close the bridge and then there would be no way for us to enter New York.

Not getting to New York would feel like defeat. The Los Angeles to New Jersey race did not have the same ring to it. For the sake of another few miles into the city the whole trip would have felt pointless.

If the bridge did close then the race would be to the start of the bridge on the New Jersey side. I had another week left in the USA and if it did come to pass that the race got shortened I would have stopped for a day or two and then ran into New York myself. At least then I could say I did it, that I finished what I came out here to do.

The meeting we had that night was quite tense, there was nothing we could do but hope that the bridge stayed open. I wanted it to be a relaxing night of celebrating the almost finish of the race with a few drinks and then sleep a little for the glory leg tomorrow. This was not that relaxing night I had hoped for. This was rubbish.

Blog entry for the morning of the last day

"Dear 4am, we need to talk. I have tried not to let it bother me for the last few weeks but now I must say something. It's not working out. It felt quite exhilarating and refreshing at the start but now after more than

two months I think the magic has ended. It's not you, it's me. You have always been there for me over these past 70 days and I appreciate that but I don't think we are right for each other. It is with a heavy heart that I say today I think we should go our separate ways. I have changed so much this summer and I think I need a change. I know you will be able to make someone else very happy someday and really hope you find that special someone, but it is not me. I hope we can still be friends and perhaps one day we will meet again and I hope that moment will not be too difficult for both of us, but for now it is goodbye. I will never forget you."

The day started with the news that it was "very unlikely" that the bridge would be closed. This was not as comforting as I hoped. It still created a rush to get to the bridge, for some reason I thought that if they did close it they would do so at noon and so I had about 6 hours to get there. It was 26 miles away. This was a pace similar to that which I had been running for the previous 3180 miles, but I did not like feeling rushed or that I had to be somewhere at a certain time.

Laurie and Gemma were crewing me today and later on we were to meet up with Bennett, the guy who stopped to say hello a few days earlier who I discovered was now Laurie's partner. We started in three waves, me being in the slowest with most of the others. Patrick was looking better than he had done previously but his second place was now under threat as Italo was putting in some really fast times and was now only about three hours behind.

I got to the bridge, bang on time and it was open for business as usual. Gemma came to run across the bridge with me and I got my first glimpse of New York, rain and clouds. I could not see the Manhattan skyline at all. The bridge was spectacular though and at the end I had only seven miles to go. With seven miles to go I always imagine our Wednesday night "three parks" seven mile club run around Hyde Park, Green Park and St James' park with the Serpentine. That's all I had left.

Remember that thing I had to do 460 times this summer? Well now I only had to do it once more.

New York was not like I imagined. It was like the opening scene in Vanilla Sky where there is no one there. It was almost deserted. Hot dog stands were idle, there was the occasional person walking and some even running but this was not the huge metropolis that I was expecting.

I stopped at my last crewing stop with Laurie, Bennett and Gemma a couple of miles from the end. I said I wanted to go alone for the last two miles. I thought at some point it was all going to hit me. I had been running for nearly 800 hours and only had about 20 minutes left. I was sure that at some point I was just going to break down, or have some euphoric moment that would represent this whole amazing summer that I had just experienced.

But there was nothing. I just crossed some roads, looked at the instructions to find a hotel as if I were a tourist and then when I saw the hotel (and everyone else connected with the race gathered outside cheering and waving) I simply jogged up to them. That was it. End of the race. 70 days, 3220 miles, 781 hours, two deserts, three mountain ranges, 13 states, one hospitalisation, dozens of friends along the way, 47 stops in McDonald's, two stone lost, 400,000 calories burned.

I wasn't making any bets on how I would feel at the end of the race. Relieved to have finished, upset that it was all over or hysterically happy. One of the feelings I didn't quite expect though was a feeling of absolutely nothing. I didn't know what to make of that. I'd remind myself that I have just run across the United States of America. That didn't seem to do it.

I was back where I had started when I got the PB in the marathon five years ago. Here had been a feeling that I had achieved what I had set out to achieve, but also a feeling of emptiness at the result. This time was different though, I had nothing else to look forward to.

The next morning I woke up around the same time as normal. I tried to lie in and sleep more but I was too restless. I got out of bed around seven am with no sense of purpose. Normally I'd be a few miles into the road by now whereas here I had nothing to do. What was the point of me now?

I checked the floods of messages that came in through my blog and on Facebook. I was so happy to read them but also disappointed that I had nothing else to give. I had done it now. What is next?

The week I spent in New York was too busy for me. I felt like I was coming out of prison and the "real world" was going by too fast. Hurricane Irene came and went, knocking over a few traffic cones during its visit. I was really looking forward to spending a week in New York, doing all the things there that I thought a tourist should do but all I wanted was to lie down in the park. I was exhausted, not physically but mentally. Things were going by so fast I just had to sit down.

The most memorable part of the week was going to Fire Island for a day trip and seeing the Atlantic Ocean. This was something I had dreamt about ever since I first laid eyes on the Pacific Ocean. In a few days I'd be flying across that ocean back to London. Back home. I was a bit worried about it though, why would anyone care about me now? What more do I have to give?

24A

WHY? VERSION 8

One of the things that the veterans did not tell me about was the post-race depression. Why would they? I have just done the most amazing thing of my life and I feel empty. This feeling of emptiness then leads to feelings that what I have just done was totally pointless.

I felt like by running across America my life had gained some sort of purpose. I loved the simple life and long to go back to it. Nothing is complicated but it is incredibly hard. You just get up in the morning, eat, run, eat then sleep. No project plans, no politics, no managing expectations, no bullshitting and no objectives. Just run what you have to each day and that's it.

It was a shock coming back to my real life afterwards where I was expected to think for myself, to decide what to do, to choose my own direction. It was hard. I didn't like it.

One of the things that really made this trip special was the attention I was getting from friends back home and strangers too. I loved writing about how each day went and loved even more that people would read it and seem to like it. I spent a few days reading back through the comments that were made on my blog and on Facebook. It started to make it all feel worthwhile.

Looking back at everything I have done it's hard to

think that there is just one thing that is pushing me along, one force that is willing me along, allowing me to endure more than I thought possible.

I've come up with so many reasons over the years trying to explain all of this and after New York I felt further way from the answer than when I started. Previous explanations of the sense of achievement, the flow, the friends made, places seen, gems collected and beautiful simplicity of running didn't seem to fit anymore as an explanation as to why I'd put myself through something like that.

On arriving at Heathrow I was expecting to see my friend Drew who was going to pick me up and take me home. I was looking forward to seeing him and spending a Sunday afternoon with friends who I had not seen for three months. It wasn't really a long time but it felt like a lifetime. I squeezed more life into 70 days than I had done in my previous 31 years.

I pushed my case through the arrivals and was astounded to see about 25 of my friends all in Serpie colours, flags and balloons all waiting for me. At first I didn't believe they were there for me, I thought they must have been waiting for someone else. It was 6 am on a Sunday morning, they must have gotten out of bed at 4. I didn't know what to say or think or do, I didn't know what order to hug people in. I was overwhelmed. I didn't even dream of a reception like this, it was magical. This was another thing Gemma had been sneakily arranging like the visit of Laurie.

I spent the next few hours having breakfast at the airport telling people everything I could remember from the trip. I then had a BBQ where I did the same, everyone was listening to me, asking questions and recalling parts of the story back to me that they were so engaged in reading over the summer. I was astonished that something that I had done seemed to strike a chord with so many people. I can talk all day and all night about my adventures over the summer and people were genuinely interested in hearing about it.

The following Wednesday I went back to the running club and looked at the map that I had placed there three months ago. One of the things that gave me hope was to come back to this room, stand in front of that map and say, "That's done". I went a bit earlier before anyone else turned up as I thought it would be an emotional moment. I just stood there for at least 15 minutes scanning over the places that were anonymous to me three months ago but now have vivid memories attached to them.

The Californian desert towns of Amboy and Ludlow where Laurie so brilliantly crewed me. The furnace of Needles on the California/Arizona border where Lesley and Dave drove 400 miles to help a stranger. Truxton and Seligman, beautiful Arizonan towns where Deb and Dave's wonderful sense of humour kept me going through the first really tough times. Crownpoint, New Mexico, worst day of my life. Somewhere near Abiquiu Lake, Bando and the best moment of my life. Guymon Oklahoma, meeting Russell and Claire for the first time and seeing Gemma for the first time in a month.

Joplin, Missouri, Alex saying "look at how your life can change" – the sharp realisation that no amount of my own suffering compares to what others have suffered. Hannibal, the birthplace of Mark Twain who told me everything I needed to know about fear. Columbus, Ohio and running a few days with Luca and D'lyn. Pennsylvania, York, Lancaster and Gettysburg that looked like home,

John Price coming for a visit and being reunited with Gemma. West Orange, seeing Laurie appear from behind a tree that felt like this amazing story was about to draw itself to a happy conclusion. Washington Bridge, three parks to go, the deserted streets of New York and then the jaunt along Broadway to complete something that I felt was a life's calling. I can see all of that and more just by looking at this large piece of laminated paper with a purple marker line drawn from one side to the other.

The post-race depression eased the more I spoke about it, the more I integrated myself back into "normal" life. I did some speaking events, some interviews, spoke to people at other races, chatted in the pub and at work and to anyone who would listen to what I had to say. It made me feel better.

And so I realised perhaps why it is that I do this. Why I signed up for my first ultramarathon five years ago. Why I thought running Badwater would be a good idea. Why I even ran marathons in the first place. What was it that got me out of that chair with 25 miles to go in the Grand Union Canal Race. What made me hobble along to the end of the Spartathlon. What was it that was keeping me upright through nearly 200 miles and four days of New Mexico. Why I slowly broke my body over ten weeks of really harsh punishment just to get somewhere that would take five hours to fly.

I realised that perhaps more than anything, the reason why I do this.

I just wanted to have some stories to tell.

I hope you liked them.

25

THANK YOU

I hope you enjoyed reading the book and hoped you got a good idea of how wonderful the world of ultra-running really is. As you will have noticed this was not a story that involved just me, there were so many people involved and I would like to thank this cast of thousands as best I can.

I will try not to go all Gwyneth Paltrow, crying as I incoherently try to thank a thousand people.

Nikolai Pitchforth, thank you for sending me that email mocking my fear of running in 25°C heat. Without that this book would have not been written, though who knows what my marathon time would be right now.

Ben Cope, Simon Bampfylde, Campbell Taylor, Gowan Clews and Lou Reeves, thank you for being in my first support crew in the GUCR. Sorry I threw the toys out a lot, I was still learning.

Thank you to the Serpentine Running Club, joining it was the best thing I ever did when moving to London.

Thank you to all the race directors in the UK and overseas. I can't remember what I used to do before I did this kind of running and I am eternally grateful for all the efforts you put in to give us these opportunities.

Thank you to all the people who followed my blog in the USA. It really helped to read your comments when I was suffering.

My Badwater crew, Laurie, Deb and Dave and Debbra you were fantastic. I was properly overwhelmed by your kindness and support in giving up your time to be moaned at by some British guy. Thankfully I saved my most grumpy moments for another crew. I had great fun and have amazing memories that will never die.

My USA running crew, Laurie again. I can't believe you signed up for yet more abuse. It made me feel so happy and relaxed to have you involved from the start. In fact you were running the show, I had it easy. I really hope to be able to return the favour someday.

Lesley and Dave. Wow, what a find you two were. It was a Geordie who got me into this it seemed fitting that a Geordie should help me out of it and blimey you guys were awesome. Running after a car with the licence plate "WHYIMAN" and listening to "Born to Run" blasting from the stereo will be with me forever. Thank you.

Debbra and Dave again, you guys are also suckers for punishment. You experience and comedy in those 6 days in Arizona were indescribable. Thank you for being part of this adventure.

The Seckers – Russell and Claire. I felt like as soon as I crossed into Oklahoma my problems were behind me and you guys played a big part in that. Thanks for running with me, telling me I look good and thanks for all the Subways J

Luca – the guy I met for only five minutes at Las Vegas airport a year earlier, thank you so much for coming along and running with me for three days. Though we had only known each other for five minutes it felt like we had been running buddies for years.

Bob Brown, thank you for answering that distress flare, I needed that.

John Price it was awesome to see you towards the end of the

race, you make the best running cookies I have ever tasted. Thank you too (I think) for introducing me to this race called "Barkley".

Laure – The Trans USA race was the greatest thing ever organised and thank you so much for putting in all that effort and you and the team certainly had the hard job of keeping everything running smoothly. The care you took for me while I was ill was amazing and I hope this book does justice for the amazing event that you created.

All of the team too were brilliant. David, the silly Frenchman, Ma Mere, thank you for amusing me throughout the journey. Bertrand, Mon Pere, Anne and Rene you were superb too.

Emilie and Berangere you came half way through the race and took to the organisation really well. Sorry that I scared you when I shaved off the beard. And thank you for taking Gemma's instructions and making me eat fruit along the way.

All of the runners in the race made the race. Rainer you are the only runner I have ever run with who I'd genuinely describe as world class. I don't think there is anyone else in the world who can run like you can and yet you run for the experience and not the records. It was a pleasure getting to know you.

Markus it was great chatting to you as we both made our way across the states and I hope to see you in Colorado sometime. Italo sharing a room with you and running alongside you for many weeks was a joy. Jenni and Anneke you were wonderful too, I never tired of that enthusiastic Dutch "CONGRATULATIONS" at the end of every stage, it was the most comforting sound ever.

Serge I can't believe you left trading in the city to go out exploring the world in this way J Of course I can understand that and thank you for inviting me along on this journey. All of he French runners and supporters were incredibly nice and helpful, despite the language barrier. I wish I had made more of an effort to learn the language.

The Japanese team were everything I expected and more. Super organised and with their unique style of wacky enthusiasm for running 1000s of miles. Thank you all for the fruit, the toilet paper, the encouragement and laughs. Mr Koshita particularly for doing it in true Japanese style, taking 0000 photos.

And of course Bando, I don't think you'll ever know just what you did that day in New Mexico but without that I would not have finished.

There are a few people I would like to thank for helping with this book.

Sam Robson, thanks for finding only 2500 errors in my original document. Rob Westaway thanks for finding another 00 that I added.

James Elson, Simon Freeman, Mimi Anderson and Robin Harvie thanks for reading the early drafts and giving me pointers on to how to improve it, particularly Simon who suggested more pages about me crapping myself.

Phew, that's a lot. Nearly there now. Just two more.

Mark Cockbain, don't you ever call me a pussy again. How can I thank you enough? I was gutted when you didn't come and felt like I was stealing your event from you. I like your style, just getting it done no matter what it takes, no complication, no fanfare, just resolve. I really hope to see you back running again someday.

And finally;

Gemma, I went to America certain that I could do this on my own, that the only way I was going to do this was on my own, that I didn't need you.

What a fucking idiot*.

Thank you for putting me straight on that, for coming out the USA at short notice and for later agreeing to be my wife. I love you more than anything.

I won't make the same mistake the next time.

---

* That was actually the working title of the book.